Relational Spaces

Relational Spaces

Daughterhood, Motherhood,
and Sisterhood
in Dacia Maraini's
Writings and Films

Virginia Picchietti

Madison • Teaneck
Fairleigh Dickinson University Press
London: Associated University Presses

© 2002 by Rosemont Publishing & Printing Corp.

All rights reserved. Authorization to photocopy items for internal or personal use, or the internal or personal use of specific clients, is granted by the copyright owner, provided that a base fee of $10.00, plus eight cents per page, per copy is paid directly to the Copyright Clearance Center, 222 Rosewood Drive, Danvers, Massachusetts 01923. [0-8386-3896-1/02 $10.00 + 8¢ pp, pc.]

Associated University Presses
440 Forsgate Drive
Cranbury, NJ 08512

Associated University Presses
16 Barter Street
London WC1A 2AH, England

Associated University Presses
P.O. Box 338, Port Credit
Mississauga, Ontario
Canada L5G 4L8

The paper used in this publication meets the requirements of the American National Standard for Permanence of Paper for Printed Library Materials Z39.48–1984.

Library of Congress Cataloging-in-Publication Data

Picchietti, Virginia A.
    Relational spaces : daughterhood, motherhood, and sisterhood in Dacia Maraini's writings and films / Virginia Picchietti.
       p. cm.
    Includes bibliographical references and index.
    ISBN 0-8386-3896-1 (alk. paper)
    1. Maraini, Dacia—Criticism and interpretation. 2. Maraini, Dacia—Characters—Women. 3. Women in literature. 4. Women in motion pictures. I. Title.
PQ4873.A69 Z835 2002
858'.91409—dc21
                                                                            2001054332

PRINTED IN THE UNITED STATES OF AMERICA

*Ai miei cari genitori,
Stefano e Laura Picchietti—
and for my husband Thomas Cragin,
with love.*

Contents

Acknowledgments	9
Introduction	13
1. Daughterhood	33
2. Motherhood	72
3. Sisterhood	105
Conclusion	138
Notes	141
Bibliography	168
Index	178

Acknowledgments

I AM GRATEFUL TO THE FOLLOWING FOR PERMISSION TO CITE PARTS of this book that were previously published, Purdue University Press, for permission to cite from my essay in *The Pleasure of Writing,* and the *Romance Languages Annual.* I would also like to thank RCS Libri, especially Rosaria Carpinelli, for permission to cite from Dacia Maraini's volumes *Crudeltà all'aria aperta* and *Mangiami pure* (both c. 1998 RCS Libri S.p.A., Milano), and Faber and Faber Ltd. for permission to cite from Sylvia Plath's poem "Mirror," published in the volume *Collected Poems.*

I would like to acknowledge the generous support of the University of Scranton for a Faculty Development Grant; and of the AAUW for a Winifred Cullis Grant and Indiana University for a Dissertation Year Fellowship, both of which facilitated work on the earliest stages of this project.

I would like to express my heartfelt gratitude to the many people who have been instrumental in helping me develop this project.

- Dacia Maraini, who, despite a busy schedule, graciously granted me several interviews and invited me to a screening of her films;
- the members of the University of Scranton's Department of Foreign Languages and Literatures, and Dean Joseph Dreisbach for their encouragement and support of my project;
- Dr. Peter Bondanella for his continued encouragement of my scholarly endeavors; the staff at Fairleigh Dickinson University Press, especially Christine Retz, for making the publishing process a pleasant experience;
- Francesca Parmeggiani, Laurel Cummins, and Margaret Flynn for constructive suggestions in the early stages of the project;
- Laura Salsini, whose friendship throughout the years has made the notion of sisterhood real in my life and whose intellectual insight was invaluable to the development of this work;

and the people to whom this book is dedicated, my parents, Stefano and Laura Picchietti, for their loving guidance through the years and for inspiring my love of literature; and my husband Thomas Cragin, for his constant support, encouragement, and loving companionship.

Relational Spaces

Introduction

"Accustomed as I was to being shut in between the walls of my courtyard, I was overcome by the sense of space."[1]

"The real problem is in identifying these marginal spaces and occupying them without permitting the system to stifle them."[2]

THE QUEST TO COMPREHEND WHAT SHAPES BOTH FEMALE IDENTIties and perceptions of the self has lead many twentieth-century Italian women authors to revisit the family and to investigate the experiences women have lived in its spaces. These authors have focused on the family as the primary site in which identity unfolds; in which, in other words, who one is develops out of the negotiation between self and other. The resulting portraits reproduce the complexities of the relational spaces in which their heroines evolve. These spaces are generally depicted through the conventional roles women fulfill in the family, and therefore highlight the relationship between familial space and gender.[3] Rather than simply repaint these roles, however, the portraits also elucidate how women actually live the identities the roles and familial relationships construct, and how the familial sphere determines a woman's sense of self.

Often, these portraits are told through first-person narratives, achieving an immediacy of expression that brings the reader directly into the folds of the heroine's private life and its subjective retelling. When viewed along a panoramic line from earlier familial portraits by, for example, Alba De Cespedes, Natalia Ginzburg, and Elsa Morante to later ones by Gabriella Magrini, Francesca Sanvitale, Carla Cerati, and Elisabetta Pierallini, the works demonstrate how women have interpreted the identity politics of postwar Italy and how the women's movement has altered their experiences. Indeed, in the earlier works the heroines' sense of self is often tragically confined to the domestic sphere. In later works, however, the heroines benefit from changes brought about by the women's movement and by the political legislation of women's rights. These latter depictions are recurrently informed by theoretical advances in feminism on issues of motherhood and daughterhood. Furthermore, in some cases they even place their heroines in the alternative relational space of sisterhood as a feminist revision and extension of the relationship between mother and daughter. Although the heroines in these portraits, like their earlier counterparts, are oftentimes restricted by their roles, new experiences both inside and outside the family offer possibilities that can help them subjectively effect both personal and social change.

As one of Italy's most renowned authors and a founder of the contemporary Italian women's movement, Dacia Maraini has been a keen observer of social realities and has produced a body of work chronicling women's experiences in postwar Italian society. To chart these experiences, she has addressed questions of identity, subjectivity, and their cultural construction. Many of her works situate the heroines in social discourses at the heart of the changing landscape of postwar Italian society. Undertaken from the 1960s to the present, the investigation of the relationship between the heroines and these social discourses has lead to the problematic site of family relationships.

In order to understand the underpinnings of women's experiences, Maraini has devoted a significant portion of her literary and cinematic production to investigating how women live in familial spaces. At the same time, her works have explored alternative relational possibilities that can allow women to redefine their identities and the way they experience relationships and the roles they circumscribe. Although critical of traditional familial patterns as confining to both women and men, Maraini's texts afford us a look at how a beneficial redefinition of the family is indeed possible, and how this revision is instrumental in developing women's subjectivity. At the same time, while at moments problematic, the works' depiction of the family is emblematic of fundamental concerns in twentieth-century Italian women's narratives on the family.

The choice to focus on Maraini's texts as documents of women's roles in postwar Italian society is significant. Maraini's works have received national and international literary awards and have been translated into numerous languages. Additionally, as focus in the literary and public arena has shifted to women's production in the decades following the start of the postwar women's movement, Maraini's works have gained critical attention as well. While several have become part of the canon of Italian studies and women's studies in the

United States and abroad, many have received recognition as cultural documents of postwar Italian society.[4]

As documents of this fertile period in women's history, Maraini's texts carve out spaces for her heroines' development from the actual and symbolic sites women have historically inhabited. On the one hand, these spaces constitute the familial relationships in which women develop—the mother-daughter and father-daughter bonds. On the other hand, they represent the diverse sites the author has chosen for her heroines' self-articulation—relational and generic sites through which their voices surface. It is in these spaces that her heroines enter new relational territory necessary for subjective development and eventual liberation in adulthood. Within the family, women are identified primarily as wives, mothers, and daughters, the two latter roles constituting the focus of this study. Maraini's works problematize the totalizing nature of these roles by challenging their construction and, through the heroines' own voices, uncovering previously hidden experiences and perceptions.[5]

The works analyzed in this study chart a trajectory that reflects the evolution of the late-twentieth-century feminist discourse on the family. In the 1960s, the feminist movement in Italy was beginning to theoretically and more thoroughly question women's roles and social status. As feminists focused at first on the rejection of the maternal role, in the 70s, 80s, and 90s they looked to the daughter as agent of change for all women, for she holds the privileged position between the domestic and public spheres. As liberatory forums of self-expression, Maraini's works (re)shape these issues within the context of a feminist understanding of their function and allow heroines to re-experience them in the newly ideated cultural spaces defined by the women's liberation movement.[6]

The spatial reality of domestic life so succinctly and insightfully expressed by Maraini's heroine Vannina in the quote heading this chapter is a central consideration in a study of roles and identity. Space is a complex term covering a multiplicity of sites in which experiences evolve. These sites might range from concrete dwellings, to canvases on which to express oneself in the visual arts, to the written page, to abstract thoughts, to relationships. This study limits its consideration of space to an investigation of the sites Maraini's heroines occupy within the family; those, that is, in which they negotiate as they strive for self-understanding, and the generic sites in which these negotiations are articulated.

The notion of familial space guiding this study develops out of theoretical considerations of the relationship between women and space. The definitions Derek Gregory and Gillian Rose develop in their studies of the complex nature of space inform this notion. Gregory's generic definition of space as both "the arena in *which* social life unfolds [and] as a medium *through which* social life is produced and reproduced" can be extended to include the family as backbone of this medium in its preparation of the individual for social intercourse.[7] Rose directly addresses the relationship between women and space, linking women's liberation with a reconfiguration of the way space is conceived. She argues that women feel "confined by space, into spaces" because they have historically not participated in its construction.[8] Women can achieve liberation, Rose contends, by redefining space and the way it is inhabited by both women and men.[9] Maraini's understanding of the spaces women traditionally populate echoes Gregory's definition, while the revisions she proposes encompass Rose's notion. Meanwhile, the way women's assumption of gendered roles in familial spaces is represented in Maraini's opus is illuminated by Judith Butler's definition of gender as a *strategy of survival* and a *legacy of sedimented acts*.[10] The performance of gender Butler describes enacts actions and roles transmitted through generations and replicated by and in the family. Familial spaces in Maraini's narratives represent a social stage upon which women enact roles they are interpellated to fulfill.

The family in which Maraini's heroines perform their roles is derived from the familial paradigm defining Western culture today. Studies that have had a significant impact on our understanding of the family in this context, such as Philippe Ariès' *Centuries of Childhood*, Elisabeth Badinter's *Mother Love*, and Barrie Thorne's edited volume *Rethinking the Family*, recognize the nineteenth-century family as a relational model defining twentieth-century experiences. Ariès identifies the nineteenth-century as the period that popularized the notion and configuration of the nuclear family. While the pre-nineteenth-century family largely functioned as an economic unit, its nineteenth-century counterpart shifted focus from a productive to a reproductive unit with the child at its center. In this configuration, the child would no longer be considered a "miniature" adult who contributes to the family's material survival, but rather deemed the family's affective center and in need of nurturing to survive both physically and emotionally. This model of the family was later legitimized by Victorian ideology. In their collaborative and now canonical study on the family, "Is There a Family?," Jane Collier, Michelle Rosaldo, and Sylvia Yanagisako maintain that Victorian notions of biology coupled with Victorian morality were instrumental in securing the perceived qualitative split between honorable public activity and menial domestic labor.[11] Badinter, meanwhile, investigates the role psychoanalysis, originating in the Victorian period, played in perpetuating this model. For Badinter, this social science theorized the dichotomy between public and domestic spheres and cemented adult roles in them: The father's work within the family diminished—it was extracted into the public sphere as it was distanced from labor in the domestic. The mother, meanwhile, remained in the domestic sphere, becoming the family member most (though not exclusively) responsible for the child's psychic development, and thus for the successful integration of the child into society.[12]

In their extensive work on the family, sociologists Chiara Saraceno and Laura Balbo regard this division as one of the signposts for understanding women's condition in modern-day Italy.[13] Their theories ascertain that the nuclear family is the foundation of our sense of self and social reality. As such, it is resistant to change because transforming the family constitutes unbalancing and altering that reality. More specifically, for Saraceno the family as institution both defines individual experiences and creates social archetypes that shape our perceptions of reality.[14] Within this framework, women's position in the family actually represents "the process of female identity formation,"[15] as the sociocultural construction of identity specifically prepares for the reoccupation of familial spaces. The link between women and the family is secured because the successful functioning of a family depends on them: They are "interlocutors of social policies" and are responsible for the "relation and interface between family and society, between the public and the private."[16] Similarly for Laura Balbo, relationships between the family on the one hand and society and the individual on the other are reciprocal ones of survival. Society depends on the family for its reproduction and perpetuation, and individuals depend on the family for their subsistence.[17] If the family's function within this scenario is altered, so are the individual and society's means of survival.[18]

These theories are of particular interest to a study of the way women's identities and experiences are perceived and portrayed and their origins theorized. In terms that directly apply to my study, Saraceno asserts that an analysis of the family institution is essential to "understanding . . . the individual's location in time and space and in social relationships."[19] An analysis that takes this concept into account will reciprocally shed light on the intricacies of those primary relationships that shape identity. Postwar Italy has witnessed significant changes in women's lives in both political and social arenas. It has seen a sharp decline in the birthrate, permitting women to enter the workforce at a much earlier time, and an increase in the number of women pursuing secondary and university degrees. These tendencies have been safeguarded in part by legislation allowing women to gain greater control over their lives. Advances in law, for example, have ensured women's entry into the workforce through the legislation of equal rights in 1977. Women's position within the private sphere, meanwhile, has been safeguarded by equality in the domestic realm (Article 143 of 1975) and the legalization of abortion (Article 194 of 1978).[20]

Maraini, along with feminist theorists, has proffered responses to the restrictive familial spaces in which women have historically developed. She has charted discourses of difference and subjectivity to propose reforms of familial relationships and highlight women's potential within them. The revision of the family informing Maraini's narratives lies at the root of feminist theories of subjectivity. When analyzed through the lens of these theories, the resulting narratives generate empowering discourses of motherhood and daughterhood. In them, the experiences are extricated from the domestic sphere and located in the public sphere, where they are rendered more visible and where their own potential for social transformation can be extended.

Significantly, feminist discourses on the family reinstate the feminine as affirming "other" against which to negotiate the developing self, positing, as Rosi Braidotti notes, "the necessity of the relationship to the other woman as . . . legitimator of the self."[21] They therefore revise the conventional notions of the mother as socializer and, therefore, as engenderer of confining relationships, and they correct conventional notions of the daughter as eventual incarnator of the mother's traditional role. Philosopher Luisa Muraro has focused her theory of women's subjectivity on a redefinition of the mother's place in a woman's life, shifting the paradigm from socializer to a symbol of women's difference and empowerment. In her groundbreaking

L'ordine simbolico della madre, Muraro investigates new spaces in which mother and daughter can interact and realize a relationship of mutual liberation. Other theorists propose the extension of this bond into sisterhood, which, according to Maria Luisa Boccia, is indispensable to processes of identity formation. This bond either transforms or compliments the mother-daughter bond and is designated by the members of the Milan Women's Bookstore Collective as sites of subjective development outside the family. The altered configuration of familial relationships of which sisterhood is an integral part constitutes Maraini's ultimate answer to the problematic reality of the conventional family.

The postwar Italian women's movement within which Maraini's work has flourished partly based its project of liberation and theory of subjectivity on the revision of relational spaces. This revision occurs on several planes, from revising history to account for women's experiences to reevaluating relationships between women. The steps taken to achieve it elucidate the focus of the project—symbolic mediation and placement, women's collectives, and symbolic mothers. The two latter components ultimately act as symbolic mediators between the individual woman and the world, because they become the cardinal points women use to reexamine both their lives and the historical legacy of other women's lives.[22] Symbolic mothers are female figures, either historical or contemporary, either recuperated from obscurity or reinterpreted within the context of a female cultural legacy. Their voices ultimately act as mediators because they are inspirational and are assumed as guides in the individual's development.

Ultimately, this revision not only affects women's identity, but also the way women express it subjectively and the way they perceive their place in the world. When developing a theory of female subjectivity, the members of the Milan Women's Bookstore Collective focused on the way women can inscribe their presence in a cultural heritage that does not represent "in words and images the relationship of one woman to another."[23] Historically, women have entered culture "without a symbolic placement": They have not inherited a written and illustrated history of women and their cultural reference of a familial relationship has not been a prominent mother-daughter relationship, but rather a father-son dyad. In order to develop a female subjectivity, the Collective contends, women must situate themselves in history by creating new points of reference, specifically constituted by relationships between women. Like their American and European counterparts, Italian feminists such as the members of the Milan Women's Bookstore Collective argue that womanhood developed out of the devaluation of women's presence in historical development. This is problematic when the development of subjectivity depends on, as Gillian Rose implies, an effective (and therefore recognized) participation in history. This lack of recognition deprived women of a legacy of female acts which would give them a sense of historical purpose and, ultimately, identity. Following the Milan Women's Bookstore Collective's prescriptive, retracing history and symbolically (re)placing women in it is a fundamental step in constructing a theory of women's liberation.

For psychoanalyst Silvia Vegetti Finzi, the practice of subjectivity entails retelling personal history.[24] This link between narration of the self and subjectivity is clearly illustrated by the Italian term for history—*storia*. The term connotes "real" historical spaces, both temporal and spatial, and "symbolic" spaces, narrating personal and/or public events. History, even in the Gramscian sense of struggle, is a story, a selected narration of events and experiences. Within this story lie countless choices for narrative content, choices that struggle to surface as or in the dominant narrative. The implementation of a practice of symbolic placement creates spaces for women in which they rewrite histories as subjects. As a result, looking back through one's own history involves redefining one's position within it. On a personal level, it involves reexamining those relationships instrumental in shaping one's identity, namely the family. On a historical level, revising History entails locating female presences, such as cultural figures, that together create a female legacy. As defined by Vegetti Finzi and the members of the Milan Women's Bookstore Collective, retelling private and public histories and effecting symbolic placement make possible the recuperation of female presences absent from official history. The new *storia* is charted along female points of reference.

This narrative process of symbolic placement into history is predicated on the recuperation of the maternal presence—both real and symbolic—in women's lives. Seen as the first and primary female figure in the daughter's life history, the mother is reconfigured as an empowering presence who serves as mediator between the daughter and the world in a process of symbolic mediation. On a personal level, symbolic mediation constitutes a subjective process that renders indispensable the primary bond with the mother in women's liberation.

Here, the daughter draws strength, not weakness, from her mother, while the mother fulfills a role that is no longer predicated on loss and subordination, but rather on strength and renewal. Maraini herself proclaims the revolutionary potential of the real and symbolic mother-daughter bond, defining it as a threat to patriarchal order and essential to a woman's renewed sense of self. The relationship is, she maintains, "a very serious threat, because patriarchy rests on the division between mother and daughter. The mother must side with the father in support of patriarchal law. If the mother sides with the daughter it is seen as a threat to the equilibrium of male supremacy within the family."[25] When extended to History, this revision occurs when historical figures are assumed as symbolic mothers in a relationship that mirrors the revised bond with the biological mother.

Translated into adult relationships, the original and now renewed maternal bond can also be symbolically recast through sisterhood. Sisterhood, investigated at length in several of Maraini's works, can form through friends, or, in a renewed scenario, between mother and daughter, whose adult roles are metaphorically interchangeable.[26] One woman is daughter to a symbolic mother, who acts as guide and helps the daughter recognize her strengths. By reformulating family relationships to include the bond between women as fundamental to women's subjectivity and sense of self, Maraini showcases the importance of the maternal and of sisterhood to the feminist movement and to the individual woman's sense of self-in-relationship.

The symbolic placement necessary to a reconstruction of *storia* is made possible through the adoption of genres that empower women by liberating their voices and allowing them to express themselves. These generic choices reflect the need to expose the reality of women's lives and to counter the frequent portrayals of women as submissive wives and conniving mistresses. According to Sally Robinson, whose work analyzes the literary interpretation of female subjectivity, women's literature can engage in a *contestatory practice of narrative*, engendering, in turn, a *contestatory practice of reading*. This type of narrative places women in a mediating space both "inside" and "outside" conventional discourses of gender. To be "inside," Robinson argues, signifies working within conventional narrative strategies; to be "outside," meanwhile, connotes a manipulation and, in essence, a subversion of those strategies to open up new or alternative sites for self-representation.[27] This "outsider" position is consonant with

Rachel DuPlessis' notion of "writing beyond the ending," in which women engage as they write works that contest traditionally prescribed endings for their heroines. Conventional narratives provide two possible outcomes for heroines' stories, the euphoric—or happy—ending, prescribed when heroines follow the designated path to marriage, and the dysphoric ending—or death—prescribed when heroines deviate from this path.[28] Women creating contestatory narratives extend their heroines' stories by either investigating what occurs beyond them, or by providing the stories with open, undefined endings showcasing potentiality.

Contestatory narrative practices evolve out of women's historical condition. In her insightful work *Le donne e la letteratura*, Elisabetta Rasy argues that for most women confinement of their written expression to the domestic sphere has meant confinement to such private and personal canvases as diaries, letters, and confessionals. Since there is no mediator between author and subject (no omniscient narrator, for example), these genres minimize the distance between writer and written, allowing the author or heroine to express herself in the first person and granting her voice immediacy.[29] But despite their private nature, these "feminine" genres help bridge the gap between the private and the public, for they have allowed women to extend their lives beyond the domestic sphere and into the public realm of readership. Contemporary authors have recuperated these genres and created what Rasy calls a *controletteratura* [counter-literature]. Through this deliberate technique, they have (re)created literary history, situating themselves in the tradition of women's cultural production and ensuring representation of their own visions not only within that history but within a more general literary context as well.

Anna Nozzoli and Carol Lazzaro-Weis have charted this *controletteratura* in 1970s and 1980s literature. According to Nozzoli, women writers of the 1970s were largely concerned with closing and eventually effacing the gap between the private and political. This endeavor included raising the public's perception of traditional definitions and representations of gender. To this end, women authors worked with such first-person generic forms as the autobiography and privileged a more "realistic" language that reflected their protagonists' socioeconomic class.[30] In the 1980s, attention to this endeavor was transformed into the more theoretical concerns of sexual difference. Reasons for this, Lazzaro-Weis argues, were the shortcomings of the "former unifying category among women, that of belonging to an oppressed class, with a common gender identification."³¹ The new angles in approach analyze gender codifications and stratifications to understand women's social and cultural status as "other."

Situated in this rich cultural and revisionary tradition, Maraini's narratives provide a formalistic and thematic link in the genealogical chain of women's authorship. Her generic choices clearly represent the refusal to shape her thematic concerns to fit rigid structures representative of traditional aesthetic concerns. This project is delineated in the poem "Le poesie delle donne" [Women's Poems], a description that loosely applies to her work in other genres as well. When a male critic contends that women's poetry lacks the aesthetic qualities so cherished in male poetry and that would render it "timeless" and "official," the poet responds, "A woman who writes poetry . . . / . . . can only make herself stick / closely to the subject because sophistication / of form is something that goes with power / and the power a woman has is always a / non-power. . . ."³²

Ultimately, these choices have a more general appeal that goes beyond the formalistic debate expressed in "Le poesie delle donne." Because they allow Maraini's heroines to express themselves through, at least in theory, unmediated voices, they provide readers themselves with points of reference for analyzing their own experiences. Maraini's work in theater offers particularly interesting insight into the way this formalistic debate eventually leads to a practice of symbolic placement for author, character, and reader/viewer. It reflects Maraini's commitment to expressing women's concerns in public forums.³³ The author's involvement in theater originally developed out of the political need to create a space of *decentramento* [decentralization], operating outside mainstream theater and bringing theater to the working-class districts of Rome. In the late 1960s, along with authors Alberto Moravia, Enzo Siciliano, and others, she founded the *Compagnia del Porcospino* [Porcupine Company] and produced several pieces concerned with the actual dynamics of theater. Several years later, she created *Compagnia Blu* [Blue Company], through which her program of *decentramento* brought theater to a working-class audience in Rome's *Centocelle* quarter. Finally, in 1973 she formed the now-defunct feminist theater group *La Maddalena* to counter women's marginalization from theater production.³⁴

With the exception of more widely known playwrights such as Natalia Ginzburg, in Maraini's early career there were few female playwrights whose voices were heard on the Italian stage. With the creation of *La Maddalena,* Maraini resolved to provide women with a collective site to write and produce plays and to learn the technical workings of theater. Within this group, she produced some of her more famous and internationally renowned texts.[35] Maraini's theatrical productions exposed and challenged the social stage upon which women have for centuries performed "strategic acts of gender." For Maraini theater offers a "clue to the present" as modern theater is symbolically linked to its origins.[36] The stage serves as a powerful metaphor for women's symbolic placement in history, culture, and society. The author herself defines it as a female form.[37] Referring to the theatrical Eleusinian mysteries and to classic works by Euripides and Aeschylus in a discussion of women's theater, she explains her position by creating an image of theater that situates it in the female body, suggestive of yet another aspect of symbolic placement in space and time: "[T]he female body contains mystery and metamorphosis, the miracle of gestation and birth. Mythology describes it to us through the first acts of Gea and the first theatrical Eleusinian mysteries tied to the cult of Demeter."[38]

Emilia Costantini underscores this practice of symbolic placement on the stage in her definition of theater as a " developing collective female consciousness."[39] Symbolic placement within this collective female consciousness is an endeavor undertaken by feminist playwrights, whose pieces are meant to raise social awareness of women's condition. In order to bridge the gap between private and public spheres and to grant their vision immediacy, they adopt styles that encourage a more direct relationship with the audience. This practice constructs new narrative spaces that break from the rigidity of traditional Aristotelian form and eliminate distanciation between stage and public, often even blurring the line between actors and audience. To achieve this, some playwrights adopt a Brechtian style, in which actors, either in or out of character, directly relate to the audience or present debates to raise the public's consciousness about specific issues. Gigliola Franco, for example, has written such pieces as *Su da brave bambine* [Come Now, Like Good Little Girls] (1978) to be performed by non-professional actors in neighborhoods and schools and to be followed by audience discussion. The main purpose of her productions is to give relevancy to her revision of the family, which sees the mother-as-indoctrinator transformed into a "feminist friend."[40] Other pieces, such as "Happening in strada" [Happening in the Streets] (1977) by Flavia Bacichi's women's collective, are meant to be performed in the streets in mime as a demonstration against traditional roles, socialization, and modes of (voiced) expression, and the rigid and confining setting of mainstream theater.[41] These presentations were designed to shorten the distance between action and meaning and actor and public. In the case of pieces like Franco's the audience becomes a maker of meaning, while in pieces like Bacichi's it becomes a virtual participant in the action by proximity to it.

While theater is an effective example of women's physical symbolic placement, it can also facilitate women's placement in historical context. Texts bringing historical figures alive through a woman's perspective, for example, are a convincing practice of revisionary history, one Maraini has undertaken in several theatrical texts. In revisionary plays such as *I sogni di Clitennestra* [Clytemnestra's Dreams], a revision of Aeschylus' *Oresteia*) (1981), *Maria Stuarda* [Mary Stuart], a revision of Schiller's *Mary Stuart*) (1981), *Sor Juana Inès de la Cruz* (based on the Mexican nun's famous letter on women's rights) (1981), and *Veronica, meretrice e scrittora* [Veronica, Prostitute and Writer], based on sixteenth-century poet and courtesan Veronica Franco) (1992), she recreates sites of symbolic placement that reveal the other side of lives that have been historically told in connection to the dominant culture. These social practices of theater are indeed valuable forms of symbolic placement. As such, they represent an important contribution to those signifying practices constituting subjectivity. In the end, through its potential to revise space, theater can be an effective tool in women's revision of relational spaces both in the private and public spheres.

Practices of symbolic placement, subjective expression, and self-representation are also explored through the cinematic medium. Maraini's work in cinema spans a variety of subgenres, from the feature-length 1969 film *L'amore coniugale* [Conjugal Love] to her work in documentary (*Aborto: parlano le donne* [Abortion: Women Speak] and *Ritratti di donne africane* [Portraits of African Women] [both 1976]). She recognizes the potential of cinema to allow her to more closely approach female subjectivity and the women she films. While her films, especially the documentaries, give women a voice, in the three films I examine in this study, the 1978 *Mio padre amore mio* [My Father, My Love], the 1978 *La bella addormentata nel bosco* [Sleeping Beauty], and the 1979 *Giochi di latte* [Milk Games], Maraini creates cinematic discourses on motherhood and daughterhood through her own gaze.[42]

While considering herself a writer who occasionally works in film, Maraini has used the camera and the profilmic territory beyond it to create sites for and visually manipulate female identity formation. The three above films challenge classic Hollywood cinema, generally upheld as a paradigm of filmmaking. This cinema constructs a linear narrative through sequential and invisible editing; focuses on the passive identification of the male and female audience with the principle male character, who advances the action and represents dominant values; and features formulaic and invisible duplication of conventional gender roles. Through the traditional cinematic constructs of, for example, time, space, and narrative which privilege the male subject, the resulting cinematic representations serve to reproduce and, consequently, reinforce values of the dominant culture. As a result, the female body is objectified and rendered the sole site of women's expression.[43]

Mio padre, *La bella*, and *Giochi* revise these conventional aspects of classic cinema by symbolically placing the heroine in a position of subjectivity in the visual narrative. They create a visual language whose syntax is apparent and does not draw the viewer into a position of passivity vis-à-vis the narrative. Rather, through such devises as symbolic editing (rather than the invisible suture of classic cinema), "real" time (rather than fictional time used to propel the plot forward), and nonlinear narrative lacking closure, Maraini's films situate the spectator in a position of contestatory viewing.

For these choices, Maraini's films can be defined as "counter-cinema," a term Claire Johnston coined to describe feminist challenges to classic cinema.[44] At the same time, as they challenge conventional modes of representation, they can be loosely categorized as "deconstructive" films, which, according to Annette Kuhn, "[speak] from politically oppositional positions or [concern themselves] with subject matters commonly ignored or repressed in dominant cinema."[45] The dialogueless *Mio padre*, *La bella*, and *Giochi* convey meaning through cinematic language by allowing "the filmic images to speak" and by focusing the cinematic discourse on a prelinguistic, purely imagistic expression of the self.[46]

In a Freudian interpretation of women's filmmaking, Paola Melchiori equates deconstructive, counter-cinema with women's fascination with images. While defining women's approach to cinema as an expression of the desire for the maternal body, her notion holds broader implications for our study of Maraini's investigation of motherhood and daughterhood. According to Melchiori, deconstructive cinema subconsciously recalls past acts in an individual's personal history, reconstructing them through cinematic narrative.[47] In Maraini's case, deconstructing and laying out the geography of the heroines' formation as (looking) subjects ultimately involves reappropriating their relationship with the mother and the father, the original site of subject formation.[48]

The revolutionary reconstruction of one's history informs Maraini's practices in prose and poetry as well, in which these signifying practices not only give thematic shape to her works, but also determine the very enunciatory act of writing. Maraini's description of the way she conceptualized writing as a child before she could read and write, "Words . . . closed in the body," is a nod to a subjective perception of the self awaiting inclusion in and as cultural syntax.[49] The "words" to which Maraini refers were signs she would draw as a child inside egg-shaped people. The egg, an ideologically charged symbol enclosing signifiers/signs, has remarkable implications for a study of women's writing. It represents a symbolic and culturally weighty female space of self-expression and re-production. Roland Barthes' notion that writing is playing with the mother's body (a notion Maraini herself refers to when asked why she writes) sheds light on our consideration of this issue when combined with Jacques Lacan's assertion that language is desire. For Lacan, language is predicated on a lack—the possible absence of the "real" objects to which it refers, the use of one word to the exclusion of others.[50] Because language represents a lack and rouses desire, the subject longs to return to the moment of fullness in her/his life, the moment in which s/he inhabited the prelinguistic sphere. Significantly, because the mother occupies it, the desire to return to this sphere signifies the desire to recuperate the maternal body. The Barthian and Lacanian notions, coupled with the Italian feminist revaluation of the mother-daughter relationship, ensure a re-experiencing of that relationship where the acquisition of women's sense of self becomes associated with a female figure.[51]

In prose, as we have seen, some of the most powerful twentieth-century texts contest women's condition through the autobiography, journal, and epistolary, and in many cases offer a revisionist image of the family. Sibilla Aleramo's autobiographical novel *Una donna* (A Woman) (1906), for example, narrates the author's contentious relationship with feminine codes of behavior and traces her progress toward liberation. Alba de Cespedes' novel *Quaderno proibito* [The Secret] (1952) is a housewife's journal that articulates her struggle for liberation from the confining reality of the 1950s domestic sphere. Oriana Fallaci's 1975 epistolary *Lettera a un bambino mai nato* [Letter to a Child Never Born], meanwhile, is a letter from a woman to her unborn child; the woman voices her thoughts over her impending motherhood. In all three exemplary cases, words are closely linked to the narrator-heroine through the use of the first-person narrative. The reader, for his or her part, is allowed entry into previously hidden private spaces of the lives of the female narrators.

In poetry, female poets have broken with formal structures and focused on thematic concerns to more directly convey meaning. Discussing the rejection of formal conventions in women's poetry, Laura di Nola divides form and content into spatial categories of the ahistorical (universal) and historical (relative): Eschewing poetry that incorporates formalistic convention, and is therefore "immobile in a time without history," for one that focuses on content signifies creating immediate exposure to individual concerns.[52] The focus, therefore, is on the personal and quotidian. Titles of poems collected in the anthology *poesia femminista italiana* [Italian Feminist Poetry] bear witness to these choices, "Sono stanca di me" [I'm tired of me], "Inno all'utero" [Hymn to my uterus], and "Un pezzo di pane" [A piece of bread].

Maraini's representation of the hidden realities captured by the titles included in Di Nola's collection is the focus of my study. Chapter 1 analyzes the development of the daughter's identity and agency in the spaces carved out for her within the family and the spaces she herself constructs outside and inside it. It subsequently examines the way in which through this construction and when voicing her concerns the daughter inscribes herself into history. The chapter is based on the premise that the daughter occupies an ambivalent place inside the family, for her identity is caught between identification—as a woman—with the mother and allegiance—as participant in social discourse—to the father. In order to understand the daughter's dilemma, I examine those psychoanalytic and anthropological theories that generally describe the daughter as occupying a precarious space between two spheres. In the case of Freudian psychoanalysis, she must develop away from a state of symbiosis with the mother toward social identification with the father, only to re-identify with the maternal role when she herself becomes a mother, the expected fulfillment of her identity as a woman. In the anthropological theory of Claude Lévi-Strauss, her exchange between two families ensures the inception and perpetuation of culture and civilization. The problematic figure of the daughter occupies a parallel intermediary space in feminist theory, only here her role within that space is subverted and rendered empowering for women, the mother included.

The daughter's discourse in Maraini's works evolves into a liberatory one that creates new relational spaces for women to occupy. For this reason, following Lynda Boose's inspiring dyad "daughter-father relationship" that undermines the secondary role accorded to her in the traditional "father-daughter" union, I use the terms "daughter-father" and "daughter-mother" to showcase the daughter's burgeoning subjectivity in familial relationships.[53] As the agent of change, the daughter inhabits sites where relational discourses intersect and where they undergo revision. In some texts the daughter contemplates her relationship with her father and mother; i.e., the 1966 poetry collection *Crudeltà all'aria aperta* [Cruelty in the Open Air] and the 1978 film *Mio padre amore mio*. Here, the discourse evolves into one in which all participants occupy subjective spaces in the relationship. In other works, such as the 1974 poetry collection *Donne mie* [My Women], the daughter becomes a woman struggling to define subjectivity in social relationships: she strives for personal growth and for change for all women through the women's movement.

Chapter 2 charts the evolution of the portrayal of the maternal figure in Maraini's texts alongside the developing Italian feminist discourse on the changing experiences of motherhood in postwar Italian society. It uses Freudian psychoanalytic theory to investigate restrictive definitions of motherhood that have shaped its image in the twentieth century, and feminist revisions of psychoanalytic theory to analyze the new potential of motherhood Maraini's works proffer. As the chapter shows, the trajectory of the maternal experience is not one that easily evolves from an image of the oppressed mother to an image of the empowered mother liberated from a stifling role, even if this trajectory traverses the women's movement from the 1960s on and is informed by its revisionary theories and practices. Rather, Maraini's depiction remains a problematic one, consonant with the difficulty of transforming such a socially, culturally, and historically weighty role that is still a much contended and embattled space.

The reality of the maternal experience is clearly present in Maraini's opus. More specifically, at the same time that the author's works provide revisionary spaces for expression of the maternal experience, the discourse they create does not consistently map out viable sites in which women actually participate in liberatory experiences of motherhood. In earlier works (the 1963 novel *L'età del malessere* [The Age of Discontent] and the 1966 poem "Madre canina" [Canine Mother]), the maternal figure is problematically drawn according to conventional notions of motherhood and is situated as someone to be rejected by the daughter. She occupies the dark recesses of the domestic sphere and lacks awareness of her oppressive situation. The familial space institutionalizes her role and creates a disempowering identity of effacement. In later works informed by 1970s and 1980s feminist theories on and practices of women's relationships, such as the film *Giochi di latte* and the poem "Demetra ritrovata" [Demeter Regained], however, the maternal figure assumes a wider ranging identity in the daughter's life. This identity encompasses the role of guide into the public sphere and into subjectivity.

Chapter 3 focuses on sisterhood against the backdrop of the Italian feminist practices of *autocoscienza* [consciousness-raising], *affidamento* [entrustment], and *rispecchiamento* [mirroring]. These practices, recalling the daughter's initial identification with the mother, create friendships between women that are based on reflection. The resulting reflective dialogue opens the individual up to new experiences and to new possibilities revealed in and through the other.

The experiences of Italian women, while not entirely parallel given class and regional differences, have been shaped and lived under similar (i.e., Italian, Western, patriarchal) institutions.[54] In the 1970s and 1980s, Italian feminists participated in practices of *autocoscienza* and *affidamento* which helped women articulate their personal histories to others. *Autocoscienza*, a collective practice of consciousness-raising, involved discovering and understanding oneself through dialogue with other women. In this relationship, women discussed personal experiences and used each other as mirrors [*rispecchiamento*] for their lives, assuming as points of reference for their own histories the lives and experiences of their female interlocutors.[55] *Affidamento*, historically practiced but not theorized until the 1980s, is an extension of *autocoscienza* and involves one woman entrusting herself to another. Offering an alternative to the exclusive identification with the father during development into the Symbolic, this relationship presents a woman as a point of reference for the individual's development. Entrustment revalorizes the maternal presence in a woman's life, a presence that becomes a very personal point of reference transcending even time—it can either be one's own biological mother or a *symbolic mother*. *Ideally*—though this is realistically not always the case—the relationship does not revolve around strategies of power, but is rather a bond of reciprocity in which the diversity between the women enriches their experiences, their perspectives of themselves and the world around them. This configuration ultimately mirrors the pre-Oedipal mother-daughter bond outside the Symbolic.[56]

Although potentially problematic, I use the term "sisterhood" as a metaphor for these practices and for women's friendships in Maraini's texts. My choice of the term is based on several factors: First, it is a historical term grounded in 1970s feminism, the period in which friendships between women were defined as political choices and in which they appear most frequently in Maraini's opus. Second, it defines what I consider to be the paradigm for women's liberation, for women's agency, and for women's identity evolving from Maraini's works. Third, it relates to the renewed "familial" spaces these works construct. The practice of sisterhood is an important part of the adult woman's exploration of self and identity. Indeed, this weighty relationship provides a significant metaphor in Maraini's work. Sisterhood, not only in the capacity of female friendships but also of female community, problematically recalls a familial relationship and, with it, a familial dynamic. However, in Maraini's production, it extends beyond the strict spatial reality of the nuclear family. While a woman's primary identity is formed within the family, where social identity is defined by the father, occupier of the public, or Symbolic, sphere of language and power, her adult identity and agency can be shaped in relation to other women, and the benefits can extend to other relationships.

I argue in this chapter, therefore, that relationships with other women are not symbolically disassociated from the family sphere. Rather, they create relational spaces that symbolically mirror and redirect the most beneficial aspects of the family. As a result, the figure of the mother is not rejected in sisterhood. On the contrary, either the biological mother or a woman who symbolically plays out the role of primary guide in the daughter's life plays a significant role in the daughter's sense of self and of social, cultural, and historical situatedness as a woman. This bond is not a one-way experience, however. The relationship between "mother" and "daughter" is one of mirroring, in which the mother becomes "daughter" to the daughter and benefits from the daughter's activity in the newly evolving women's movement. Moreover, the relationship with the father can benefit as well. As seen in several works, the daughter's agency and sense of self as a woman allow her to revise the bond with the father into one of two (different) relating subjects.

The conclusion recapitulates the major points of this study while positioning Maraini within the context of the growing focus on women and the family. As women occupy more powerful positions in society, the family undergoes substantial revision in both the way it is lived and depicted. Not only has stricter legislation been passed that ensures women's rights both inside and outside the family, and women's groups are continuing to direct their work through grassroots organizations, but women's literary and cinematic portrayals of the family continue to command an impressive position within the cultural landscape. Within this context, Maraini's exploration of women's experiences continues to uncover unsettling realities. At the same time, however, its focus on the family persists in redefining the relational spaces women occupy.

1
Daughterhood

> If we can . . . recapture the feelings and thoughts of the daughter, we will be able to chart the internal geography of femininity. . . . It was the experience and the institution of daughterhood that prepared us to know ourselves as women.[1]

> Is it but . . . a tardiness in nature / which often leaves the history unspoke / That it intends to do?[2]

DACIA MARAINI'S TEXTS FEATURING THE DAUGHTER CREATE A discursive space in which the daughter negotiates between her understanding of her own experiences and the cultural story defining the daughterly role. The works analyzed in this chapter are chiefly written in the first person, both as an autobiographical act of self-expression and as a way to initiate a public dialogue within the social and cultural metanarrative of daughterhood. Earlier ones focus primarily on the father-daughter relationship. Later works, however, also revise the relationship with the mother, rejected in some postwar feminist texts as threatening to the daughter's happiness and psychoanalytic development, but later deemed essential to women's liberation in feminist theory.

The narratives examined in this study investigate the origins of the daughter's story and the anxieties arising from her position as an intermediary figure between mother and father, domestic and public spaces. As they chart the daughter's experiences within the family, they expose problematic issues in the daughter's life arising in and from the family. At the same time, however, they also reveal the daughter's own reaction to her situation and her deliberate revision of her cultural story. In works written before the 1970s women's movement, Maraini's daughters resist a relationship with the mother, clearly a result of the absence of an alternative cultural matrix to the mother's role as indoctrinator and enforcer of patriarchal laws. With the perspective of a more developed feminist ideology, however, the daughter revises her narrative through the very act of rereading and rewriting.

When inspired and reeducated by the women's movement, the daughter understands that the development of subjectivity lies in reinstating a mutual, loving bond with the mother and with other women, a subversive act challenging the mother's subsidiary role in the adult daughter's entry into the public sphere. "Many daughters," Maraini asserts, "have the father as their emotional reference point because often it is the father who mediates between culture and the maturing daughter. It is the father, not the mother, who moves freely in culture."[3] While feminist theory concentrates more often on the mother's place than the father's in the daughter's life, Maraini's texts also highlight the father's position as central figure in the daughter's development. Significantly, this focus serves a subversive function as well. Through rereadings of both maternal and paternal bonds the narrating daughter redefines her relationship with both mother and father, so that the two figures do not frustrate her quest for liberation, but rather factor eventually as key participants in her development as a liberated woman.

If we investigate the theoretical discourses defining daughterhood within its familial context, we find that the daughter appears weak and coopted into a patriarchal system of gendered roles and relationships. In its historical configuration, the family has regulated daughterhood and ensured the daughter's development into submissive sociocultural roles. Consequently, this identity might at first reading seem problematic for feminists to assume in their project for women's liberation. As a symbolic identity, however, it contains possibilities for renewal and change. Indeed, in feminist considerations of daughterhood, the daughter's location between the domestic and public spheres is considered a privileged social position. Although her identity is defined by the domestic roles she is interpellated to fulfill, it also contains the possibility of engaging in activities in the public sphere that showcase her individuality and intellectual capabilities and through which she can effect change.

When developing a theory of female subjectivity, the members of the Milan Women's Bookstore Collective maintain that it is necessary for women to redefine and create alternative spaces to inhabit, and to replace themselves in history by establishing new symbolic frames of reference, specifically constituted by relationships between women.

In this proposal, the Collective does not explicitly emphasize the link between this symbolic (re)birth and daughterhood. However, the task of determining a symbolic placement for women does indeed rest *symbolically* on the daughter figure, whose identity is determined either by the relationship with a biological mother or by a symbolic relationship with a female historical figure, or symbolic mother. As symbolic daughter, she is born out of a cultural matrix that determines her identity as a woman; as biological daughter, she is born of a woman who plays a physical and social role in shaping that identity.

Extending the Collective's proposed pattern and constructing spaces for a feminist redefinition of womanhood entails a woman's repositioning herself as daughter in social and cultural relationships and/or writing the daughter's story from a subjective point of view. Such a revision permits women to investigate their development into their feminine identity and to redefine the trajectory of their (re)birth. This renaissance is central to an analysis of women's literary representations of womanhood and the development of post-war Italian feminist theory. When writers and theorists explicitly place the "daughter" in the configurations of relationships outlined by the Collective, they reveal the potential of daughterhood to be a revolutionary identity both within the family and outside it.

Although on a theoretical level it can be a fortuitous location, this intermediary position can also present existential problems. The access to realms both inside and outside the family causes the daughter to bear the tensions existing between them. On the one hand, she is prepared within the family to fulfill such expected roles as motherhood and wifehood. On the other hand, the public sphere of intellectual pursuits and careers is no longer outside the realm of possibility for her. But her entry into public institutions such as education and the work place can lead to complications. Given such realities as time constraints and physical and psychological demands, it can be difficult for her to juggle her public duties and her domestic ones. On the level of personal relationships, this entry sets her on a trajectory often requiring the rejection of either the opportunities available in the domestic realm or the ones available in the public sphere.

The tension the daughter bears is highlighted by her location within the Western family saga as well, where her role often represents an intersection between nature and culture. Occupying the position Claude Lévi-Strauss has found to be essential to the existence of culture, she has the potential to unbalance the very structure of society.

Her mere presence, especially as a member of the women's movement, reminds us of the power contained in her position between two traditionally divergent "realities" of being. To surmount this threat, cultural theories have generated definitions of daughterhood designed to ensure stability.

Feminist studies of her place in Western culture argue that the daughter has been largely absent from official culture because traditional patterns of daughterhood validate her absence in the form of her nonaction, or nonsubjective participation in its inception of culture.[4] This assessment of the daughter's story reflects in part the place defined for her by Lévi-Strauss' theory of structural anthropology, which describes the relationships comprising society and a civilized state. In an exogamous system of exchange between kinship groups, it is the daughter who ensures the passage out of a natural or uncivilized state of marriage within a kinship group into a complex cultural system regulated by the prohibition of incest. As the "supreme gift" from one group to another, she does not control cultural means of production, but rather occupies the position between nature and culture.[5] While Lévi-Strauss' theory reads her exchange as what makes culture possible and preserves it, Freudian psychoanalysis has formulated a theory of daughterly development supporting women's extraneousness from culture. Not only does Freud maintain women's entry into heterosexuality and motherhood as evidence of normalcy, but he also defines their psychic state as incapable of achieving cultural currency. A woman must transfer her primary desire for an exclusive relationship with the mother to the father. This transference advances her development into "normal femininity," because it prepares her for the heterosexual union in which she becomes a mother and through which she ultimately completes the cycle of femininity. This cycle, however, places the daughter in a bind. In one of his few studies dedicated to female sexuality, Freud argues that since girls do not fully evolve out of the Oedipal complex, their superego, or ability to participate in the construction of social regulation, "cannot attain the strength and independence which give it its cultural significance."[6]

In these scenarios, the positions the father and mother occupy vis-à-vis the daughter become problematic. The father's privileged sociocultural position creates an impasse in his relationship with the daughter, in that especially in Freudian and later Lacanian psychoanalysis he stands as both socializing presence and governing symbol of the heterosexual union the daughter should enter into in adulthood. As Maraini herself explains, when the daughter endeavors to gain an independent identity within the family, she is anchored by the social law the father represents: "This is a father's society, in which imagination, eroticism, fantasy, and means belong to the father. Even the language we speak is patriarchal. Everything refers back to the father."[7] For her part, the mother is regarded as a figure similar to the daughter because she is a woman. However, despite being a foundation for understanding and solidarity, this closeness infuses the relationship with tension. The mother, a socializer like the father and the one generally held responsible for the daughter's development into femininity, represents their generational differences in sociocultural outlook and the figure the daughter must abandon in the process of individuation.

These configurations have historically been depicted in literary representations of the family, where we often see the daughter struggling to negotiate a space for herself. Perhaps not surprisingly, more conventional depictions reflect the structural anthropological description of the daughter's location. In such exemplary narratives as Luigi Pirandello's play *Sei personaggi in cerca d'autore* [Six Characters in Search of an Author] (1906), Maria Messina's collection of short stories, *Casa paterna* [Father's House] (1991), and Alberto Moravia's novel *Gli indifferenti* [The Time of Indifference] (1929), the daughter occupies a tenuous position within the family and holds no, or very little authority. Pirandello's piece peels away the psychological layers, or *masks* comprising social identity—the daughter's included. Moravia's novel, meanwhile, considers changes in interpersonal relations developing in interwar Italy, transformations impacting the daughter's outlook. Perhaps because they capture women's experiences as daughters, Messina's short stories are more insular, focusing on the way family shapes a daughter's possibilities and choices. Within the textual economy of the three works, the daughter, especially in Moravia's work, is a modern figure in her subversive attitude toward her role. However, despite her bold characterization she still ultimately bears the tension between domestic and public realms, her tale denied the desired euphoric ending.

The daughter in *Sei personaggi* is the figure on whom the incest taboo, so central to the anthropological definition of culture, is marked. While the explicit representation of the taboo is not an innovation of Pirandello's work, the portrayal of the consequences of the transgression of sexual mores within the context of modernizing Italian culture opens a window onto the daughter's position within the changing sexual politics of the period. In this period of Italian history, the first phase of the women's movement was struggling for women's rights in areas of education and labor. Meanwhile, women authors such as Matilde Serao, Grazia Deledda, and Sibilla Aleramo were putting female voices on the cultural map and often expressing women's experiences through autobiographies, bringing the personal into the public sphere of readership. Within this context, Pirandello's play creates a powerful image of the daughter's potential to unbalance the status quo.

In the play, the daughter is stepdaughter (called simply *la figliastra*) to the male protagonist, who, nevertheless and tellingly, is called "the father" [*il padre*]. After a long absence, the two meet again, without at first recognizing each other, when she is eighteen years old and working as a prostitute. The encounter occurs in the sexualized setting of the daughter's workplace, and even though she comes close to but does not ultimately transgress the incest taboo, the stepdaughter destabilizes the familial situation both through her physicality and through her assessment of the situation, "But is it possible . . . to expect from me—'afterwards'—that I act like a modest lady, well brought up and virtuous, in agreement with his damned aspirations 'to an unfailing moral fortitude'?" (61). The daughter's threat to moral convention comes not only through her presence, but also through her own participation in the reconstruction of the scene in front of her family, the actors who are to reproduce the scene, and the viewing/reading public. Through her explicit interpretation of the encounter she constructs meaning for herself within the narrative and ultimately threatens the cultural authority her father and the play director represent, "but I want to represent my story, mine!" (96).

In Messina's collection, the daughter's subversion does not rest on her sexuality, but rather on her awareness of her stifling situation. In the first short story, "Casa paterna," originally published in 1911, the daughter Vanna bears the tension between her father and husband's house, her father and husband's authority. Virtually abandoned in the domestic sphere by her lawyer husband in Rome, she escapes to her father's house, daring to venture back to her native land alone. However, once back, her family does not make her feel welcome, as her authorized place is with her husband. Both father and husband are virtually absent from the tale. Their authority does not need to be represented, however, because their presence is already marked by Vanna's role as daughter/wife, and by the father's house and repeated allusions to the husband's. Caught between these two authorities ("Now that she was rejected by her paternal house, she grasped at her husband"),[8] Vanna commits suicide. "L'ora che passa" [The Passing Hour] (1918), meanwhile, represents the effects of the daughter's indoctrinated obligation toward the family. Although desirous of independence, the schoolteacher Rosalia remains bound to the family and pays the price for her repressive situation, "A voice inside her warned her not to abandon the family. Her entire youth sacrificed to the family. There was no more pain in her heart, but just a calm melancholy" (51, 55).

While Pirandello's daughter represents a tragic figure of sexual politics, and Messina's stories depict the oppressiveness of family obligation, the daughter in Moravia's novel reflects the social and sexual tensions produced by the changing mores of the interwar period. In this period, the developing women's movement focused on gaining political and social rights. At the same time, however, the social and economic crises growing out of World War I hindered the advancement of women's participation in the public sphere. The Fascist regime's campaign for restabilizing postwar society included the enforcement of conventional gender categories and the advancement of programs promoting the traditional family roles of mother and wife.[9] In Moravia's text, the disruption of gender roles resulting from the social and economic changes brought on by WWI inform the novel's depiction of the daughter Carla. More specifically, Carla represents the destabilizing force of women's sexual emancipation. Her modern attitude toward sex produces tensions within the family: Her active pursuit of an affair with her mother's lover makes evident the daughter's threat to propriety. At the same time, it highlights and accentuates the mother's own ambivalence toward gender regulation, which stems from the tension between her age and maternal role and her desire to live a sexual relationship.[10]

Feminist portrayals of the daughter in the family saga, meanwhile, examine the other side of this threat. They assume the daughter's story as focal point of the narrative, questioning the regulation of daughterhood and at times even exploding the primacy of the family over the individual. In the autobiographical text *La mela e il serpente* [The Apple and the Serpent] (1974), for example, Armanda Guiducci approaches her personal history through psychoanalytic and historical analysis, retracing the sociocultural development of her story as daughter within the family. In Teresa Ancona's *Una famiglia normale* [A Normal Family] (1974), a marriage of fiction and psychoanalysis, the daughter is the subject of a spiraling psychological drama that pits her against the stifling feminine attributes her mother espouses. Meanwhile, in Gabriella Magrini's *Lunga giovinezza* [Long Adolescence] (1976) the protagonist's identity as an adult woman is analyzed and interpreted through the momentous relationships shaping social identity, most notably the daughter's relationship with her mother and father.[11] Collectively, these texts underscore the importance of deconstructing and revising the daughter's story as they investigate the development of her identity within the family.

Often, works featuring the daughter focus primarily on her relationship with either the father or the mother. The greater focus on one rather than the other creates a more in-depth view of the daughter's movement within it, and carves out a literary space not only for the daughter, but also for the bond's evolution. In works focusing on the daughter-father relationship, the emphasis frequently lies on the daughter's desire to reconstruct the relationship with her father in which he no longer represents an unattainable symbol of social authority.

Works such as Gianna Manzini's autobiography *Ritratto in piedi* [Portrait Standing Up] (1971), Mariateresa Di Lascia's novel *Passaggio in ombra* [Passage into the Shadows] (1995), and Maria Luisa Aguirre D'Amico's novel *L'ombra del padre* [The Father's Shadow] (1997) showcase the daughter's admiration for and dedication to the father. Manzini's text is a subtly rhapsodic memoir of her father, who is her gateway to the world and to writing, her life métier. Although the relationship is indeed, and perhaps naturally defined by moments of joy and moments of tension brought on by the daughter's resistance to the father's authority, he is the figure with whom she measures her life.[12] Di Lascia's novel, meanwhile, recounts the young Chiara's longing for her father, who periodically abandons the family. The daughter's bond with her father is developed both by contact with him and his family, and through the act of epistolary correspondence. The events constituting the relationship and the daughter's yearning define Chiara's first-person account of her youth.[13] Similar to these two works, D'Amico's text investigates the daughter's desire to solidify the relationship with her father. The father in this novel, however, is largely absent, a present absence that casts a "shadow" on the daughter Eva's past and future decisions. This tale, which pits the daughter's relationship to her father against the backdrop of an unsuccessful marriage and unhappy periods spent outside Italy, provides the most clear understanding of the culturally problematic nature of the relationship.[14] That the father in D'Amico's text is an elusive figure and still plays a major role in the daughter's story speaks to his position in the daughter's story. The father's twofold social identity is revealed through the daughter's mnemonic journey: He is at once a figure who can move freely within and give shape to social discourse and he is the primary male figure in the daughter's life upon whom she bestows her burgeoning love. In foregrounding this figure in the daughter's story, all three works uncover the cultural dynamics shaping the relationship.

In works in which the daughter's relationship with her mother is foregrounded, a more strained and ambivalent bond is depicted. Unlike the father, the mother remains a known figure, the one whose similarity to the daughter and presence in the domestic sphere render her a constant point of reference in her offspring's memory. When the daughter contemplates this relationship, the mother becomes a problematic figure for the domestic destiny she represents. Indeed, this fact renders her a less sought-after and desired figure, as is the case in such works as Sibilla Aleramo's seminal *Una donna*, focused entirely or in part on the quest for the paternal.

In these works, however, the tension marking the relationship is often also accompanied by a turn towards the mother, as the daughter recognizes her own potential to help the mother achieve some degree of liberation. In some works, such as Francesca Sanvitale's novel *Madre e figlia* [Mother and Daughter] (1980), and Fabrizia Ramondino's novel *Althénopis* (1981) and play *Terremoto con madre e figlia* (1994), the importance of the daughter-mother relationship to the daughter's history is explored. In these texts, the narrating daughter regards the mother, if not always in a positive light, as a figure who inspires for its potential to give and to survive life, and who ultimately functions as a reference point for her history.

In other narratives, such as Alba De Céspedes' *Quaderno proibito* and Carla Cerati's *La cattiva figlia* [The Bad Daughter] (1990), the daughter revolutionizes female identity as she moves freely in both domestic and public realms and distances herself from the traditions her mother represents, not necessarily from the mother herself. Although in *Quaderno* the daughter-mother relationship is troubled, the daughter Mirella unveils to her mother Valeria new possibilities available in the public sphere. Mirella's sexual liberation is problematic for Valeria. However, the daughter's judgment of her mother's entrapment in the domestic sphere is informed by her own experience in the public arena and a relationship with a man based on both sexual pleasure and intellectual compatibility. Mirella's exhortation to her mother to ponder her situation voices Valeria's repressed awareness of it: "Think it out: What sort of life do you have with Papa?" (34). In Cerati's novel, meanwhile, the daughter invites her mother to accompany her to work one day. This symbolic gesture ultimately exposes the mother to a public discourse to which she is not normally a party: "I brought her with me to a debate on love. The average age of the women present was forty-five; only my mother was old. I saw her attentive, curious."[15]

In their readings of daughterhood, feminists infrequently dwell on the redefinition of the father's place in the daughter's life, focusing instead on the mother as they strive first to create a female-gendered frame of reference. Luciana Percovich and Anna Maria Piussi's challenge to traditional relational paradigms presents both the physical and symbolic reinstatement of the—a—mother-figure into the adult daughter's life. This act of female solidarity arises by the daughter's own hand and becomes a visible sign of the creation of a feminine lineage and a cultural matrix within which the mother and daughter exercise mutual guidance. Piussi and Percovich advocate revising and revalidating the daughter's relationship with the mother as a way to reconstruct representations of female experiences. Revision of the mother-daughter relationship directly challenges the traditional psychoanalytic configuration of women's development, insofar as it has conventionally been defined for, rather than by, women. Piussi sees the daughter's search for the mother figure as a quest for reestablishing female authority in her life.[16] While we shall see in chapter 2 that the mother can represent a problematic figure through her role as enforcer of conventional configurations of gender, the daughter can place her in the new cultural and social heritage she herself designs. Female reference points reconfigure the primary female figure as a symbolic guide for her developing identity as a woman in an age of feminist awakening. When the daughter (re)reads the mother's role in her life, she endows it with a new authority, for while traditionally the mother leads her into the domestic life that she enforces, the daughter now assumes her as a guide into a burgeoning female culture. The balance of power the daughter witnesses in social discourse is therefore seen through the mother. For Percovich, the recognition of the mother's potential value as an authority figure is a subversive act that privileges the daughter's position as intermediary between familial spaces and public sphere.[17] The daughter brings into the public sphere knowledge of the workings of the mother's domestic sphere and can address the needs of this domain through legislative changes and cultural transformation in attitude and language.

As interpreter of the familial sphere, the daughter occupies a powerful position to readjust the balance of power exercised there. This readjustment, therefore, should ideally result from a revision of family relationships. But a rescription of these relationships is a delicate process demanding external as well as internal support. In their depictions of the daughter's interpretation of these bonds, Maraini's narratives remain conscious of the powerful societal and cultural forces determining them. In earlier works, Maraini's daughters are aware of their situation but lack the tools and support to immediately change it. Their only means of escape from their cultural story is, literally, to escape the confines of family relationships. In later works, we see that the familial sphere has changed little, but that the daughter can participate in its reconstruction.

Maraini's early novel *L'età del malessere* [The Age of Discontent] (1963) is poised between the conventional 1950s, in which the daughter's successful entry into womanhood consisted of assuming the conventional ideals of femininity, and the rebellious late 1960s, a period in which student movements and second-wave feminism rebuked bourgeois ideals of the family at the heart of the social rebuilding of postwar Italy.[18] *L'età* features as protagonist a young woman whose development into adulthood undercuts the gender myths of 1950s Italy and foreshadows the later cultural changes generated by the sexual revolution of the late 1960s. Seventeen-year-old Enrica's actions reject the image of innocence and virtuousness ascribed to her as an adolescent. In this transitional position between adolescence and adulthood, her actions are performed in a state of semiconsciousness, which in later works produced at the height of the feminist movement develops into purposeful action. Enrica's tale creates a complex picture of the daughter's developing sense of self through her relationship with her family and her growing drive for self-actuation.[19]

L'età del malessere examines the difficulty the daughter encounters when struggling to define her identity within a milieu that perpetuates a discourse of conventional femininity. Yet this early work subverts the stifling ideals of womanhood by creating a daughter who evolves out of a state of impassivity to exercise agency. When she finally takes action and escapes at novel's end, this daughter creates a (matri)lineage with Aleramo's earlier autobiography by reflecting the ending of its predecessor. This reflection, in turn, foreshadows the heroine's escape at the end of Maraini's own *Donna in guerra* and *La lunga vita di Marianna Ucrìa* [The Silent Duchess] (1990), thus extending the genealogy of feminine escape from confining milieux. While this lineage in 1960s, 1970s, and 1980s Italy reminds us of the sociocultural failure to provide alternative possibilities within the family and domestic sphere, it nevertheless grounds the heroine in a cultural legacy that showcases agency.

The inability of literary characters to exercise agency has been invested with symbolic significance as they react—or fail to react—to external crises from which they feel alienated. In moments reflected in twentieth-century literature, such as the interwar years in Moravia's *Gli indifferenti* and the post-WWII economic crisis in Beppe Fenoglio's *La paga del sabato* [Saturday's Pay] (1969), this inertia is evidence of an existential crisis in which individual action has no meaning within a larger sociohistorical context.[20] The action thus becomes a nonaction, as the male protagonists are prompted by the pressures evolving out of their increasing sense of displacement in an ever-changing and impersonal world.

In Enrica's case, her (re)action is not determined by an external (historical) crisis, but rather by her body and sexuality, the physical signs of women's presence in the world. When she discovers she is pregnant, she decides to illegally terminate the pregnancy. Her act, especially in a moment when abortion was illegal, is transformed into the will for self-determination she previously lacked. Although Enrica's reaction is indicative of the representation of women's action as stemming from the body, it is significant that on the eve of a cultural and societal transformation for women it should originate from her physicality, the symbolic site of political battles over women's reproductive rights. As Enrica's decision distances her from her mother's generation, it and her decision to leave also foreshadow women's (re)action in the form of demonstrations, sit-ins, and *autocoscienza* groups in the feminist movement of the late 1960s.[21]

As with other Maraini texts from pre-1970, the daughter's burgeoning womanhood and consciousness develop in such internal spaces as the family, her boyfriend's bedroom, her older friend and employer Signora Bardengo's house. Understanding her increasing sense of entrapment and unease in her daughterly identity, the young protagonist's awakening culminates in an escape from the family. As part of her quest to construct a sense of self, not limited by the cyclical development back into domesticity her parents, especially her mother, exemplify, Enrica must confront and eventually unravel the intricacies of the traditional image of daughterhood.

This process entails specifically determining the nature of her relationship with her mother and father. But while in works appearing after *L'età* that feature the daughter's story, in which Maraini focuses on the elusive relationship between daughter and father, a pressing concern stemming from her own autobiography, in this text it is the daughter's relationship with her mother that most clearly illustrates the daughterly role the young protagonist experiences. Enrica's first-person account of her mother's life reveals to the reader how she reads the reality of a role earmarked for her. Using a minimalist style lacking outward emotion to express her thoughts, Enrica's representation of the mother reveals her unwillingness to subsume her self under a devastating role. Enrica's mother Teresa is a self-sacrificing woman who forsook her aspirations to attend university, subsumed her identity under the roles of mother and wife, and now succumbs to the consequences of that restriction—a death of body and spirit with symbolic meaning for the heroine. As a result of her description of this deterioration, Enrica eschews conventional motherhood and the fragmented female identity Teresa represents.

The mother-daughter relationship serves as a prescriptive for the daughter and as a perpetuation of the institutionalized female role and women's confinement to the domestic sphere. For the daughter, this situation generates a difficult relationship, because at the moment the mother's guidance could most be propitious, the daughter must reject her in order to avoid entrapment within the restrictive role and if she is to redefine the role.[22] In order to ensure that Enrica adheres to the socially mandated path of daughterhood and therefore adeptly "survives" in social discourses, Teresa teaches her about courtship and marriage, the ultimate gateways for her return to the domestic realm. When Enrica returns from a visit to her lover Cesare's house, Teresa delineates the prescription for achieving marriage. It is defined in terms of male desire, " 'You must be cunning. Make yourself desirable. And above all, don't give him anything'."[23] In a culturally telling and significant moment, Teresa's instruction underscores the anthropological definition of the daughter as "the most precious possession," " 'A girl like you must think about marriage. She must make herself *precious*' " (37; emphasis added). This prescription of female behavior fragments the daughter's identity. On the surface, it seems to endorse a woman's control of courtship. In reality, it rests on the premise that sexuality is a woman's currency for marriage and socioeconomic stability and status. It sets the stage for women's sexual subservience.[24]

While Enrica's movement away from the mother mirrors the psychoanalytic narrative of daughterly development, Maraini's novel also elucidates an alternative side to this development. This alternative results in the same movement but with more meaningful conclusions for a feminist analysis of daughterhood. The importance of playing out a scene in the daughter's visual sphere lies in the governance of perception: The mother's body is first captured within the specular (mirror) frame and then transmitted linguistically to the reader, the same Lacanian sequence of steps—image to word—constituting identity development. In literature, the specular image has been invested with a similar sort of psychological power to unfold meanings which a character would not normally perceive.[25] Enrica's progression toward a conscious exercise of agency is enhanced by the spatial depth the mirror projects. This depth of image expands and extends the daughter's perception of herself. Although it follows the Lacanian step in her symbolic development, this rejection of the mother ultimately symbolizes her conscious refusal to accept the mother's social destiny.

This destiny, therefore, is reflected through the mirror as it is inscribed on and identified through the mother's body, the cultural locus of female identity and inextricable from the spatial reality of the domestic sphere. Significantly, reflection back to the daughter creates a dual reality, both physical and imaginary. Thus the daughter in the imaginary stage of Lacanian development can visualize herself, for proximity, in her mother's body. This visualization allows her to foresee through the image the roles and spaces that (female) physicality will inhabit, "I could see myself in her place, with a man sitting in my father's place and a kitchen just like this one" (39). Awareness of this mirroring function in the daughter-mother relationship, then, informs the daughter's literary narration of her story, as in Cerati's *La cattiva figlia*. Like Enrica, Cerati's protagonist recognizes the mother as a mirror onto womanhood and resists the predetermined role it represents, becoming the "cattiva figlia" [bad daughter] of the novel's title, "I don't want to end up like her, that mirror in which I saw myself reflected these last few years."[26] Built around and in the domestic, Cerati's protagonist endows recollections of the relationship with tension to maintain a distance between herself and the woman who has always striven to "bring me back to what she considered my primary duties" (31). The similar *rapprochement* between Enrica and her mother, then, develops, again, in the visual sphere. Here, the daughter captures the physicality of motherhood through the optical frame as Teresa undresses; but unlike Lacanian individuation, in which the self distinguishes itself from the other, the result of Enrica's visual perception of the mother is the recognition of their similarities and her eventual refusal of their existence.

Visualizing the mother's body, which renders the private a reality for Enrica, however, also provides the daughter with a sense of womanness she had never before perceived. As a final moment in Enrica's contemplation of herself and her mother, the mirror reflects her developing perspective on her own life. When she wraps herself in Teresa's robe, she looks in the mirror and sees her mother: "I saw mother with two black circles under her eyes and a tired and bloated body that showed through her bathrobe. . . . I was like her. I made the same gestures" (119). Up until this moment Enrica has not attempted to comprehend the circumstances defining her mother's life, to question whether Teresa was truly indifferent to everything, or whether indifference was merely a reaction to her confinement and to a fatalistic sense of female duty. The young heroine's potentially dangerous choice to terminate her pregnancy marks a significant step in her development as a woman, both as an act of agency and as currency in the daughter-mother relationship. Her situation brings her closer to her mother in experience. This projection onto the mother of her own decision reveals the daughter's movement toward understanding her mother's legacy, even abandoning the negative image of the mother's body, "Maybe she had also tried to abort. . . . I saw her immersed in a boiling hot bath" (91).[27]

Despite Enrica's act of agency and an awakening to her body and to an understanding of her mother, the specular process involved in this development is ultimately negated by paternal authority when projected through the father's optical frame. When Enrica enters the kitchen, her father thinks he sees Teresa, collapsing her image/identity with the mother's. His visual reference for the daughter—his wife—reminds Enrica of the potential limitations her body and the domestic sphere symbolize. The father's assessment causes Enrica to resist its implications and to subsequently make a valuation of herself that is necessary for her final liberation, "I was *like* her" (emphasis added), separating her identity from the mother's.

The father's role in Enrica's articulating her individuation represents the extension of the symbolic into the daughter's life. The paternal figure at once represents patriarchal order and the order of language and, therefore, expression of one's self. Although in his own way loving, he provides an unsettling portrait of the father-daughter relationship. Unlike the mother who voices her opinion on her daughter's life, he remains detached, consumed by his hobby of building intricate Byzantine birdcages, and gradually descending into alcoholism and misery. While the novel's portrait of the father engenders pity, it also reveals his symbolic and potentially devastating role in the daughter's socialization. The father, an aging man inept at maintaining his job or control over his family, fails to try to understand his teenage daughter, and (therefore) to establish a communicative relationship with her. Channeling his energy into building the complex cages, he symbolizes the restraining effects of the domestic sphere on all members.[28] While the father has historically regulated gender as head of the family, Enrica's father's cage building represents the paternal role in containing her within the symbolic spaces of daughterhood as she becomes progressively self-assured and self-aware.[29] With their intricate design of towers and cupolas, the aesthetic appeal of these beautiful and delicate spaces belie their metaphorical meaning: Behind their cathedral facade lies a repository of patriarchal values that have determined women's lives for centuries.

The protagonist's final decision to begin her life anew and to become fully self-sufficient results in part from her reflections on her relationships with her mother and father, as well as through a subconscious awareness of her situation. While she "seldom . . . recognizes the portents of her dreams,"[30] a powerful one she has at her mother's deathbed brings together the two familial motifs of the novel, the restrictive effects of women's prescribed roles (in this case motherhood and its transcendence to the daughter) and the traditional paternal role in their regulation. In her dream, Enrica collapses her father's Byzantine cages with her mother's womb, thereby containing the space of procreation within the confining spaces of patriarchal order. While at first Enrica herself is trapped in one of the birdcages, upon awakening she realizes she was actually inside her mother's womb. The womb, though an affirming space for life ("smelling of flowers") and a part of Enrica's own body, also delivers her into a life of institutionalized roles ("cold like a church"). This awareness is carried through to her mother's funeral and revealed in a symbolic discussion of zoo cages. When discussing caged zoo animals with Carlo after Teresa's funeral, Enrica contends that one does not adapt to everything. While revealing Enrica's appreciation of the mother's inability to adapt to the entrapping traditional maternal discourse, the statement also emphasizes her awareness of the confining reality of motherhood. Together with her dream, it reveals her own awareness of the limitations of the roles to which she is socially mandated to adhere. Her growing consciousness of the destructive effects of institutionalized roles compels her to reject them.

Like the ending of later Maraini works informed by feminist tenets of women's liberation, Enrica's escape at the closure of *L'età* represents a turning point in her developing independence and consciousness. She recognizes the entrapping potential of the family and other conventional and limiting relationships such as the ones experienced with male suitors. As a result, she sets off on her own, proffering an open-ended "contestatory" resolution to a story in which familial relationships remain unaltered.

While *L'età* investigates the impact of the family and domestic spaces on a young woman's development, the 1966 poetry collection *Crudeltà all'aria aperta* represents in part Maraini's reconstruction of her own *storia* as daughter within the familial context. The autobiographical poems, published fortuitously at the beginning of postwar Italian feminism, are based on experiences that constitute Maraini's identity as woman and poet. To give shape to her life narrative, the poet originates her daughterly story in mnemonic moments, which reconnect her present to her past and mend her personal genealogy by reconstructing her history as a woman. The different moments with which she chooses to define her history are primarily familial relationships. As a result, like in the works discussed above by Manzini, Di Lascia, and D'Amico, the daughter's reconstructive project is once again defined by her quest for the father, elusive both in reality and in her memory.

The effects of the daughter's incomplete history is most understood in this poetry collection, where, focusing primarily on the daughter-father relationship ("I started by writing poems that were all about him"),[31] Maraini experiences difficulty remembering her past and hardly ventures beyond the point in which she identifies with her father and develops into adulthood. While glimpses of hope for recovering her memory do appear in *Crudeltà*, her struggle to recount her *storia* will later progress beyond this early collection to encompass the return to the mother and social sisters through a more theoretically defined feminist discourse. In this early collection, meanwhile, the daughter overcomes her lack of memory by writing a personal account that is available to a wide public, and by transforming this lack into a subjective refusal of the fragmentation of her identity and of the past—that is, of her absence from history as woman, poet, and biological and symbolic daughter.[32] This act of agency assumes a central position within the collection, a gateway between painful recollections of daughterhood and her adult experiences as mother, writer, lover.

Explorations of identity and their underlying awareness of the process of inscribing the self into a cultural genealogy include a primary focus on Maraini's development within the intense and loving relationship with her father. Significantly, the father occupies a place in this process as executor of the public sphere; that is, of the realm of official history and culture. The poems to which I will pay particular attention are exemplary of this set up, affording an in-depth perspective of Maraini's recurring concerns as both daughter and author.[33] Throughout the poems, the daughter attempts to "recapture" her father, elusive both because he is at moments absent from her life and because he inhabits the sphere of public affairs. And, more importantly for our purposes, she reads the import of that relationship to her past and her sense of self.[34]

The poems filter the father-daughter relationship through visual spaces of the adult daughter's consciousness, grounding it in symbolically charged images that define the bond. These portraits, in turn, reveal the difficulty of her exploration of identity, which remains easily contained within conventional, cultural images of the relationship. This dynamic is described in "Cordelia," a poem that appropriates as signifying metaphor the famous bond in Shakespeare's *King Lear*. Here, the daughter clearly and succinctly locates memory, her relationship to her own past, within the father-daughter space. Because her memory at this point originates from this emotional bond, it remains governed not only by the reality of the father's elusiveness, but also by the cultural precepts controlling its nature. Acknowledgment of his inattentiveness to her needs or unwillingness to participate in her explorations of her self coupled with her desire to recapture the father leaves holes in her subjective development.[35] The daughter's memories remain incomplete because her assumption of the father as love object lacks the cultural articulation that would lend her memories validity, "I was drunk with astuteness and / false chastity ... but you know / that when you walked like that, in front of me, / your legs enclosed by your corduroy pants" (27; sic). This truncated memory results in the daughter's fragmented history and symbolic death of those parts of her life she considers essential to her story.

For its intimate character and frankness about the father-daughter relationship, *Crudeltà* is a landmark work in women's writing. It constitutes a piece of the relationship's genealogy. In the opening poem "Bagheria," which frames the origins of her story, the daughter struggles to reconcile the jealousy induced by her father's absences and the social taboos regulating her emotions. The central question (literally line 43 of 87) of "Bagheria" is the English phrase "father, how can I love you?" (7). Uttered in an*other* language in which the English *love*, unlike the Italian *amare*, can be used in multiple contexts, the question coyly conceals the nuances of the daughter's understanding of the forbidden answer.[36] This question infiltrates the mnemonic process and sets the question of the daughter's love apart from other recollections of life in Bagheria and Rome. It also informs, along with the pain and desperation brought on by memory, the collection's title, *Crudeltà all'aria aperta*.

"Bagheria" contains what the daughter considers the salient elements of her story, from her passion for the father, to his role as socializer, to the underlying absence of the mother. Although she introduces here her desire to "recapture" the evasive father and her weak memories, she returns first to the maternal Sicilian villa where Maraini grew up after the war. Bagheria, identified as the "culla materna" (maternal cradle) in the poem "Villa Valguarnera," provides the poet with concrete images serving as springboards for her memory. These images include idyllic physical surroundings ("grass vineyards banana trees"), her aristocratic family genealogy ("there was grandfather's portrait ... which alluded to past wealth"), and aspects of daily routines ("the dog without a tail ... the cowherd's daughters"). These memories of the maternal villa are nevertheless devoid of the maternal. The mother will be represented only in the poem "Madre canina" (analyzed in chapter 2), which, in a nod to her role in the daughter's psychosocial development, acts as gateway between poems on the poet's childhood and adolescence and her life as lover and writer. Here, the daughter's memories rest instead on specific episodes in the relationship with the father and, therefore, on these chosen *paternal* points of reference for her history.

In scripting her *storia*, the daughter's complex reaction to the father's roles is informed foremost by the tension existing between her culturally problematic love for him and his regulatory determination of the course of their relationship, already present in "Bagheria." The aspect of the relationship that most colors the daughter's memory is her unrequited love ("wasn't I in love with a man who made me / mad with jealousy?" [9]). Through this enunciation she leads the reader into territory not typically charted. But the fact that she chooses to articulate this feeling highlights aspects of her daughterhood that culture, to survive in its conventional structure, finds necessary to repress.

The daughter's unbalancing act of trespass therefore creates an underlying tension within the texts of *Crudeltà* that is itself kept in check by memories of the father's role as socializer. "Bagheria," for example, is an impassioned plea for love that is undermined and repressed by his position as educator, "you taught me that going against the world was a terrible sin" (8). As this education evolves and the daughter matures, her memories confuse her desire to love the father with anger at his control and disillusionment with his duality as loving father and stern educator.

In the collection's second poem, "La rosa del buon senso" [The rose of common sense] the daughter develops into the rational world of patriarchal order through this instructive process. She uses metaphors of voice and vision to express her transition and the tension developing between her sense of self, struggling to be articulated, and her father's regulatory function. Silence and vision are syntactical elements of the daughter's story, elements already present in *L'età* and visually explored in the film *Mio padre amore mio*, discussed below. The suppression of voice and vision, representing the daughter's tenuous relationship to and position in culture, is finally subverted through the act of writing, through which she expresses her consciousness of the father's complicity in her repression: "I almost understand why my voice is corrupted by and weak from resentment . . . I think I contemplated killing you" (10–11). Vision is an optical metaphor recurring throughout her daughterly tale and presenting a counterpart to her silence. The appropriation of the gaze, of the field of vision through which she, like Enrica in *L'età*, can judge and assess before she speaks, is an act of agency resulting from indelible past experiences, as she expresses assertively in the poem "Zinnie," "my child's eye was wide open, without being able to see, but still seeing that which, once seen, it can no longer not see" (33). The tension and challenge created by the daughter's vision and expression and culminating in the blossoming of the daughter's "rose of common sense," reflects her frustrations with the limitations placed on her gender.

In the poem, the metaphors of vision and voice are collapsed into one entity, so that her vision becomes the mouthpiece for her developing voice. Tellingly, the father's function as regulator is centered on the optical metaphor. It calls into play a field of perception that in the visual arts, especially cinema, has been traditionally considered outside women's purview.[37] The daughter's judging gaze will not find its full voice until it appropriates the camera in Maraini's works of the 1970s. Instead, in "La rosa del buon senso" it becomes the locus of the tension between father and daughter. While in "Bagheria" the daughter's vision is privy to her surroundings, even to those not culturally suitable for her ("the cowherd's daughters masturbated behind bushes" [8]), it is safely ensconced in the maternal realm. Once older and as a participant in the public sphere, her presence and judgment become a threat to the sphere's survival. As socializer, the father governs and oversees the adolescent daughter's vision, that prelinguistic domain where assessment and construction of meaning first occurs and in which identity is first discerned, and mediates her perception of the world.

The daughter's developing field of vision parallels the father in both its recognition of the outside world and its conformity to the status quo. Although the father's own vision clashes with social injustice, his reaction is one of containment, of disavowal of his own consciousness, and eliminates the irritation in an act of self-regulation, "you feared the stunned and chaste eye inside of you / and you covered it with a finger" (10).[38] As an act of repression, this gesture is extended to the daughter and to her own growing awareness of her self and of social injustice: "you put a hand on that [judging and resolute] eye / so that it would appease its oblique and astonished stupor" (10). For the father, the daughter's judging gaze, which articulates her evaluation of his actions, is an act outside the "normal" and conventional bounds of what is within her purview to judge. For the daughter, her act of "insanity" (insania), as she defines it, counterbalances his "common sense" of the poem's title. It represents the madness and hysteria attributed to women when they attempt to tip the balance of gender. The regulation of the daughter's eye and, by extension, "insanity," affects her memory and the articulation of her story, again creating holes in her perception of her history. As she attempts to declare her "insane" vision, her voice falters, plagued with doubt. When, however, as her father's daughter, she finally capitulates to assume a regulated role, her insane, perceptive vision is "silenced," "the rose of common sense blossomed vigorously between my lashes and eyes" (11).

The maturing daughter's judging eye evolves into an assessment of cultural production in the poem "Il circolo di Chaplin" [The Chaplin Club], where she subverts the institutionalized knowledge and value systems introduced in "La rosa." Cultural production esteemed as high art and the father's equally abstract value system are undercut by the daughter's burgeoning sexuality. Both the father's location in abstract ideals and intellectual pursuits and the daughter's biological presence are drawn along established gender lines, and the poem purposefully underscores the conventionality of this configuration. The daughter consciously interjects with concerns about sexuality both because it is an immediate concern to her sense of self and because she is countering the asexual and therefore unreal ideals (i.e., Beatrice and Laura) patriarchal aestheticism has created. While the poet, her father, and her father's childhood friend Hans admire sculpture in Rome, view the avant-garde films of the *Circolo Chaplin*, and listen to discussions on the artistic value of cinema, Hans makes advances to her and she reciprocates. The father remains remarkably detached from his daughter's experiences, instead concentrating on the art around him, or on forms that can be easily regulated. Like her eye in "La rosa," the more mature daughter continues to stand outside the order her father admires, occupying instead the more mundane and physical "tricks and / absurd human truths." She reproaches her father for having divorced himself from basic human concerns and distanced himself from her experiences, which ultimately cannot be systematically controlled. By breaking the proper code of behavior and allowing her voice and sexuality to surface during the cultural excursions, the daughter renounces the laws that govern the unchanging, static beauty of what the father cherishes: "Hans and I had sex . . . / while you . . . described . . . the red cupolas . . . / look at the perfect / symmetry of those forms" (20–21). The daughter cannot be contained by the aesthetic laws locked away in a past. Indeed, the harmonious aesthetic they regulate cannot withstand her presence and is, tellingly, in decay in this prelude to a period of social upheaval in Italy.

Through her mnemonic voyage across her past in *Crudeltà*, the daughter records her changing voice and vision, a change that later will be informed and accelerated by her participation in the 1970s women's movement. Through the painful and at once loving memories of her father, she is able to discriminate between the idyllic moments of her childhood relationship and the more sobering instances of her adolescence when her sexuality threatened the social balance the father exemplifies. She recognizes the paternal role in the loss of her memory, her history, and her voice through his symbolic governance of expression. This realization finally ushers the daughter into adulthood, and opens her up to perceptions of her self that she will later articulate through other works.

The regulation of womanhood and the reaction to social modifications of behavior is a recurring topic in women's literature. From Alba de Cespedes' *Nessuno torna indietro* [There's No Turning Back] (1938) to Alice Ceresa's *Bambine* [Little Girls] (1990), investigations of the institutional control of young girls' behavior are considered fundamental to understanding the origins of women's social identity and charting a theory of women's liberation. In their examinations of institutions regulating conduct, De Cespedes and Ceresa's texts allude to their roles as, as they would be described by Althusserian theory, *ideological state apparati*.[39] Both works recognize the education system, for example, as designed to maintain and perpetuate the behavioral ideals of a society and its culture; and a symbolic or real family, meanwhile, as the mediator of these ideals in the private sphere.

Like these works, Maraini's 1970 play *Il Manifesto* depicts the effects of institutionalized regulation of behavior and examines the consequences of ideological indoctrination on the daughter. More specifically, in the scenes centered on the protagonist as daughter, it focuses on the role language plays in this regulation. The play constructs this role by presenting interaction between daughter and father, symbol of linguistic authority, and foregrounds the daughter's own reaction to the linguistic entrapment in femininity. This reaction evolves symbolically through silence—a nonlanguage—the use of profane language and, ultimately, the protagonist's response through the feminist manifesto she dictates.

Language in Maraini's play is an instrument of subversion. Through the daughter's appropriation and manipulation of language to express her demands and convictions, the work integrates the most popular feminist response to socialization at the time—the manifesto. In this instance, the manifesto, rendered live for the theater public, represents the way women's theater of the 1970s made feminist ideals and issues a physical presence through street performances. Maraini's play expands critical issues explored in the autobiographical *Crudeltà*, such as women's silence and the family's role in its perpetuation, and informs them with ideas culled from the early years of the women's movement. It links contemporary feminist arguments on women's subordination to an analysis of the protagonist Anna Micolla's development and eventual assimilation of feminist ideology to bring about change.

Anna's own account begins with the family, the origin of her identity, and with her birth, in which her father, more so than the mother, plays a prominent role. The foregrounding of the father's role in Anna's nativity is not incidental, nor is it an indication of the daughter's preference for or clearer memory of the paternal figure. Rather, the emphasis on the paternal at this early stage sets the tone for her development as daughter and immediately discloses what constitutes the symbolic basis of her struggle as a woman in patriarchal society.

Anna's birth provides a metaphor for the social and cultural divestiture of women's control over procreation and the severance of the pre-Oedipal bond between mother and daughter. An antithetical account to Athena's birth from her father's head, which conferred significant political and social power upon the goddess, Anna's own birth, happily originating from the mother, is quickly controlled by her father, who ushers her into the subordinate status against which she will die fighting. It is the father's act of separation, crude and rudimentary, that succeeds in bringing the daughter into the social order of which he is authority: "I was a strong, silent, hungry little girl and / for days I sucked on my father's fingers / waiting for the joy of milk."[40] Anna's succinct words outline her slow yet inevitable indoctrination, a passage based on the daughter's resignation and surrender of her desire to assume the mother as guide into social discourse.[41]

Anna's education within the family encompasses linguistic prescriptions for her behavior in the public sphere and mandates the passive abdication of the desire for agency to the father. Her passage into the sphere of social interaction charts the daughter's education into a category of alterity that defines her female identity as problematic, as potentially threatening to social order. Control of this identity is centered on the most obvious sign of a woman's presence in social discourse, her body and thus her sexuality.

In this phase of her Pygmalion-like education, this regulation is articulated through language in the public sphere, where to remain inside the category of "proper lady" Anna cannot openly express her sexuality. Already as a five-year-old Anna is taught by her father to be "good" and to "preserve" her virginity for her husband: " 'Women must remain good. . . . A woman has something between her legs that must always remain hidden. . . . And no one must touch it. . . . You must pretend that it is a little dead thing buried under the ground, that will awaken only when . . . you marry a good young man' " (193). This notion of sexual "silence" is further extended to her voice: " 'I taught her how to keep her mouth shut. My daughter will not talk to anyone until she is married' " (195). The implications of the father's assertions reveal his exertion of governance not only over his daughter's sexuality, but also over her participation in social intercourse. By collapsing the daughter's voice with her gendered role and sexuality, and by attempting to repress her sexuality until she is married and under the authority of a husband, Gaetano implies that she, a woman, expresses herself exclusively through her body, which falls under male tutelage.[42]

Anna's unwillingness to participate in her father's lesson on sexuality undermines the traditional symbol of female acquiescence: She appropriates her sanctioned silence as a sign of opposition. This act of rebellious expression prompts the father's friend Piro to call Anna a *puttana* (whore), later defined by Gaetano as " 'one . . . who speaks dirty, who laughs when she shouldn't, who doesn't obey anyone and follows her own head' " (198). In the face of the linguistic control exerted over her and the men's articulated dominance of social discourse, Anna's silence represents a linguistic present-absence that reflects her position within it. It connotes an enunciation formulated outside the realm of utterance. While the men's attitudes restrict

Anna to a sexual role, her counter-rebellion subverts her subordinate status, creating a genealogical link to Maraini's other daughters and—on the theatrical and social stage—a conspicuous subversion of regulation of her voice and self-expression.[43]

Anna's presence in the male-dominated social arena evolves from silence to punctuated participation when she erupts onto the father's cultural space and (mis)appropriates "his" language. In her study of daughterly acts of rebellion, Lynda Boose notes that, among other possibilities, the daughter's trespass into "the father's linguistic space" is "a vision of social inversion that must be vehemently quashed" (34). In Maraini's play, Anna threatens the men's cultural space by using language traditionally restricted to male interaction, including sexuality, and, in essence, seizing phallic power. In response to Gaetano's friends' sexual innuendos, Anna's choice of improper, sexualized language functions as a willful manifestation of the father's equation of her voice to her sexuality, " 'Damn! . . . Why don't you tell him to go fuck himself' " (196).[44]

But Anna's ultimate "threat of insurrection" occurs at play's end, when she assimilates language into a feminist rebellion, drafting a manifesto of women's liberation and organizing an uprising in prison. While in chapter 3 I will more extensively examine Anna's self-articulation in light of its connection to sisterhood, it is important to note here that by penning her manifesto, she transforms her indoctrinated silence and behavior and her life experiences into a rebellious linguistic expression of women's liberation. The manifesto redefines the tenets of femininity the father has tried to inculcate in her and sets the stage for women's public expression.

In literary projects such as the autobiographical *Crudeltà* and the fictional *Il Manifesto*, the daughter appropriates language to articulate her vision of the world and to inscribe herself into a larger cultural context extending beyond the family. In Maraini's case, the works can be plotted along a trajectory of appropriation that culminates with other first-person accounts, such as the poem "Demetra ritrovata" and the autobiographical novel *Bagheria*. In the case of cinema, the daughter repossesses the mediating gaze and the camera becomes her "mouthpiece."

The cinematic eye becomes an extension of the daughter's vision of the daughterly story that can only be partially mediated by the conventions of language, symbol of the patriarchal order challenged by her presence as a maker of meaning. In the 1978 film *Mio padre amore mio*, the daughter visually reconstructs her *storia* through an interpretation of numerous scenes previously described in *Crudeltà*. She relocates them in the visual spaces regulated by the father in the poetry collection. To do so, she returns to the optical metaphor of visual language to reconstruct a story that counters the visual narrative of classic cinema and establishes her as physical presence on the cultural stage.

Episodes originating from, once again, the daughter's memory and from her present situation comprise the film's syntax. In keeping with the autobiographical elements the daughter privileges, the narrative revolves around the daughter-father relationship and neglects the maternal figure. The film's non-linear arrangement points to the problems associated with reconstructing memory. It also underscores the difficulty of defining the role the bond played in determining the course of her history and, therefore, the subjectivity with which she retells it.[45]

Before turning to an analysis of the film, a brief linear plot summary will facilitate discussion of this complex work. The film opens with a shot of the daughter applying clown makeup in preparation for a play. While preparing her face, she visually reminisces about her relationship with her father, which, while idyllic and peaceful in childhood, becomes burdensome in adulthood as the daughter's maturing sexuality tests the boundaries of their love. Feeling that the father has betrayed their relationship when he takes a lover, she symbolically murders him. This separation caused by parricide—the daughter's volition—is underscored by two momentous episodes in her life: her departure for a Catholic *collegio*—a negative memory; and her participation in the women's movement—a constructive moment in her adulthood. The film culminates with a shot of the play for which she has prepared throughout the film. In the end, she contemplates her reflection in a mirror, re-identifying herself alone in her specular image.

In this as in other Maraini films, editing disrupts the seamless sequence of images defining classic cinema. Classic cinema encourages and enforces viewers' suspension of disbelief and therefore their identification with the film's protagonist, generally male and an exponent of dominant cultural values. Maraini's film, in contrast, creates a subversive daughterly discourse with images that often shock the viewer's notion of cinema as well as of the father-daughter relationship. When discussing the way women depict their experiences, Luce Irigaray defines a "radical" system of representation to illustrate the process they undertake. Because women have historically had access to conventional means of representation only through "mimicry," Irigaray contends, language and traditional (visual) images are powerless to "translate all that pulses . . . in the cryptic passages of hysterical suffering-latency." The alternative—revision, or even eradication—permits women to manipulate these means and express their personal experiences, "*Overthrow syntax* by suspending its eternally teleological order, . . . by modifying continuity, alternation."[46] In its rejection of the classic style of filmmaking and its proposal of a "counter-cinema," *Mio padre* becomes the counter-*storia* that visually represents formally silenced experiences. The *different* syntactical elements that comprise the film represent the daughter's authorship of the cinematic narrative, her residence in the newly defined discursive spaces she manipulates to recount her story.

In order to foreground the daughter's hand in production, the film reveals its artifice, fracturing viewer identification and the notion that a film reproduces "reality" and constitutes an effortless transcendence of meaning from screen to spectator. The purpose of Maraini's text is to represent the daughter's perception and reading of both her self and her position in the narrative, and to render her expression of this understanding a unique currency that counters conventional cinematic language. The text achieves this through specific techniques: Symbolic montage makes evident the protagonist's mnemonic process by suturing past and present images, while the application of stage makeup, the daughter's application of specific color to herself and her father, the use of repetition, and deliberate breaks in action foreground the film's construction.

These elements are played out during significant moments in both cinematic and life narrative, and highlight the daughter's determination of meaning. While red objects, symbols of love and anger, dot the daughter-father landscape, her deliberate painting of the father in some of the film's most weighty scenes reveals her inscription of meaning in the relationship. During scenes of parricide, she paints "blood" on the father's forehead and shirt after shooting him. Repetition of this deliberate act of inscription and of deliberate breaks in action, in which the father, just shot, gets up and walks off screen, imply that his murder is a symbol within the configuration of the daughter's cultural story: The parricide represents the separation, we could say, sanctioned by the social and cultural laws governing the relationship. These elements that highlight the film's artifice all foreground and symbolize the weightiness of the elements of the relationship in the daughter's mind and uncover the daughter's interpretation of her *storia*.

Just as significant to the daughter's narrative are scenes in which she applies clown makeup, and which appear several times during the course of the film. In these, the daughter brings to the surface layers of social identity acquired over time and uncovers the artificiality of gender performance.[47] As a syntactical element of her identity, color, added on screen by the daughter's own hand, acts like a conspicuous hieroglyphic, undermining the Freudian definition of women's sexuality as mysterious. In her construction of the clown persona, the protagonist ultimately deconstructs the "riddle" of women, which according to Freud only men are able to solve.

Socialization has camouflaged the daughter's perception and vision of herself and is mirrored by the specular image before her, instrumental, again, in the Lacanian development of identity and in the development of a social persona. This mirroring situates her in an ambivalent position: In order to participate in social intercourse she must assume specific attributes of a subservient feminine role. However, it also lays bare the gradual layering of socialization onto the daughter's face. Because the daughter herself executes this symbolic layering, the mirror promotes her growing self-awareness and reflects her interpretation and willful subversion of the development into femininity. The daughter conspicuously assumes the facade of a clown while reading her *storia*, so that the specular image—the clown—evolves to represent her social identity. The Freudian "hieroglyphics" and the "riddle of the nature of femininity" are represented by the geometric figures that at moments cover her face. In her reconstruction of her *storia*, images of the theatrical persona created to make people laugh interrupt it, serving as a reminder of the possible consequences of women's attempts at subverting their socialization. Laughter here serves as a nonverbal communication supplanting (but also making blatantly evident) women's silence. The daughter's donning of the laughing clown mask, a *seemingly* mild subversion of the daughterly discourse, actually exposes what Irigaray sees as the pattern for womanhood, in which women's articulation of needs and desires is perceived as an "innocuous" demand that *"merely make[s] people smile."*[48] In the film, the juxtaposition of the laughing clown mask that will indeed make people smile with the daughter's unfolding story reveals her understanding of her fragmented identity.

As is evident in these scenes, the daughter's interpretation creates an intersection for two textual narratives—the cultural story of daughteronomy, to borrow Sandra Gilbert's term, and the daughter's self-created *storia*. The filmmaker manipulates elements from the former to infuse the latter with meaning, all the while highlighting and undermining these elements to expose the role they play in her conventional story. The action that permeates the film and anchors the two stories is parricide. While countless feminist theorists have described Clytemnestra's murder as the symbol of the foundation of patriarchal culture,[49] Maraini's protagonist attempts symbolic parricide several times within herself to chart a countertrajectory to the path set by the Aeschylian matricide. This countertrajectory allows her to pave the way toward a culture that validates her subjectivity, represented at film's end by her participation in the women's movement and in a play about her own story.

The culminating moment of the film's and, therefore, daughter's narrative is her participation in the "Take Back the Night" march for women's rights. The protagonist places herself amidst women who struggle against their subordination, sanctioned by, for example, the educational institution the daughter enters in the film and the social institutions governing her relationships. While not made as explicit in this film as in such works as the poetry collections *Donne mie* and *Mangiami pure*, both of which deal in part with her integration into social order, the fact that this scene is included in the film can only imply that the reconstruction of the daughter's story and her subsequent performance of that story on the social stage have been made possible by the enlightening effects of the women's movement on her consciousness. Thus, while separation from the beloved father is the result of unpleasant moments, participation in the women's movement allows the daughter to begin her process of self-exploration. The geography of daughterhood is therefore mapped out on two levels, the film (the *other* side) and the theater (the Pirandellian social mask unmasked). She ultimately achieves awareness of her situation by performing on an*other* stage, erupting as presence onto the patriarchal stage.

Reconstructions of the daughter's cultural story often result in internal explorations of the self—intimate psychological narratives. Accounts of the daughter, such as those by Teresa Ancona, Carla Cerati, and Fabrizia Ramondino, typically investigate her subjective reactions to relationships in her life that define her as a daughter. Placing herself in the relationships and, ultimately, on the literary stage of narration, the daughter's internal life becomes part of a larger cultural and indeed sociohistorical context in which she becomes a maker of meaning. The daughter's entry onto this historical stage ultimately makes evident her presence as subject.

Her entry therefore demands the exploration of her daughterly ancestors to create a background history for her present story. Consequently, charting this genealogy necessarily requires investigations of mythic narratives that define models of daughterhood embedded as meaning in Western culture. Several feminist theorists considering women's subjective reconstruction of their female identities emphasize the value of revision of myths. The mythic models they examine predate the "scientific" psychoanalytic and anthropological narratives that have referred back to them in their own constructions of meaning, unveiling the genealogical sedimentation of culture. Luisella Veroli, for example, stresses the usefulness of these myths as historical resources for women exploring their own life narratives.[50] In her own examination of the "tactics of revisionary mythopoesis," DuPlessis argues that women poets revise mythology to "attack . . . cultural hegemony as it is." She defines these tactics as "narrative displacement," which, in turn, emphasizes "otherness" and focuses on the "marginalized."[51]

In chapter 2 we will consider the value of revising and reinterpreting the Aeschylian myth of Clytemnestra to a reconceptualization of motherhood as an empowering experience. For daughterhood, one of the preeminent models of the daughterly experience in Western culture is Homer's "Hymn to Demeter." The hymn recounts the myth of Demeter, goddess of agriculture, who despairs over the loss of her daughter Persephone to Hades, god of the underworld, only to rejoice at her return. This rich tale contains elements central to the daughter's development, chiefly her relationship with the mother and her initiation into heterosexuality, two benchmark elements for a feminist reconstruction of daughterhood. In the 1978 poem "Demetra ritrovata," Maraini's revision of the Homeric text in *Mangiami pure*, the poet draws out her own story of daughterhood, focusing on the road back toward the mother and forward to a community of women.[52] By rereading Homer's classic text, Maraini creates a new mythopoesis for the daughter based on the "genealogical sedimentation" of womanhood.

Because mythology is shaped out of a culture's ideological sedimentation, revision unravels that sedimentation and exposes hidden stories.[53] Feminist analyses of the Demeter-Persephone myth point to the daughter's enforced absence and the interdiction of the maternal in her life as markers of her story.[54] By focusing on Persephone's tale from the point of view of the daughter's search for the mother, Maraini's version not only extricates her from silence, but also reinstates the maternal presence into her life.

As revision, "Demetra ritrovata" not only places the original text on a genealogical map of women's culture, but also refocuses attention on the constructive role women play in identity formation. Maraini's poem applies a feminist vision to the female protagonists: The daughter is the motivator of the action, embarking on a journey to rediscover the maternal in her life. The mother becomes the source of her life, the person who reinstates women in the daughter's life and mediates between the daughter and her future. In the adult daughter's life, this maternal role is extended into female friendships, which do not eradicate the mother's presence from the daughter's life, but rather continue its benefits of solidarity and love through entrustment.

In Maraini's text, the daughter's journey back to the mother does not, tellingly, begin with an examination of the pre-Oedipal relationship with her. Instead, it opens with a meditation on when the love for her father began. This contemplation mirrors the daughter's journey in *Crudeltà*, but aims for a different, woman-centered relationship. This intense love began in the maternal "casa borghese" (bourgeois home) in Bagheria. While vestiges of the maternal home already echo in the daughter's mind in the *Crudeltà* poem "Villa Valguarnera" ("Bagheria, maternal cradle, *adle*" [22; emphasis added]), in the daughter's memory the invasion of paternal love into the maternal house casts the love as a force drawing her away from the mother. Reasons for separating from the mother at this point may be twofold. First, the daughter may not remember the early bond with her mother, given her age at the time of transition; and later, the image she has of the mother is one of submission and denial, as represented in the fictional *L'età del malessere* and delineated in the autobiographical "Madre canina." Second, the daughter intends to subvert the regressive cyclical development mapped out in traditional narratives of female development. For her, cyclical movement would imply closure, finiteness, the completion of a journey (back) into domesticity and the end of the possibility of renewal. Instead, by beginning her poem with musings on the father, her movement back [*ritrovare*] is actually a movement forward toward the mother, a "writing beyond the ending" of traditional models of development through subjective mediation and consciousness.

Filtered through the daughter's memory, the daughter-father relationship is first (re)cast in an idyllic framework devoid of tension ("It all began in those days / of childhood splendor among peach trees in flower / and small mint sweets"),[55] then marked by her relationship with the father and the men who symbolically replace him. The daughter divides the two movements toward the father and, later, husband into "infanzia straniera" (foreign infancy) and "addolescenza infiammata" (impassioned adolescence). The foreign elements of her infancy emphasize the daughter's movement away from familiarity with the mother into a position within the world of the father and other men. Like Anna in *Il Manifesto*, this entrance into the public sphere of paternal authority casts the daughter as *other*. Only later, in adolescence, as her identity as a woman is set and sexualized does her attention become focused on the men in her life.

In the daughter's mind, the beginning of the daughter-father bond is marked by genderlessness, a lack of assimilation of social roles and qualities earmarked for their genders. At this point, she lacks identity as a woman ("I did not know I was a woman" [5]), while the father still does not enforce his own masculine authority ("you had not yet blossomed into the world / of virile and sun-filled fear" [5]). As the daughter slowly assimilates her gendered role, however, the relationship becomes contextualized within an intellectual framework traditionally attributed to the male domain.[56] It is at this point that she "loses" her mother and abandons her sisters. During these "times of moral development" into participation in social discourse, she even transfers to the father vestiges of the maternal left behind ("he caressed my cheeks / with milky fingers" [6]) and recognizes her birth not from her mother's womb, but, like Athena originating from Zeus' head, from her father's mind. Not only does the father, the "god-man," physically beget his daughter, he also intellectually molds her, ordaining her entrance into the intellectual sphere he himself occupies by historical right.[57]

The daughter's initiation reveals the consequences of losing her mother, abandoning her sisters, and being subsumed under an institutionalized identity. Silence, placidity, and fear are all conditions which embody her prescribed role in the social configuration of gender. In her discussion of the father-daughter relationship, Luciana Percovich asserts that the daughter becomes disillusioned in the identification with the father, because as her identity represents a threat to social order it is contained.[58] In this submissive position to the "Law," the daughter's subjectivity and will are domesticated. The world she enters is a "world / of virile fear," a place which, as the linguistic juxtaposition implies, is threatened by the daughter's presence: Fear of subversion is recast as symbolic virility to mask the faultlines the daughter's presence makes evident. Her domestication, then, ensures a renunciation of subjectivity and agency: As her footsteps quietly, cautiously follow the father, her eyes, no longer agents of her gaze, become fearful and demure.

The daughter describes her induction into social discourse using unsettling images of violence to portray both her experiences and the rupture from the primary state of oneness with the mother. Consistent with Homer's version of Hades' rape of Persephone, she metaphorically depicts this intellectual initiation as a physical violation in which she was left "pregnant with male knowledge," as a sacrifice illustrated through the metaphor of transubstantiation. In a moment that evokes the injunction of the collection's title, *Mangiami pure* [Go ahead and Eat Me], Proserpina's very body becomes sacrificial bread and wine. The "little girl with the white body / of bread" (7), as she earlier describes herself, now sacrifices bread—her very self—in fulfillment of the tenets of her gendered role. She is the Lévi-Straussian foundation of culture, the basic daily bread of established order.

While the Zeus/ Athena myth symbolizes the father-daughter relationship and its subversion of a maternal element in the daughter's development, the Demeter/ Persephone myth provides the framework for the daughter's relationship with her mother. Under the "leggi democratiche" [democratic laws] she still upholds, Atena-turned-Proserpina clashes ideologically with Demeter. For Proserpina, who until now has existed in the father's domain, both mother and abandoned sisters occupy a space of uncertainty and mystery as they engage in ideological warfare with paternal authority. Not interested in communality with women and in their struggle for change, Proserpina enforces the peace underwritten by the "democratic laws" to maintain the status quo and to commit symbolic matricide, ridding herself of the maternal presence in her life. Belonging to this subjugated group would mean certain defeat ("the embrace of the defeat she wants / the embrace of feminine truth" [10]), and the admission of the daughter's inability to enforce the rules of her gender as dictated by patriarchal order.

At the crossroads of her development, the daughter's complicitous participation in the social order the father represents is ensured by the cultural assessment and definition of the gendered roles they fulfill. She therefore perceives the mother, as Maraini defined her twelve years earlier in the poem "Madre canina," as one who cannot prevail, whose social position holds no currency in social discourse, and whose degenerated body reflects a history of submission and disempowerment. The daughter's complicity to the laws of gender, therefore, becomes a calculated act to disassociate herself from her mother "for too much resemblance" (10). In the initial phase of her passage she rebels against those qualities that represent both the traditional containment of women in the domestic sphere and their reproductive role. Unlike the father, who occupies the public sphere of intellect, science, philosophy, and art, the mother's relegation to the domestic sphere is naturally determined by her body, and her role essentialized as integral to the domestic realm. In telling images of what lies at the heart of women's social repression, the daughter succinctly portrays the mother's situation with descriptions charged with double meanings, representing the fragmentation of the mother's identity. For example, the daughter describes her breast as "full of hot soup," replacing breast milk with hot soup and shortening the distance between the mother's work in the domestic sphere as daily nourisher of the family and her body. Similarly, the image she crafts of the mother's "bed of blood and spices" refutes the feminist interpretation of women's blood as a sign of difference. At this juncture of her development between mother and father, Proserpina reads the mother's blood not as a symbol of strength and difference, but only in terms of her corporeal and spiritual defeat, which renders her "vanquished and witless."[59] For this reason, she resists subjecting herself to a role that has historically kept women outside the realm of authority and agency.

Proserpina's definition of the subordinate status of women ultimately threatens the trajectory of her "normal" psychoanalytic return to the maternal/domestic sphere. Her process of returning back to the mother, therefore, represents a conscious effort to reconfigure women's development. It will eventually demand the daughter's reinterpretation of the signs constituting womanhood. Only when the daughter contemplates the trajectory of her relationship with Demetra does she recognize that being inducted into the social realm of daughterhood and womanhood signifies sacrificing the maternal bond. Symbolically, she describes this situation as a "winter penury": Not only does Demetra render the earth physically bare at the loss of her daughter, but the separation gives rise to a symbolic and spiritual winter in which the daughter loses "the first knowledge of warmth ... tenderness, mutuality" that Adrienne Rich considers indicative of this primary relationship.[60]

For Maraini's readers, the ultimate motivation for the daughter's return is problematic, however. It is not Proserpina's embrace of her social sisters that propels her reassessment of the presence of women in her life. Rather, it is her dispossession by the father. This recurring autobiographical element subverts the feminist ideal of a self-motivated change. The impetus for change at first makes Proserpina wary of the implications of unity (*abbraccio*) with other women, who represent powerlessness within social order. Recognizing the daughter's precarious situation, Demetra threatens to wreak havoc on earth if Proserpina abandons "the mother, women's laws / the arms of her solitary sisters" (9).

When she finally does rediscover her mother and social sisters, she must reunite with them in the Irigarayan "darkness" where "they lie abandoned." Her father, still occupying the spaces the daughter has sought to inhabit and in which cultural and social authority continue to be exercised, lives in the world of letters. Her mother and sisters, on the other hand, inhabit a "secret forest," the site of the exclusive Eleusinian Mysteries instituted by Demeter for her reunion with Persephone. It is a place not governed by patriarchal authority, but rather the site of a return to the imaginary sphere and of women's exercising of the symbolic as subjects. It is the site of darkness in which the ability to create life—not only new life, but also the lives of women out of historical oblivion—is celebrated as a form of agency. Maraini describes the importance of the daughter's bond with women as a reconstitution of one's self, "It can be an encounter, a confrontation, and sometimes a clash, but there is almost always a request for affection, for recognition, tenderness, there is this need of the other woman as a part of ourselves."[61] Within this context, Proserpina answers the question Luce Irigaray herself poses in relation to the loss of the mother-daughter bond: "And where are we to find the imaginary and symbolic of life in the womb and the first *corps-à-corps* with the mother? In what darkness, what madness, do they lie abandoned?"[62]

The return to the mother and to other women engenders the hope for a "new order" in which women rejoice in their womanhood. The poet alludes to the Homeric separation of earth and hell to illustrate the traditional division between the male and female spheres, while at the same time appropriating it to illustrate the new existence and power fashioned out of women's solidarity. Although equating the female sphere with the earth and the male sphere with hell, Maraini in no way links women to nature or demonizes men. Rather, she draws on the Homeric division to depict women's existence within conventional culture and their existence in a culture in which they may exercise agency. Therefore, while the conventional configuration of their existence, in which they are silenced and subordinate, is indeed an "inferno," the new configuration, in which they metaphorically reestablish the primary relationship with the mother, is centered on women's creativity and on their power to procreate life.

This new model reflects the one prescribed by 1970s feminism through such women-centered activities as *autocoscienza* sessions and women-only retreats. Although beneficial to women on a personal level, however, these activities proved ineffective in their separateness from the sphere of political activity. Just like the failings of *autocoscienza*, "Demetra ritrovata" does not extricate the daughter's union with her mother and sisters from the "secret forest." On the one hand, this localization highlights the inadmissibility of this alternative authority into patriarchal order: The women's activities in this separate sphere allow them to constitute a new order that embraces alterity as a social, cultural, and political currency. In this regard, the poem places the women on a literary genealogy that begins with the Homeric "Hymn" and exposes them to a public readership. On the other hand, however, Maraini's text never extends beyond that moment in readership that brings Demeter, Persephone, and their social sisters out of the darkness of the secret forest to define the impact their solidarity will have on the feminist movement and society in general.

Nevertheless, this journey back to the mother and forward to her social sisters, the daughter's act of rereading and rewriting revises familial spaces and her script, "writing beyond the ending" of a more personal, psychological development. Unlike the movement toward the father, which mandates abandoning the mother as guide into the sphere of intellect and reason, the return to the mother does not demand forsaking the father. Without advocating separatism, it allows the daughter to love her father without fear, submissiveness, or silence. The father is no longer the threatening authoritative symbol of women's subordination, but rather a regenerated figure born out of a new social order. With the balancing of the father's place in the daughter's life, the earlier, exclusive love for the "god-man" is now displaced by a reciprocal love not of a god, but of a human being. At the same time, the daughter reads the myth as a key to constructing a model for women's solidarity. By reevaluating her relationships and by entering into propitious relationships of sisterhood with other women, Proserpina has reawakened from her "sonno impaurito" (fearful sleep). Thus, just as Percovich recognizes encounters with women as "the discovery of the world, that finds in us the look of signification,"[63] Proserpina has regained her subjective gaze.

Maraini's reconstruction of daughterhood and her challenge of the conventional relational spaces this figure inhabits inform the daughterly discourse in the works examined in this chapter. In these works, the author reflects on the daughter's cultural story to shape her present *storia*, and examines the way conventional precepts of daughterhood affect women's development and sense of self. As we have seen in the discussion of women's authorship, feminist theorists advocate the subjective recreation of the past and the location of women in a genealogical framework that legitimates their intellectual/cultural activities. Although in her autobiographical works Maraini is often besieged by memory lapses caused by the pain of recalling the unrequited love for the father, this personal approach allows her to subjectively recapture her own *storia*. Like other women authors, such as Sibilla Aleramo and Armanda Guiducci, who have informed their works with autobiographical references to their relationship to daughterhood, Maraini appropriates this subgenre to reshape her history into a story on daughterhood that is not only self-revealing but also revealing of cultural daughteronomy.

At the same time, the daughterly discourse informs her fictional works as well, as her characters embody this cultural daughteronomy, suffer from its limitations, and finally draw strength from their experiences to break free and start anew. In the fictional scripting of the daughter's story, Maraini focuses on the social prescriptions regulating it. She explores the daughter's entrapment in the conventional daughterly discourse and, eventually, her escape. This sense of entrapment becomes literally apparent in the birdcages in *L'età* and the apartment and prison in *Il Manifesto*, two exemplary texts in which the daughter's liberation includes reflections on confinement and on escape engineered by their own hands.

As part of the daughter's escape, Maraini explores the social benefits of her participation in the women's movement. A chronological overview of the works discussed in this chapter will afford a glimpse of the evolution of this issue in Maraini's works. Although both Enrica of *L'età del malessere* and the protagonist of *Crudeltà all'aria aperta* cannot yet enjoy the fruits of the 1970s women's liberation movement, their self-awareness, gained through experience and reflection, ushers them through journeys toward independence and maturity. Anna Micolla in *Il Manifesto*, however, draws from her experiences as daughter, lover, factory worker, and thief to pen a manifesto of women's liberation grounded in contemporary feminist ideology. Finally, in the autobiographical *Mio padre amore mio* and "Demetra ritrovata," Maraini applies tenets of the women's movement and a feminist-inspired revision of genre and myth to explore ways in which the daughter may free herself from the stultifying effects of daughteronomy. While in the film she challenges the rules of classical filmmaking to retell her story as she remembers it and as she feels shaped her life, in the poem she rereads the "other side" of a classic text to lay out the trajectory of her personal discourse as daughter, ending with the embracing of mother and social sisters.

From the silence and fear that shaped the early daughters' sense of self, to the freedom and reform that defines the later daughters' outlook on life, Maraini's discourse on daughterhood provides an insightful look into the evolution of women's struggle for the expression of their thoughts and desires. With amazing foresight already in 1963 and especially in 1966 with *Crudeltà*, Maraini has set a course for the understanding of daughterhood and the daughter's desire that will not allow her readers to look at the question of daughteronomy in the same way again. If, in our own revised reading, King Lear is truly correct when considering Cordelia in the lines heading this chapter, history will indeed be put back on its course as daughters express their own *storia*.

2
Motherhood

All human life on the planet is born of woman.¹

In a new world envisioned by some feminist theory, . . . a born-again maternity should offer wider possibilities to the individual, possibilities for integrating lives, creating new lives. While requiring activity and community, . . . these possibilities would not . . . denigrate as lacking the sex whose body was, for all of us, the first experience of plenitude.²

We don't have to give up being women to be mothers.³

IN RESPONSE TO A QUESTION ON THE MOTHER'S POSITION IN WESTern culture, Maraini remarked,

> the mother is a losing character in this world, and it is therefore necessary to get close to her, to try to understand her, to try to also understand the inherent contradictions in guaranteeing the laws of the father and at the same time bringing a daughter into this world. These are contradictions because the father's rules are often against the daughter, against the daughter's freedom, and the mother finds herself lacerated by this division. This laceration causes sickness, unhappiness, self-hatred and hatred towards her daughter. If a mother is a woman subject to the father's authority, she won't rebel against the father. Only a woman who already feels liberated can do so.⁴

This portrait of the mother as a figure caught between the drive to destabilize conventions limiting women to confining roles and her cultural role as bearer of tradition reflects the problematic familial position she inhabits in the private sphere. It mirrors as well the points of departure for feminist analyses—both theoretical and literary—of motherhood.

The mother is the figure traditionally relegated to the background of the conventional family story. Although as procreator she stands at the origins of life, culturally she is rendered subordinate to the social laws governing both private and public spheres and remains confined to the domestic sphere. Here, her identity and selfhood are played out through the maternal role, whose function is to perpetuate social law through her children. The role places the mother in a conflictual position marked first and foremost by her disassociation from a sexual identity not linked to reproduction. This disassociation, as Julia Kristeva contends, has stripped women of their own articulation and management of the experience of motherhood, and has been reinforced by depictions of motherhood that proffer maternal self-sacrifice and asexuality as ahistorical ideals. In this scenario the characteristics of self-sacrifice and asexuality mark the successful fulfillment of motherhood and eliminate threats to the conventional role.[5] These qualities have also been legitimized by scientific, philosophical, and psychoanalytic theories which closely link women's social role with the biological, reproductive function of their bodies. Together, they create what Kristeva defines as "the module of a biosocial program," ensuring that there is no rupture in the ideal and that the content of the role is not compromised.[6]

A compromise in the system would change roles in the family and, by extension, the public sphere. Women's liberation and women's entry into the public sphere has, therefore, caused a re-evaluation of this program and, consequently, the family. Studying the changes in the postwar Italian family in *Sociologia della famiglia*, sociologist Chiara Saraceno faults the development of the nuclear family, propelled by nineteenth-century industrialization and intensified in the period of economic rebuilding of the 1950s and 1960s, as the reason for the mother's isolation in the domestic sphere. She notes, however, that this economic prosperity also fostered change, creating an inverse relationship between families' financial growth and birth rates. The continued decrease in these rates was the result of women's greater control over reproduction and their entrance into the workforce in ever growing numbers. This shift from the domestic to the public sphere, Saraceno further notes, had an effect on the way the maternal role was perceived, especially by daughters. Significantly, the daughter in this period started challenging her conventional education into a passive femininity as she adopted the mother's participation in the public sphere as normal. This shift in perception was fueled by a growing feminist consciousness and a revision of family laws, which guaranteed legal equality between spouses in the household.[7]

Despite these cultural and political changes, however, the mother's continuing central position as primary educator and nurturer remains a legacy of the patriarchal family. The reason is due, in part, to the difficulty in eradicating longstanding cultural paradigms whose shift destabilizes power and alters notions of the self in society. In his groundbreaking study of the modern family, *Centuries of Childhood*, French historian Philippe Ariès identifies the cult of the family from which this legacy developed. The focus on the nuclear family intensified with the growth of the bourgeoisie in the nineteenth century. The expansion and political strengthening of this social sector lead to the deeper schism between private and public spheres, in a sense privatizing family life. As a result, attention fell on the children, no longer seen as available labor as they had been for centuries before, but rather more typically seen as the focus of a burgeoning nuclear family. This new family culture also more clearly defined the division of labor between father and mother, husband and wife. The father was the family provider, working outside the home; the mother became the children's primary educator into social law as well as the primary source of their emotional well-being.

The divisions Ariès identifies have roots in Aristotelian theory and were upheld in the nineteenth and early twentieth centuries by, among others, the theories of G. W. Hegel and Sigmund Freud. The parameters set by these dominant theories have created a basis for what Saraceno describes as the mother's education into the domestic and her complete assumption of the maternal role in the name of morality and social responsibility.[8] The Greek philosopher Aristotle claimed biological evidence for the division of male and female into the public and domestic spheres. The importance of his theory to feminist considerations of this division is that it is widely responsible for laying the scientific groundwork for Western models of women's social and political participation in both realms.[9] In *De Generatione animalium I & II*, Aristotle positions the male as active generator and the female as passive receptacle, thus determining a qualitative difference between the contribution of the sexes to the procreation of life. The male provides the "form and source of movement," while the female furnishes the more base "matter." For its spiritual and intellectual properties, the male contribution to society is evaluated as "better and diviner" and "more excellent." The female contribution, on the other hand, provides the material from which life is made, but not its form or generative impetus, and is thus deemed less consequential.[10]

Hegel's *Phenomenology of Spirit* (1807) provides metaphysical support for the division Aristotle delineates. Hegel places women at the center of the family, whose law he defines as an intuitive and god-given "universal substance." This divine essence renders women's situation ahistorical and immutable, and obliterates any distinction between individual women in its emphasis on the unchanging natural role of motherhood. According to Hegel's theory, men can move freely in the public sphere, determining and shaping events. For their part women cannot exercise subjectivity, "[remaining] alien to the particularity of desire."[11] More specifically, they cannot exercise the individual choice and action fundamental to citizenship in society and in the world of ideas, where meaning is created.[12]

The definitions outlined by Hegelian philosophy were later reinforced by Freudian psychoanalysis, which charged the mother with the even more fundamental task of ensuring the child's psychic well-being. Echoing Hegel's division of the domestic and public spheres, Freudian psychoanalysis places much of the responsibility of the child's development on the mother. In her important and widely read study of motherhood and its social and cultural definition, Elisabeth Badinter faults psychoanalysis with "making the mother the central character in the family" and therefore attributing to her the child's psychic stability.[13] In this configuration, the mother is the object *against* which her offspring must develop in order to form the ideal social identity. As infants, male and female children identify with the mother. However, when the male child recognizes that he has the phallus—the symbol of power—the mother, who has none, represents the possibility of its loss. The girl, on the other hand, upon seeing the similarity between herself and her mother, blames the mother for "refusing" her the symbol of wholeness. Therefore, the girl searches for a replacement of the phallus she desires. Freud translates this desire into a desire for a baby, thus conflating women's "normal" sexual development and motherhood and making motherhood an integral part of femininity.[14]

Italian feminists devising projects of women's liberation have delineated theories that free the maternal experience from these restrictive models. Those whose theories on motherhood offer a broad working base for an analysis of the maternal role in literature, among whom

Luisa Muraro, the members of the Milan's Women's Bookstore Collective, Luciana Percovich, and Paola Melchiori have favored a social definition of mothering designed to reinstate motherhood within the realm of women's agency. At the same time, while often still focusing on the mother-child relationship, their theories have privileged the mother's role in identity formation and have not tended to evade essentialist notions of women's biological identities as bearers of children. Rather, much like their French counterparts Julia Kristeva and Luce Irigaray, they have turned their attention to the empowering potential of procreating human beings both from a biological and cultural perspective. This constructive view of motherhood provides a starting ground for a new maternal identity. By admitting the power in the relationship between women and biological reproduction, they bring this capacity into the arena of debate and change. Not only do they demand the creation of new social, cultural, and political discourses beneficial to all women, but they also extend maternity into a symbolic arena of cultural (re)generation.

The theories resulting from these challenges assume the point of view of the daughter in search of her mother(s). While certainly problematic when attempting to reconfigure the mother as agent, positioning the daughter as agent of this transformation recognizes her location between the domestic and public spheres and her management of the tools necessary for effecting this change.[15] As a result, the theoretical and practical trajectory mapped out for women's liberation is a return back to the mother, the point of origin of female identity. This return is not regressive, as Freudian psychoanalysis would have it, but rather progressive: It represents a defiant move forward to the recognition of both the mother as primary female figure and the role she plays in shaping a woman's life. This return has contested the sociocultural identification of women solely as mothers, while at the same time acknowledging both the negative and positive effects the mother has on the daughter. The mother does indeed fulfill the culturally mandated role of transmitter of conventional notions of femininity to the daughter; she prepares her, after all, for participation in the society to which she belongs. However, she is also recognized as the female figure the daughter can refer to when recharting her own identity as a woman.

While the feminist project for women's liberation names the mother as the chronological starting point of women's history, the definition of "mother" is multilayered, reaching beyond the biological to encompass the cultural and symbolic as well. The paradigm for women's liberation constructed by the members of the Milan Bookstore Collective, for example, focuses on the Symbolic Mother, a cultural-historical figure from whom women can draw inspiration, someone who serves as reference point for a new woman-centered cultural map. Recalling Kristeva and Irigaray's theory of the maternal prelinguistic sphere, Luisa Muraro's proposed return includes the acknowledgment of the mother's role in language acquisition. As outlined in her landmark study of motherhood, *L'ordine simbolico della madre*, this return results in the acquisition of one's ability to express oneself and to subjectively create meaning. For Luciana Percovich, the assumption of the mother as reference point is a political choice based on women's desire to redefine their identity. Like Muraro, Percovich deems this act essential to defining women's culture.[16] For Paola Melchiori, the "mother-daughter / daughter-mother" dyad explodes the social hierarchy the family historically contains while it accentuates women's ability to create relationships of reciprocal learning. Here, the symbolic mother transcends the essentialist maternal experience and makes evident the limits of biological motherhood, limits imposed not only by society, but also by extension the relationship with the daughter, whose very identity itself determines its boundaries.[17]

Feminists focused on revising maternal experiences have for the most part engaged in a polemical debate with the standardized classifications of gender delimiting motherhood. The debate, as we have seen above, has been largely informed by both essentialist and constructionist definitions of womanhood. Briefly, the essentialist perspective maintains that maleness and femaleness and the gendered roles ascribed to them are "essential," derived from a biological, and therefore absolute and irrefutable foundation. With regards to motherhood, nurturance and other characteristics ascribed to the role, such as self-sacrifice, are instinctual. For the constructionist, gender differences are the result of characteristics and roles created in a particular culture, resulting in historical, multilayered, mutable experiences. Motherhood in this scenario comprises qualities determined by a specific milieu, so that a characteristic such as nurturance becomes defined for the fulfillment of a culturally mandated notion and purpose.

The differences between these two views on gender and, for our purposes, motherhood, have created what Diana Fuss labels an "impasse" in feminist theory, "predicated on the difficulty of theorizing the social in relation to the natural."[18] This impasse, as Fuss and Teresa De Lauretis have both concluded, is the result of feminists' not unfounded fear of women's being limited to and by essentialist categories of gender. The restrictions imposed by gender roles have disenfranchised women and removed prescriptions regarding the body from the mother's agency.[19] The mother is therefore excluded from the production of the conventions and regulations that define motherhood, the spaces she inhabits, and the governance of her own body within those spaces. The mother's role is, once again, merely supportive, rather than creative.

This impasse can, as Fuss maintains, be defeated and a truly freeing theory of women's liberation constructed. French philosopher and constructionist Simone de Beauvoir maintained that a woman is made, not born, refuting the limiting notion that "woman is womb."[20] Certainly essentialism poses a threat to the struggle both to achieve liberatory practices and to defeat the ahistorical perspectives of Aristotelian, Hegelian, and Freudian theories. As Luce Irigaray shows, however, a theory of women's liberation is far too complex to reject outright a perspective that, joined with other possibilities, can have constructive meaning for women. In her influential work *This Sex which is Not One*, Irigaray deconstructs women's sexuality in light of the patriarchal culture that has historically defined it. Rather than reducing it to essential wholeness, she defines female sexuality as a plurality and women as subjects producing plural meanings. Irigaray's polemic against sexual difference is that as a constructed system for defining maleness and femaleness in biological categories it has the potential of reducing women to "being only the indispensable compliment to the only sex."[21] Women's plurality, their complex and multilayered sexuality, and the pleasure derived from it are not reducible to one specific physical area—as Freud would have it, the penis versus the clitoris. Rather, because women's bodies have multiple erogenous zones, the plurality causes the individual to be "indefinitely other in herself" (and perhaps even *different* within herself), to be a complex sexual subject. Although this notion suggests that women's identity and expression is biologically determined—an essentialist view—Irigaray's theory refuses both the confinement of women to a single identity, purpose, and experience, and the fragmentation that divests the maternal role of desire and agency. Rereading both essentialist and constructionist positions, while keeping present De Lauretis' warning to "[take] the risk of essentialism seriously," we can conclude that a truly liberatory experience of womanhood can include the awareness and practice of the biological and symbolic potential of motherhood: A woman creates both life and ideas, develops both social beings and meanings with cultural currency.

Within these theoretical debates, Italian feminists have endeavored to achieve the marriage between womanhood and motherhood, the recognition of the mother's sexuality, of the need to create a holistic identity of womanhood in which a mother is not devoid of agency, pleasure, or desire.[22] Their efforts enlighten our approach to the portrayal of motherhood in Maraini's literary production. Italian women authors who are contemporaries of Maraini, among whom Elsa Morante, Natalia Ginzburg, Oriana Fallaci, and Francesca Sanvitale, and especially since the 1970s, have attempted through their work to "give life back to that mother, to the mother who lives within us and among us."[23] They have recognized in this dictum the reciprocal nature of the mother-daughter relationship. This relationship of "mutuality," as Adrienne Rich defines it, extends beyond the biological to encompass the Irigarayan feat of giving birth in the symbolic realm. Recognition of this bond signifies identifying the relationship as a complex one: The biological mother gives birth—both physically and symbolically—to the daughter, for as mother she not only procreates a physical being, but also introduces her to the world of symbols with which she as daughter will create meaning. As a result, the adult daughter, as we have seen in chapter 1, gives symbolic (re)birth to the mother, who in turn becomes a daughter, living Melchiori's duality "mother-daughter, daughter-mother."

With their depictions of the mother's story, Italian women authors have responded in part to the more conventional portraits of motherhood in Italian literature. Some exemplary twentieth-century portraits depict the mother in a strictly essentialist familial role, where her participation in the narrative is determined by and limited to the maternal identity. Most often, the parameters for the mother's portrait are set by her biological role, her Hegelian exclusion from political debate, and by the psychoanalytic understanding of her position within the family. The mother or maternal figure is generally drawn along the conventional lines of sacrifice, social introversion, fortitude, and asexuality. If she questions or performs actions undermining these desired qualities, her position is rectified or she disappears from the narrative. The narrative cannot withstand the tension the mother's actions create because the woman cannot divorce herself from her maternal identity. The text therefore works to restabilize the relationships circumscribed by motherhood.

Elio Vittorini's 1941 novel *Conversazione in Sicilia* [In Sicily] and Italo Calvino's 1947 novel, *Il sentiero dei nidi di ragno* [The Path to the Nest of Spiders] are two canonical works whose momentous portraits of the mother reveal the intricacies of the cultural discourse on motherhood. In both texts of filial development, the mother must remain within the prescriptions of her role and the son must eventually abandon her for both psychic and narrative development to occur. Vittorini's allegorical tale showcases the mother's role in her offspring's subjective development and preserves the expected subordination of her desires to the maternal role. The mother Concezione [Conception] inhabits a sort of dreamscape nestled in the narrator Silvestro's memory, constituting a mythology of his past. She is her adult son's mnemonic gateway to his childhood roots and Virgilian guide through familial territory, occupying the "underground" site Luce Irigaray recognizes as the mother's historical fate for her relegation to the background of the adult child's life. As guide and prompter, then, Concezione helps her son reconstruct his adult identity. Indeed, she more specifically becomes "procreator" of his past and of meaning within that personal history, a role represented by her very name.

Despite the mother's centrality in this narrative of development, however, expressions of her sexuality can threaten to destabilize her maternal identity and, as a result, her role in the son's development. Accounts of her extramarital relationships cause the mother's sexuality to seep through the narrative, and as a result must be contained. In the novel, the stories of Concezione's relationships are reduced to an interrogation by the son that, while friendly, nevertheless underscores the social unease of confronting the mother's sexuality. Concezione had dalliances with two men when her husband pursued affairs with other women. Her recounting of her sexual encounters are the result of Silvestro's conversation, not of her own intentional expression of these experiences. She is hesitant about introducing the matter into their exchange. Because the conversation brings this element of her womanhood into the familial arena, it is quickly located under the son's discursive tutelage. This frame is constructed by Silvestro's interpretation of events and ultimately undermines Concezione's own willing participation in the dalliances: [S]: " 'I imagine he must have raped you!' [C]: 'Raped me?' " (81–82). Although at first reticent about discussing the matter, the mother's simple exclamation serves to reestablish her agency in her extra-marital relationships. It also counters the son's assessment and subtly reveals that she herself desired the consensual relationships. Silvestro marvels at her attitude because she stands as the object against which he (re)constructs his personal narrative. His journey through familial territory assumes—a priori—stable and recognizable roles.

In Calvino's novel, the young protagonist Pin's Freudian rejection of the maternal figures in his life is depicted as necessary to accede to paternal order. This order is represented by war, a male concern, and in particular by the male members of the Resistance movement. The depiction of the maternal figures in this work shows how alterations of the conventional maternal image are considered destabilizing forces in the fabric of Western civilization. As they introduce sexuality into the narrative, the text's two female characters unbalance androcentric order and threaten the very success of the Resistance. Despite their sexually threatening position within the text, Pin's sister Rina La Nera and the married Giglia are nevertheless at first represented as potential mother figures for the young motherless protagonist. Both women, however, fall short of this role, and their failure justifies the mother's ultimate demise. Rina has always shunned conventional domestic work and, as a prostitute working with the Germans and the Fascists, she embodies moral depravity. She cannot, therefore, be assumed as Pin's mentor into adulthood. Giglia, meanwhile, is the most obvious maternal figure, but assumes an ambivalent role that is defined by Pin's willful resistance of a relationship with her. As she introduces the element of sexual temptation into the partisan group, she draws attention away from the fighters' cause and from Pin's instruction in this cause. For their problematic identities, therefore, both women must be abandoned as maternal figures for Pin's development to occur and for Western civilization, in the guise of war, to succeed.

Unlike these more conventional portrayals, the narratives women authors have produced have not resisted the mother's foray into the forbidden territory of sexuality and self-definition. Rather, they have allowed her experiences within it to develop and to be articulated. Although not all resulting characters succeed in their challenges of the traditional maternal role, the texts are invaluable assessments of the relationship between women and cultural expectations.

Because they must contend with a myriad of cultural factors embedded within motherhood, the portraits I examine are not always constructive and do not necessarily convey hope for an enriching experience of motherhood that is not restrictive and oppressive. Oftentimes these representations are created within a narrative in which the daughter is subject, a difficult reality in the struggle to give mothers a voice. Indeed, striving to carve spaces of her own, and in order to liberate her identity from the restrictions the mother exemplifies, the daughter tends to either reject the mother or criticize her without offering hope for a mutually beneficial reconciliation.[24] In those texts, however, where the mother is the narrative's central character, her own understanding of her situation informs the depiction. The motives for the mother's actions are not necessarily questioned or questionable. Rather, they are understood within the context of the sites she inhabits in her role, and reflect women's positions in the historical periods in which the texts were produced.

In Natalia Ginzburg's short story "La madre" [The Mother], the title character lives out a poignant tale of entrapment in a stultifying role and rejection by her family. Published in 1957, this text reflects the attitudes toward women of the immediate postwar era, which saw, as Saraceno points out, an intensified link between women and the domestic sphere. Ginzburg's protagonist represents the tensions between the conservative attitude toward motherhood and the slowly changing lexicon of women writers and such early reformers as *UDI* and *Demau*. The polemic is judged, as historian Michela De Giorgio notes, a "social question," for its introduction into the public sphere both of politics and readership.[25]

Ginzburg's 1950s mother eschews convention in both appearance and behavior: She smokes, she goes to the movies in the evening, she keeps a disorderly room, wears makeup, and appears younger than other children's mothers. She has created a life in which womanhood and motherhood coexist in her identity. The family's views and pronouncements on her transgressions, however, create a schism between the two, deeming the mother a wholly ineffectual member of the family. The laws applied to her are governed by her father, the family patriarch, who reproaches her for going out evenings. The father's attitude and judgment is upheld by the children, who feel burdened by the mother's difference from conventional mothers.[26] The protagonist's worthiness as a mother is determined by the family's judgments and by family members' conceptualization of their relationship to her. The identity sites she is therefore allowed to occupy are circumscribed by the family and she, as a woman, dies a sort of sociocultural asphyxiation.

In Oriana Fallaci's landmark 1975 epistolary novel, *Lettera a un bambino mai nato* [Letter to a Child Never Born], the mother inhabits the space of first-person narrator who subjectively articulates the meaning of her experiences. The letter of the text's title, addressed to the child she is expecting, constitutes the mother's considerations of diverse social and cultural discourses on motherhood. It creates meaning out of her experiences and opens the literary public up to the debates her letter showcases. The narrator-mother, who recounts her story to her embryo, breaks the silence of a woman's experiences during gestation and responds to the roles those around her construct for her to fulfill. Her boss's reaction to her pregnancy, for example, reflects the Hegelian separation between domestic and public spheres: He does not think the protagonist can successfully carry out her already flourishing career in journalism because her thoughts will be hampered and divided by her primary, biological function as mother. The doctor, espousing an essentialist view, presents the mother's allegiance and devotion to her child as instinctual and natural. The protagonist challenges these restrictive perspectives by waging a campaign for the integration of motherhood into her already intense, thriving, and rewarding intellectual life, rather than perpetuating the stifling division between the two areas of her life.

The author, however, recognizes the complexity of motherhood, and does not fall into the trap of pitting one "side" against the other. In an alternative perspective of women's positions in these circumstances, the protagonist also takes on her liberal girlfriend's rejection of the beneficial possibilities of motherhood. Her resistance to her friend's support of an abortion and negative view of motherhood sheds light on the ambivalent position the friend represents and women face. The friend's position of an either/or dichotomy mirrors the doctor's and boss' in its divisiveness. The friend, like the protagonist, is pro-choice and advocates protection of women's rights, but her extreme position within the novel renders her advice restrictive as well.

The mother, instead, focuses on the life she is procreating and on the potential of that "child" itself to promote a philosophy of human rights in the future. The experiences she articulates in her letter provide her direction in her child's education. Like Carla Lonzi's proposition that mothers should raise men respectful of women's rights and desires, Fallaci's protagonist sees motherhood as the possibility of procreating and raising a child who will contribute to society by altering those elements that have rendered her experiences and other women's experiences so defeating.

Franca Rame's 1977 play "L'uomo incinto" [The Pregnant Man] considers pregnancy from the point of view of a pregnant man in order to highlight and satirize the stereotypes that undermine the value of women's prenatal experiences. In the play, a forty-five-year-old wife, her eighteen-year-old daughter, and her industrialist husband (*Industriale*) are all pregnant. The two women represent generational differences in the way pregnancy and motherhood are perceived. For the unmarried daughter, the pregnancy should create a bond of friendship with her mother. She resents her mother's continual referral to her as *bambina mia* (my child), because her impending motherhood brings the two women closer in experience. The mother, on the other hand, not aware of her daughter's pregnancy, occupies an uneasy position within the narrative, for she maintains a traditional attitude toward motherhood and toward the relationship between the sexes, even though this attitude undermines women's choices, hers included. She considers herself too old to have children and will not accept her husband's proposal of termination, and refuses to admit that an unmarried woman such as her daughter could have children. She also refuses to support her daughter in her criticism of her father, even when the *Industriale*'s position renders the mother's position subordinate,

> [DAUGHTER]: In other words he suggested that you get an abortion.
> [MOTHER]: But your father has his principles, his morals.
> [D]: Well, of course, because he's not the pregnant one.... He's the boss!
> [M]: Remember he's your father! (106).[27]

This conversation contains cultural elements familiar to the reader: the father/husband's authority, the daughter's revision of that authority, and the mother's defense of that authority.

These reference points, however, are turned on their head when the situation crosses genders and a male voice articulates the experience of being pregnant.[28] Rame provides several stereotypes used as signposts in the depiction of pregnancy, nausea, cravings, and knitting. The *Industriale*'s understanding of these states highlights the levity with which pregnancy is typically portrayed in Western culture. After spending a November night searching for watermelon to satisfy his craving, for example, he notes, "I didn't find one, but I found an old lady knitting . . . and I was overtaken by the desire to start knitting myself. . . . So I knit like crazy the whole night . . . and I made a lovely little scarf" (109). The *Industriale*'s reaction to discovering that he is pregnant is to seek an abortion, a hypocritical exception he makes even as the president of an anti-abortion league, justifying his demand with the tale of Adam and Eve, "I'm not a woman. . . . I wasn't born to suffer . . . and to give birth with pain! I didn't steal the apple, I didn't make a deal with the devil" (112).

The *Industriale*'s succinct version of the tale emphasizes the foundational elements of the Western account of women's reproduction. It highlights women's culpability in the sex act (the apple, the devil), which results in pain through pregnancy and childbirth. This judgment is present in the way the daughter and mother must deal with pregnancy: The daughter's pregnancy is the result of a transgression of the moral laws of marriage; her mother's state is the result of carelessness (the pregnancy can make fatal an already existing physical condition) and the basis of the mother's feeling of shame. Pairing these reactions with the father's absurd situation showcases the bind of pregnancy and motherhood for women, one created more by sociocultural convention than by the physical state of gestation.

The mothers in these works by Natalia Ginzburg, Oriana Fallaci, and Franca Rame all confront restrictive attitudes on motherhood while developing sites in which to subjectively define women's experiences. Ginzburg's short story centers exclusively on the mother's experiences in the family as she transgresses social mores to avoid subsuming her desire for enjoyment outside the home under her role as mother. Her family's condemning attitude, however, makes it impossible for her to live fully in both spheres. Fallaci's epistolary text becomes the venue for the mother's personal account of her experiences and her subjective assessment of the social debates on motherhood. Rame's brief one-act play cleverly intertwines diverse discourses on motherhood to reveal the cultural viewpoints shaping the experience. Although different in approach, all three works showcase the conflict between the struggle for a subjective expression of motherhood and the powerful conventions regulating it.

The maternal figures in Maraini's works showcase either conventional experiences of motherhood or alternative ones made possible by the cultural context feminism defines. These figures originate from Maraini's exploration of this role since the 1960s and are situated between the traditional maternal role and the new maternal discourse proposed by the women's movement. While this positioning can prove problematic for women who feel ambivalent toward the conventional role, it nevertheless prompts us to rethink the potentials of motherhood and understand the predicament of an unrevised role. For this reason, the author's maternal figures provide a compelling portrait of motherhood forged out of women's history. In earlier works, Maraini analyzes the mother's position within the family as well as the social disempowerment through which the role is enforced, calling the role women's "sole social expression."[29] The outcome is the depiction of a motherhood that has a dubious and often tragic nature: The mother not only fails to express her sexuality, as Teresa in *L'età del malessere*, but she is also caught between the desire for bonding with her adult daughter and the transmittance of patriarchal values sanctioned by the maternal code. These texts contemplate what Adrienne Rich defines *the essential female tragedy*—"the loss of the daughter to the mother, the mother to the daughter."[30] Works produced at the height of the feminist movement, however, such as the 1978 film *Giochi di latte*, create maternal figures instrumental in the daughter's symbolic placement. At the same time, they suggest the possibility of a new maternal experience that does not fragment a woman's identity, but allows her to live out her potential as both woman and mother.

When Maraini published "Madre canina" in the 1966 poetry collection *Crudeltà all'aria aperta*, the women's movement had just begun to define its ethos and its program through published manifestos and newly organized women's groups. The first group to have a substantial impact on this definition was *Demau*, which issued its now canonical "Manifesto" in the same year. This position paper highlighted the problematic nature of women's familial roles and specifically the division of labor, and subverted the notion of the problems women bring to society by raising the question of the problems society brings to women. In outlining these issues, the group's vision extended to the socio-political spaces within which women's identities and roles are determined. Its work, meanwhile, set up a functional paradigm for women's liberation and, by extension, for authors concerned with creating revisionary and revolutionary texts that would bring women's experiences into the public sphere of readership.[31]

When read against *Demau*'s model and inquiry, "Madre canina" is shown to be a narrow portrait of motherhood that asks what problems the mother poses for herself and for her daughter. It does not propose change, but rather is an exposition of the mother's own complicity in her subjugation. While *Demau* augurs the new feminist daughter's central role in addressing issues of women's liberation and in bridging the chasm between domestic and public spheres, micro- and macrohistories, Maraini's daughter-poet's description of an "inexistant" and "guilty" mother reflects the daughter's ambivalence toward the maternal figure she is culturally destined to become. As a result, the poem delves into the emotional rift between a daughter who is awakening to feminist consciousness and the mother who has quietly acquiesced to a stultifying role.

The mother's image is perceived as a painful, ambivalent one, created out of a dominant cultural model of female existence. Conventional properties of motherhood are highlighted through its traditional attributes derived from the ideal of courtly love, "purezza," "dolce" (purity, sweet).[32] Historically, these attributes of muted sexuality and passivity were an outward manifestation of a nonthreatening feminine ideal or mystique, as depicted by such celebrated portraits of the feminine as Dante's Beatrice and Petrarca's Laura. They are a woman's currency in a patriarchal system of gender in which contained sexuality is preferred. Their attribution to motherhood in a post-Freudian culture reflects the culture's continuing unwillingness to recognize the sexual component of motherhood and a mother's sexual persona. When Maraini's poem couples the above qualities with the terms "senza storia" (without history) and "inestistenza" (nonexistence), the reality behind the image is revealed: Relegated to the private sphere for centuries, and dutifully fulfilling her role, with her *storia* unwritten and untold, the mother is displaced in history and therefore excluded from "official" existence. At the same time her absence from *storia* also belies her social and cultural destiny. The absence creates the illusion that the mother's purity is essential, ahistorical, a given and irrefutable part of her identity, of her Hegelian universal substance.

"Madre canina" is the daughter's sometimes contemptuous attempt to comprehend the complexities of the woman who generated her and prepared her for social integration. It encapsulates her vision of the maternal, between tradition and fragile potentialities. Significantly, this poem occupies a central space in the poetry collection and, consequently, in the daughter's development charted by the collection. In this spatial capacity, it represents the space the daughter must traverse in order to progress from her cherished relationship with the father to womanhood. Within this scenario of the daughterly evolution, the mother symbolizes the dichotomous identity which the daughter must confront in order to achieve the liberation to which she, in the mid-1960s, aspired. The maternal portrait the daughter creates teeters between a tenuous pathos and aversion. It nevertheless anticipates aspects of motherhood central to its reconstruction in later feminist discourses.[33]

The problematic nature of the fulfillment of the traditional maternal role is depicted through concrete images, and the juxtaposition of contradictory concepts, nouns, and unexpected adjectives. The maternal experience is framed by concrete elements constituting recognizable sociocultural reference points for the reader. The poet reconstructs the mother's physicality through elements originating from the daughter's memory but based on the maternal body, "menstrual odor;" "tired cheeks;" "disconcertingly white hips;" "red . . . morning nails;" "consenting throat;" "cunning teeth;" "friendly mare's breasts." Although these pairings may at first reading seem unusual, the basic physical elements they contain are familiar as attributes of a woman's physicality and therefore create a context from which to draw meaning. The menstrual odor links the mother to other women in their biological reality, while her mare's breasts recall both her nurturance and daily labor; the tired cheeks and disconcertingly white hips recall her physical state after working; her teeth are cunning because they hide "nervous rage" that "crowns her breast" by not articulating consciousness of her situation, while at the same time articulating the daughter's education into femininity.

Even though it highlights only the problematic aspects of motherhood and provides only glimpses of its beneficial possibilities, Maraini's poem still retrieves the maternal figure from the oblivion sanctioned by her domestic role, and, in a moment that does follow *Demau*'s prescription, demystifies the maternal experience. This poem was written at a moment in Italian women's history when consciousness of the reality of the conventional role was just beginning to inform the political movement. While Maraini consciously foregrounds elements that are primary factors in the new maternal discourse she envisions, her portrayal of the mother in "Madre canina" remains a deliberately realistic depiction of the traditional role.

Bringing the maternal presence and experiences of motherhood into public consciousness and inscribing it into history became an imperative of the women's movement during the 1970s. In the 1960s and 1970s, the focus was on women's experiences in the domestic sphere and polemics were mounted against the discomforting notion of essentialism. The psychoanalytically supported notion of motherhood as biological destiny proved a theoretical and practical hurdle to surmount in the struggle for reproductive rights and for the recognition and practice of motherhood as the empowering potential to create both human life and a female-centered—if not all-inclusive—symbolic order. By the late 1970s, feminist theory ventured into the symbolic arena of motherhood as a relational link not only between biological mother and daughter, but also between women across generations and cultures. This link encouraged women to journey through their personal and cultural pasts to integrate the mother into their "official" history.

Within Maraini's body of work, two short films, the 1978 *Giochi di latte* and the 1981 *La bella addormentata nel bosco,* provide a visual landscape of motherhood as seen through the lens of this perspective. The films' portraits reveal a more gentle understanding of the mother and the role she carries out as procreator in the daughter's life and as manager of the domestic sphere. *Giochi* develops a new vision of motherhood designed to embrace procreativity as a legacy for the daughter. *La bella*, meanwhile, does not create a model that revolutionizes the maternal experience. Rather, it alters our perception of motherhood by exploring the mother's desire, a source of tension in conventional narratives.

With *Giochi di latte*, Maraini transports the maternal image into visual scenes occupied by both mother and daughter. The film takes place in a park, inhabited by an old statue of an ancient goddess, and confronts the mother's dualistic nature as both woman in the daughter's life and educator into her restrictive role. In a discussion of this film, Maraini clarifies this position,

> This mother is a character based on a duality. On the one hand, she transmits the father's laws. On the other hand, she nurtures and gives life, and the two things cannot be perfectly reconciled. They are the reflection of reality. We live in a culture that contains both these things. The traditional role within the family contains sacrifice, and it also contains motherhood as a gift, as ability to create life. Women must face these two historical tensions.[34]

The film confronts these two images and in the end displaces the mother's role as socializer. While it opens with a scene that establishes both the mother's role as socializer and procreator, it closes with a shot that affirms her empowering potential as guide through the newly defined cultural legacy the film proposes.

The film's opening scene sets the context in which the displacement will take place. The visibly pregnant mother and her young daughter walk hand-in-hand through the park, stopping to contemplate the weathered statue. While the physical proximity between the two main characters emphasizes the close relationship between mother and daughter, the statue foregrounds the femaleness of their bond and adds an atavic dimension to it. This third presence revises the familial father-son-mother triad by extending it into new relational spaces, the genealogical line of mother-mother-daughter. The configuration is further highlighted by milk flowing from the statue's breast, a more powerful and life-affirming symbol than the animalistic "mare's breasts" of "Madre canina." Since the pregnant mother herself already stands as the bearer and nurturer of life, the statue links her generative function to a cultural heritage represented by, as Maraini defines her, "a deity, a great goddess, Gea," the earth mother.[35]

Before definitively restoring the feminist model of the mother-daughter relationship, however, the film, in a moment of realism, introduces the mother's role as defined after Apollo's decree. It presents the mother as transmitter of conventional values through two similar shots. In both, the mother adjusts the young daughter's hair. As the mother and daughter walk through the park, the camera zooms in on the back of the daughter's head and gives an extreme close-up of the mother's hand at work on the daughter, an action repeated several times.[36] Repetition peels away the symbolism of the mother's action and underscores the forcefulness of her gesture. The gesture is repeated in two distinct shots, and in both it is isolated and emphasized through extreme close-ups. The mother's action imposes control on the daughter's "errant" hair, and reshapes it to fit the proper image of what her appearance, and thus the daughter herself, should be (feminine) and do (act properly).

In the film, these two shots intersect with more powerful images of the mother's ability to create and nurture life, thus emphasizing the more beneficial potential. Right after the first of these shots, the camera moves to a close-up of the daughter, who contemplates her mother's pregnant belly. The camera then moves to the mother's laughing face. These two images undercut the picture of the mother adjusting the daughter's hair. Although in the first scene the mother socializes the daughter, in the second both she and the daughter bond through laughter, a sign of understanding and of the daughter's inheritance of the rich female legacy the mother and goddess represent. Knowledge is therefore transmitted from mother to daughter: not only the codes of feminine behavior, but also and more significantly for women's liberation, the understanding of their potential as women, as subjects of a new maternal discourse. As both smile at each other, as their bond grows, the stream of milk from the statue's breast grows heavier and becomes absorbed by the earth, which will renew and perpetuate its life-sustaining potential. As the film ends, the camera gives extreme close-ups of the mother and daughter who once more contemplate the statue's lactating breasts. Mother and daughter walk off together, sharing the knowledge of their mutual confirmation.

Inscribing a liberating motherhood onto history and constructing visual spaces for the mother to inhabit can include the revision of traditional tales containing gendered paradigms replete with rewards for "good" behavior and punishments for "bad" behavior. As we have seen in *Giochi di latte*, the mother and daughter are placed into a historical setting. The setting is constructed to provide the mother-daughter relationship with a place of its own, containing physical signs symbolizing the bond's cultural legacy. The film *La bella addormentata nel bosco* revises the Sleeping Beauty story by replacing the virginal protagonist of the original with a mother figure. It deconstructs the fairytale, a process that leads back to the family, the original site of subjective formation and socialization. The result is a film that reconstructs a maternal discourse out of elements from the other side of the myth's (un)reality and out of the fairytale's excess.

This excess is the mother's elided reality within conventional narratives, a reality that often underlies them but is not allowed to surface.[37] The film exposes the encoding of women's sexuality in the tale by examining the relationships in the domestic realm that result from the euphoric relationship of marriage to Prince Charming, but that are never read beyond the tale's ending. The original tale would like us to believe that the heroine's salvation lies in achieving marriage to the Prince, that the union with the Prince represents the reward for her "good" behavior, and that the promised "ever after" results in a happy life. *La bella* contrarily reveals that the "ever after" within the domestic sphere fulfills a duality—both the problematic site of familial tensions and the site of feminine desire.

While the original Princess' identity and success are determined in part by her beauty, in the feminist cinematic revision the heroine's identity is motherhood and her desire is delimited by her children and housework. In the original tale Sleeping Beauty awaits awakening by a young prince—a sexual awakening resulting in admission into a social hierarchy of which she is beneficiary. In Maraini's film, the heroine is confined to the domestic sphere. She is not restricted, however, to the conventional aspects of motherhood played out through domestic labor and in relation to her son and daughter. Instead, as its title suggests, the film focuses in large part on the heroine's desires as a woman, thus suturing the split between mother and woman marked by the inadmissibility of desire in the maternal identity.[38]

La bella addormentata nel bosco examines these two aspects in two different moments. The examination at first suggests their incompatibility, but in the end shows through the heroine's cheerful demeanor how they are successfully integrated in her life. The film employs diverse shots to create a multilayered Irigarayan image of motherhood. The context of the protagonist's existence is carefully crafted through deliberate use of "real time," which pits the mother's dreams against the tediousness of her daily activities. The film takes particular care to represent domestic activities in their full temporal scope, to not only present their place in a "realistic" portrait of housework but also to showcase their symbolic value within the heroine's narrative.[39] Each frame isolates elements of this work. Close-ups highlight the confining parameters of the domestic space, focusing on both the creative potential of this sphere and the repetitive tasks constituting it. In several scenes throughout *La bella*, the camera focuses with extreme close-ups on the mother's work, zooming in on the tools of her household labor. By isolating each movement, the camera pieces together a cinematic syntax of the mother's enterprises. Thus, for example, the camera provides a close-up of soapy water in a bucket; of the mother's hands, "housewife elegant" in pink rubber gloves; of her mop, one of the implements of her trade; and finally on her hands as she cleans the floor. Similarly, the camera showcases the raw materials the mother uses to produce the food necessary to sustain her family. This isolating technique foregrounds otherwise invisible and consequently devalued aspects of the mother's daily narrative, and transforms them as well into part of the film's syntax. In this capacity, the images gain a symbolic dimension and convey the protagonist's unverbalized thoughts and repressed desires. For example, when the mother uses onions and tomatoes to prepare lunch, alternating close-ups of her dreamy countenance and the objects with which she works invest the objects with sensuality. While her hands physically work the food, her mind wanders to the outside field that later serves as the stage for her fantasies. This careful interchanging of images creates a tactile sensation linked to the protagonist's thoughts.[40]

In the film, motherhood is, as we have noted, physically played out in domestic spaces. Consequently, relationally and, it follows, psychoanalytically, it is played out in the familial sphere. Through the mother's relationship with her son and daughter, *La bella* explores and exposes women's identity and position within the family. Although the husband—the symbolic reminder of social law—is not present, his absence does not result in a development between mother and child. Other Maraini works proffer sisterhood as a solution to this predicament, because it allows women to explore and develop facets of their lives outside the immediate family. In this film, however, the mother never progresses beyond her spaces within it. The family itself anchors her desire, so the film cannot resolve the tension between the sensuality with which the mother endows her work and the environment within which she carries out that work.

The mother's dreams do offer a subversive version of the relationship with the son and daughter, although, as Maraini notes about this film, "even in her dreams her children bring her back home."[41] This split between relationships played out in the physical realm and relationships played out in a dreamscape potentially creates a dilemma. Contained within the private sphere, the familial relationships revolve around a traditional maternal figure. Having acceded to the public sphere, the adolescent son and daughter disregard the mother, remaining instead absorbed in each other's antics and popular music. Tellingly, as they happily play the song "I Can't Get No Satisfaction," they do not recognize its implications for the mother: Confinement to the domestic sphere ensures her satisfaction will not be realized because deprived of its potential fulfillment in other sites. Satisfaction can only be achieved in the heroine's dreams, which, by unfolding in spaces outside the immediate home, symbolically liberate her.

Liberation of the mother's desire turns conventional expectations on their head. Traditionally, the cinematic narrative is appropriated by the male gaze, both, again, the gaze of the male protagonist, who promotes textual action, and the male spectator, representative of the film's male subject. The female characters are thus contained within this dualistic male gaze and consequently objectified. Maraini's version of Sleeping Beauty subverts this set up by taking the mother's exploratory gaze as its point of view. For her spectator this position is significant, especially in a film about a woman's liberation. In their introductory essay to *Off Screen*, Giuliana Bruno and Maria Nadotti note the importance of appropriating female pleasure from the male gaze in constructing critical discourses on cinema. While as the object of the male gaze it is negated as a subjective experience, its reappropriation by the female gaze brings it into the realm of female experience and construction.[42] The critical model Bruno and Nadotti propose works as well in considerations of a film's internal narrative. By releasing its heroine's fantasies through her own subjective interpretation, *La bella* guides the spectator through her inner self.

As a revision of the Sleeping Beauty story, Maraini's film challenges the spectator as it questions the conventional narrative of motherhood. The spectator is placed before the heroine/mother's desire and participates in its subversiveness. The heroine's two-part dream recounts the Oedipal story, this time undermining its androcentric narrative, and refigures the mother-daughter relationship from one of socialization to one of procreation into subjectivity. In the first part, the son as a masked Prince Charming arrives on a white horse to awaken his mother/Sleeping Beauty. In the second part, the mother awakens and nurtures her dead daughter back to life. In both, the film's structural language frees the mother's experiences. While, as we have seen, close-ups of objects that make up the heroine's work convey the narrowness of her existence at the same time that they are sensualized and gain value in her life, the alternation of long, medium, and close-up shots within the mother's dream sequences orchestrates the liberating fulfillment of the sensuality contained in these objects. Long and medium angles give breadth to the action while close-ups primarily frame the mother's exploratory gaze. For example, in the first fantasy sequence, long and medium shots frame the arrival of Prince Charming. Later, the camera moves to a close-up of the mother's eye as she unmasks her son. Without resorting to a subjective-point-of-view shot, the film showcases the heroine's own gaze and perception of the unveiling. In the second dream, medium shots frame the mother's awakening of her dead daughter and her subsequent nurturance. These medium frames allow the mother-daughter relationship to fully unfold uninterrupted.

As in other Maraini works, the content and structure of these two dream sequences displace a conventional psychoanalytic paradigm of relationships. The mother's dreams subtly frustrate this model by proposing the reintegration of the pre-Oedipal and Oedipal bonds in adulthood. While in the domestic scene the film implies that the son and daughter have successfully abandoned the mother to enter the Symbolic sphere, the mother's fantasies reveal her desire to recuperate the original bond of reciprocal love and nurturance of their childhood. The film traverses forbidden territory when revealing the mother's desire, especially when replayed within the Oedipal bond with the son. It does not, however, unleash its heroine's fantasies into the socially dangerous territory of incest. Instead, it structurally maintains the distinction between the "real" mother watching the fantasy unfold and the "fictive" mother living the fantasy. While serving the purpose of subverting the consequences of her children's development out of the Oedipal phase, this distinction also layers the mother's gaze and empowers her as promoter of the narrative action, a fact the film highlights by immediately returning to the mother inside the home. The representation of the mother's gaze and her creative potential in the home and as procreator constructs revisionary images in women's culture. At the same time, by focusing on the mother's relationship with her progeny within this culture, this film, like *Giochi*, redefines the bonds from a maternal perspective.

Like in *La bella*, in the 1981 play *I sogni di Clitennestra* Maraini also revisits an age-old tale, this time recreating an ancient myth significant to theories of familial relationships. The text revises Aeschylus' *The Oresteia* and examines what occurs when the bond between mother and daughter is not restored. The Greek author's work was chosen to represent women's struggle against the restrictive precepts of motherhood for its importance in mythological history as chronicle of the passage from matriarchy to patriarchy.[43] Maraini's play reinterprets the Aeschylian myth from a woman's perspective to disclose Clytemnestra's power as queen and mother and its subversion by the literary and social patriarchal text.[44]

As revision of Aeschylus' text, *I sogni di Clitennestra* transposes the Greek Clytemnestra to present-day Prato, recontextualizing her concerns as both woman and mother. The new myth examines how

Apollo and Athena's favorable judgment of Orestes' matricide in the original work redefined motherhood and affected the experiences of the modern-day protagonist, Clitennestra. As a mother in contemporary society, Clitennestra must embody the social laws of motherhood, renouncing her sexuality and upholding and transmitting conventional morality within the family. When she strives to define her own identity and redefine the maternal role from a woman-centered perspective, she comes into conflict with the more restrictive role.

While Aeschylus' text represented the historical transition from matriarchal to patriarchal society, Maraini's play constructs a female genealogy with Clitennestra as symbolic mother and reference point for women's liberation. By paralleling events in the modern heroine's life with events in the Aeschylian queen's life, Maraini's text assumes the Greek Clytemnestra as female-gendered frame of reference. It subverts Clytemnestra's powerlessness by claiming her as an ancestor for women. Clitennestra, the object of patriarchal society, identifies with Clytemnestra, the subject of matriarchal society. However, while *The Oresteia* focuses primarily on Agamemnon's murder, his children's reaction to it, and the favorable judgment the gods pass on Orestes' matricide, *I sogni di Clitennestra* maintains a feminist perspective by focusing on Clitennestra and motherhood.

In order to showcase Clitennestra's concerns and her conflict with the control exerted on motherhood, Maraini's play highlights and alters elements of the Greek play to articulate the mother's condition. The play's oneiric structure turns on the transcendental qualities of dreams and fortifies the lineage between the two Clytemnestras and the similarities between the two texts.[45] Because it obscures the distinction between dream and reality, Maraini's text increases the collective quality of both Clytemnestra and Clitennestra's experiences and imprints them onto a cultural continuum. Clitennestra's dreams allow the Greek Clytemnestra's experiences of motherhood to transcend time and to become an experience common to, but not exactly analogous for, Clitennestra. The dreams in Maraini's play underscore the fact that women's endeavors to rewrite history are strengthened through the recognition of this history's collective nature.

To further enhance the connection between Aeschylus' Clytemnestra and Clitennestra, several speeches anchor *I sogni* to its foundation. The play is framed by two speeches, almost direct citations from Aeschylus' piece and appearing in *The Eumenides*, the third part of *The*

Oresteia. Here, Apollo and Athena's judgment transforms the Furies, born "from the womb of mother night" and avengers of matriarchal law, into the complacent and docile Eumenides of patriarchal law.[46] These speeches introduce and conclude Maraini's play as urgent calls to women to reclaim and defend their empowering potential to create life and meaning. Delivered by Clitennestra, the initial soliloquy introduces her perspective of the son's matricide and calls forth the Furies to awaken and vindicate the ancient matriarchy. Moreover, as it stresses the importance of dreams as a locus for collectivity, it solicits women to learn from her story and recognize it as part of their cultural heritage.[47] Meanwhile, the closing speech is delivered by Moira, a prostitute who personifies the Erinyes, or Furies. It is an adaptation of the final speech given by the Furies in *The Eumenides* and closes the play with a message not of defeat but of hope for women.

When Orestes breaks matriarchal law by murdering his mother in *The Oresteia*, his matricidal act provokes the anger of the powerful Furies, but is nonetheless judged legal by Apollo and Athena. In *I sogni*, Clitennestra is embittered by Apollo and Athena's symbolic judgment, which results in the transformation of motherhood into an institution defined in patriarchal terms. In the Greek text, this separation is sanctioned by Apollo and Athena when they proclaim that the "*man* is the source of life," while the mother is "just a nurse to the seed" (260). In Maraini's text, Agamennone, Clitennestra's husband himself supports this view in an Aristotelian exposition of procreation: "our good comes from this head . . . I gave birth to you through my own creativity. Your mother . . . contributed her body. I contributed truth."[48] Clitennestra's battle against this disenfranchisement reveals the difference between motherhood as woman's procreative choice and motherhood as woman's destiny. Like the Greek Clytemnestra, Clitennestra conceives motherhood as a choice resulting from women's agency and strives to redefine it as a "social power."[49] Her awakening is prompted by incidents that speak to the split feminists challenge between mother and woman. Not only is her participation in motherhood initially undermined by those in her household, but expressions of her sexuality are deemed inadmissible for a mother and immediately corrected.

All of Clitennestra's roles—wife, mother, worker—come under the patriarch's tutelage, preserved by Orestes and Elettra. Indeed, Agamennone's authority extends to his daughters, and therefore to Clitennestra's relationship with them. When he forces Ifigenia to marry, he ignores the mother's objections. Divested of her power to save her daughter, Clitennestra's reaction to Ifigenia's death, like Clytemnestra's before her, is one of frustration and anger.[50] Ifigenia's relationship with her mother was a loving bond, a celebration of their generative, female sexuality and of their collective womanness, "they kissed each other, mouth to mouth; they poured each other milk, tongue to tongue" (37). Since this exclusive female relationship threatens social law for its foregrounding of feminine unity and power, Agamennone's sacrifice of Ifigenia ultimately preserves familial order.

This act of familial preservation also transcends to other parts of Clitennestra's life. She boldly exercises her right to experience a sexual relationship with her lover Egisto. Through Clitennestra's self-assertive attitude in reaction to her divestment of rights within the family, the play explores the ideological clash between the traditional definition of motherhood as an asexual role and the feminist revaluation of a mother's right to sexual expression. For feminist psychoanalyst Silvia Vegetti Finzi, sexuality is an integral part of a feminist discourse on motherhood, which includes "redefining the erotic dimension of women."[51] Like Aeschylus' Clytemnestra before her, Clitennestra rejects the confining image of the pure, asexual mother, as she reaffirms her right to have a sexual relationship and to continue to assert her vital maternal potential: "I am forty-five years old . . . and I am not dead yet. . . . I make love to a living person. I give life to life" (35, 36). Despite her family's objections and her neighbors' opinions, Clitennestra lives with Egisto, becomes pregnant, runs the household, and claims rights over the cottage textile industry built on her labor for ten years. However, this self-assertiveness and revision of the maternal discourse brings Clitennestra into conflict with her two surviving children, who consider it a threat to the family. Elettra and Oreste refuse to accept their mother's transgression of the social rules of motherhood, even though they wholly accept their father's relationship with his American lover Cassandra. Thus, for her violation of moral code, they impose their will on their mother, stripping her of her household rights.

As her power is curtailed in the domestic sphere, Clitennestra attempts to express herself in the public sphere. She first met Agamennone when she was a fourteen-year-old prostitute. When she seeks to assert herself outside the home and reenter the public sphere again, her only venue of expression, given her socialization, is to objectify her body. The sexuality her family tried to repress is released through her "talking dirty" ("parlare sboccato") and exhibitionism. These activities, not admitted in the home and certainly not acceptable for a mother, ultimately emphasize the socially mandated split between the mother and the sexually assertive woman.[52]

The containment and neutralization of the mother's sexuality is often assured by family members, whose attitudes toward motherhood may remain conventional while they themselves might redefine their own roles to allow for changes in sexual mores.[53] Through the conflicting relationship Clitennestra has with her daughter and son, Maraini's play bares and critiques the psychoanalytic principles defining family bonds. In contrast to her "rebellious" mother, Elettra represents patriarchal order, acting as the father's mouthpiece. She fulfills the successful passage from girlhood to womanhood prescribed by Freudian psychoanalysis, by transforming her active pre-Oedipal identification with the mother into a passive one for the father: "How I loved this idiotic mother, who disobeyed paternal law. . . . [But afterwards] my heart was firmly closed in my father's hands" (37–38). She therefore renounces her "female-gendered frame of reference" to accept subservience to paternal will. Elettra will not tolerate Clitennestra's unwillingness to concede to patriarchal law. Her polemic is centered on the family and, in essence, represents the play's response to the daughter's psychoanalytically mandated return to identification with the maternal when she herself fulfills her womanhood by becoming a mother. This cultural preservation of the family becomes, through Elettra's words, a condemning judgment of the mother's assertiveness. Her assessment of Clitennestra's situation holds aspects of the mother's sexuality and womanhood up against familial law. Like the children in Ginzburg's short story, Elettra condemns Clitennestra's transgressions while affirming her own non-threatening asexual identity, now rooted, again, firmly in the family: "I would have preferred you . . . with a body dedicated to the family, ready for any sacrifice" . . . (33), and "I am neither woman nor man. I am the family" (36). Elettra disapproves so vehemently of her mother's privileging her sexuality, and her passage into the symbolic sphere is so complete that she herself, unlike the Aeschylian Electra, proposes to Oreste that Clitennestra be "murdered," an act that in Maraini's play corresponds to Clitennestra's institutionalization in a psychiatric hospital.

Clitennestra, on the other hand, bemoans her daughter's decision to side with the father rather than bond in womanness with her as Ifigenia did. While Elettra demonstrates a yearning for the traditional, self-sacrificing mother, Clitennestra longs for the mutuality shared between mother and pre-Oedipal daughter. Elettra's renunciation of her love for her mother and her new "allegiance" to her father not only frustrates Clitennestra, but also brings the two women into ideological conflict. Like her relationship with Elettra, Clitennestra's relationship with her son Oreste is doomed in the end by his own acceptance of patriarchal law. Oreste reads Clitennestra's assertiveness, anger, and new sexual relationship as a privileging of her sexuality over her role as mother. For him, as for Elettra, the two identities cannot be reconciled, "a mother who is not a mother is not a woman" (35). But unlike Elettra, who at play's beginning has already acceded to the symbolic order, Oreste's embrace of social convention is complicated by the maternal love he finds difficult to refuse. Oreste claims that his disapproval of Clitennestra's relationship with Egisto is based on her age and on his respect for Agamennone. But his lover Pilade recognizes the Oedipal love implicit in his reaction: "You're jealous, like when you were a boy and you'd hide behind the door to spy on her" (27).

Regression to this phase of love for the mother is, of course, forbidden by the social law, as it would undermine social order. The son's fear of this possibility is expressed in a dream. The notion of the transcendence of myth through dream highlights the symbolic link between Orestes' conscience and the psychoanalytic precepts that have shaped the cultural codifications of the family saga. After confronting the Gorgons, Oreste dreams of strangling Moira, the prostitute with whom he has just had sex. In the dream, he is prosecuted by her companions, the three Erinyes. On trial, Oreste admits his horror at the prospect of being swallowed by the prostitute: "I was small, lost inside her . . . and she swallowed me. . . . I killed her to free myself; she wanted to kill me" (50).

Oreste's fear of and aggression toward the Fury Moira is indicative of his relationship with his mother. The text sets up this analogy by introducing Clitennestra's own dream, parallel to Oreste's. In this dream, Clitennestra replaces Moira, so that while Oreste strangles Moira in his dream, he strangles Clitennestra in her own dream. As a prostitute, Moira represents Clitennestra in her previous career, and as "fantasma della madre" (mother's ghost) she represents Clitennestra as mother. This twist reveals how Oreste's Oedipal love for his beneficent, nurturing mother, whose breast he once wanted to suckle, becomes fear of the sexually assertive woman, first represented by the prostitute Moira, then by Clitennestra herself. Thus, Oreste's double murder, the ancient matricide visualized in his mother's dream and the murder of the Fury Moira, aids his ultimate passage out of the early relationship with the mother. Oreste's symbolic matricide, supported by Elettra and spurred by his dream, translates into the committal of the defiant mother to a psychiatric hospital.

This institutionalization, then, serves to correct the threat of the mother's sexuality. Control of the mother in the psychiatric hospital is depicted through two sets of figures who symbolize repression, three patriarchal nurses who represent the domesticated Eumenides, and the psychiatrist. To ensure that the mother's struggle does not subvert Apollo's symbolic judgment, Clitennestra is supervised by the *Prima*, *Seconda*, and *Terza Infermiera* (First, Second, and Third Nurse), antitheses of the three prostitutes-Erinyes. The nurses' role is to domesticate the rebellious mother by enforcing and reinforcing social and moral indoctrination. They guarantee that Clitennestra respect the laws regulating motherhood and the mother's body by administering a sedative and electric shock treatment. The psychiatrist, who also serves as indoctrinator, is Atena, Zeus' daughter and a scientist. As Atena she derives her lineage from the "motherless" Athena, whose vote cast in favor of Orestes' matricidal act helped legitimize Clytemnestra's murder. But as the psychiatrist, she draws her lineage from Freud, the father of psychoanalysis.

Atena imposes psychoanalytic law to transform Clitennestra's transgression into conformity and submission to the social law. This action places the two women into a conflict representing the feminist challenge to psychoanalytic paradigms of femininity. To Clitennestra, a mother struggling for her female identity, Atena has been completely coopted by patriarchy. She has not experienced connection with the maternal figure: "You never knew your mother. Your father did everything by himself. And after nine months of thoughts hatched in male hatred you were born" (55–56). On the other hand, to Atena, Clitennestra's struggle is a sterile, futile rebellion, because her real and acceptable place is the private, not the public sphere. In an effort to assert her subjectivity, Clitennestra defies psychoanalytic law by masturbating, an activity considered by Freud a failure to accede to the prescribed heterosexual relationship. Citing psychoanalytic theory, Atena concludes that Clitennestra has failed to transform her active, liberated "masculine" sexuality, based on self-fulfillment and the knowledge of her own body, into a passive, repressed "feminine" one. She admonishes the mother for her assertiveness, reinforcing the psychoanalytic opposition between female passivity and male activity, by delivering a diagnosis informed by conventional Western philosophical and psychoanalytic discourses,

> Do you know what your aggressiveness [and] your sexual obsession . . . are? . . . [E]nvy of virility. You don't accept your feminine side, your sweetness, your passivity. You want to rival men, with power and you become . . . hysterical. (54–55)

Alone, Clitennestra reflects on this betrayal by her female doctor and recognizes the collective quality of her dreams, which brings her into communion with other women. Indeed, her speech is a testament to the hope fostered by collectivity, which in other Maraini works will be fulfilled through sisterhood, "Women of my dreams, don't betray me. . . . In some part, among dead dreams, I will continue to live, to continue to dream" (58). Her final speech stresses the adversity women face when they violate their socially mandated roles. At the same time, it enjoins women of the past, present, and future to unite in their struggle for subjectivity. Without this support, and divested of the maternal, creative power she once possessed, Clitennestra dies, vanquished by the very forces she strove to overcome.

Maraini's examination of the complexity of the maternal discourse parallels the emergence of the women's movement. While her earlier texts explore the subordination of the mother to the family, her later works examine a discourse informed by the changing perspectives on motherhood in postwar Italy. These works fashion a maternal discourse based on subjectivity, choice, and the rejection of the imposition of motherhood as women's social and biological destiny. Thus, while the mother in "Madre canina" suffers from the lack of support for her condition, in later works the mothers benefit from supportive relationships with other women or knowledge drawn from symbolic placement within a larger historical context, as Clitennestra's text asserts.

Maraini's narratives are documents of the physical and emotional turmoil implicit in the conventional maternal role. The author strives to approach the mother, as Irigaray would have it, and understand how she has inhabited the culture that for centuries has subjugated her. The mother in *L'età del malessere* and in "Madre canina" suffers physically and lives a relationship with her daughter that deteriorates under the weight of the mandated embodiment of a restrictive maternal experience. The daughter/narrator of these works engages in an important and innovative stance which allows her to define her own position within the family and to use familial relations as spaces in which to rebuild her own identity as a woman. Although the mother assumes an important role within this revision, the return to the mother and the reformulation of her role relegates her to a secondary status nonetheless. Indeed, although she represents a primary focus, it is the writing and polemical daughter who determines the return and, essentially, the mother's existence in her new relational spaces.

Through the play *I sogni di Clitennestra*, Maraini rewrites an ancient myth to unfold a discourse on motherhood on the stage, using the theater as symbolic placement for Clitennestra's body— traditionally confined to speaking through motherhood. By structuring her play around Clitennestra, the reincarnation of the Greek Clytemnestra, Maraini reveals the symbolic effect Apollo and Athena's judgment has on her protagonist today, and underscores the consequent enduring social and cultural conventions surrounding motherhood. Maraini interprets Aeschylus' *The Oresteia* to focus on women's evolution from the matriarchal subject to the patriarchal object. Her heroine reasserts both her sexual and maternal potential as woman. And, even while defeated, she solicits women to unite and redeem motherhood's empowering potential. In this way, *I sogni di Clitennestra* inspires women to reject the notion of motherhood as their social and biological destiny and retrieve motherhood as their procreative choice, "glorious from the womb of Mother Night" (112).

Through her films, Maraini creates a cinematic language that foregrounds both the visual reality and potential of motherhood. Her films bring to the light the figure traditionally relegated to the domestic sphere. Although in *La bella addormentata nel bosco*, the mother's cinematic discourse principally evolves in the kitchen, the reconstruction of the fairytale reveals that aspect of the traditional story elided by dominant culture. In this capacity, the domestic realm as site for the construction of the heroine's desires points to the reality, not fantasy, of the traditional maternal discourse. The film's movement to exterior spaces as sites for the unfolding of the mother's desires only serves to underscore this fact. With *Giochi di latte*, this site is transformed into a symbolic historical space, in which mother and daughter contemplate the genealogical aspects of their procreative capacity as women. With Rich's notion of "mutual confirmation" between mother and daughter complete in this film, Maraini shows that through the changes in maternal discourse brought about by the women's movement, there is indeed hope for a future in which women's exercising of the maternal role stands at center stage of a new family story.

Although these portraits of motherhood do not exceed the boundaries of the daughter's own interpretation and articulation of the maternal (*L'età* and "Madre canina"), the domestic sphere (*La bella*), and an exclusively feminine context (*Giochi* and, to some degree, *I sogni*), they do allude to the possibility of altering the maternal experience. The two 1960s works and *La bella addormentata nel bosco* have not ventured beyond the conventional role, even though the film does explore the mother's hidden desires. *Giochi di latte* and *I sogni di Clitennestra*, on the other hand, do contemplate a new maternal discourse, and *I sogni* in particular identifies this possibility in the creation of a community of women. It is this relational context, in which bonds of sisterhood develop and unfold, that informs some of the more reformative of Maraini's works.

3
Sisterhood

A woman bends over me, / Searching my reaches for what she really is.... I see her back and reflect it faithfully.[1]

in the calm of my airy head I embroider / threads of thoughts / ... / I filter ideas through / the spider's web / that envelopes my brain / ... / shall we embroider together?[2]

MARAINI'S 1978 POEM "RICAMARE" [EMBROIDERY] APPROPRIATES the traditional female task of embroidering as a metaphor for the historical oppression of women in the domestic sphere the mother inhabits, and recasts it as an empowering symbol of women's liberation. As representative of a common historical occupation, the act of embroidery symbolizes the confinement of female creativity to the domestic and, as an emblem of this creativity, represents the limits this sphere places on women's self-expression. The poem's ultimate transformation of the act of embroidery into a call for solidarity, however, recuperates it as a symbol of Maraini's own vision of a sisterhood of female subjects. Indeed, situating the poetic subject's own participation in this task in both a historical context of women's culture, rendered by the Arachnian imagery, and a current feminist discourse on women's liberation relocates and inscribes her personal *storia* within the larger context of a historical female community. When we extend this metaphor to the works examined in this chapter, we find that the embroidery of a rich and complex sisterhood of women creates a new space for their heroines' life narratives to evolve.

The poem's image of a sisterhood arising from the gendered spaces women have historically inhabited is a telling one for our investigation of the relational territory charted in Maraini's works. As we have seen in chapters 1 and 2, the daughters and mothers who populate these texts occupy familial spaces that can limit their potential to the archetypical roles of daughterhood and motherhood. They inhabit these spaces through a cyclical development that can (re)contain them within the domestic sphere: The family, again, is both the original site of their development into gendered identities and the site in which they can eventually be reintegrated to fulfill the adult roles of mother and wife.

Although the family in this historical configuration does indeed prove problematic for women, Maraini nevertheless revisits it to investigate potential sites for women's liberation. The reconstituted family she envisions is a symbolic network of relationships through which women can redefine their identities along newly appointed points of reference. As we noted in our discussion of daughterhood in chapter 1, a cross-cultural feminist discourse has revised the role the mother-daughter bond plays in women's lives and has highlighted its potential as a new space for the development of a wider ranging symbolic order. In the paradigm we find in Maraini's works, this regenerative relationship transcends the nuclear family to encompass the union between social sisters. It is reintegrated into the lives of her heroines as both a renewed social bond between adult mother and daughter and friendships among women.[3]

When played out in the works examined in this chapter, sisterhood extends beyond the strict spatial reality of the family and uncovers relationships historically hidden but essential to a practical design for liberation. In their diverse configurations, female friendships enrich the heroines' lives because they reveal to them different perspectives and experiences of womanhood. While the mother serves as a point of reference outside the paternal Symbolic sphere, friendships with other women *ideally* create a new *symbolic* family of subjects. The result is the revision and reconfiguration of the meaning and practice of familial relationships in women's lives.

Friendships between women have historically been accorded a secondary status as separatist spheres privileging female companionship over familial or heterosexual bonds. Interestingly and perhaps even paradoxically, this exclusivity has presented a threat to the conventional family. Although providing a space in which women could express themselves, they were seldom deemed a significant social relationship, since they developed in the private sphere. Because of these conditions, women theorists have assumed female friendships as measures of women's social status, attributing their ancillary status to women's marginalization. For Simone De Beauvoir, for example, the friendships have historically served as a "behind the scenes" site for the "exchange [of] confidences and recipes" and to prepare women for participation in society.[4] For Rossana Rossanda, meanwhile, their secondary status is the result of women's isolation and disenfranchisement.[5]

The two theorists' assessment of the social status of female friendships mirrors the role the relationships have been historically assigned in their literary depictions. As a literary topos, female friendships have served to advance the heterosexual coupling around which the plot traditionally revolves. Although in this case they help the heroine negotiate the pressures of fulfilling social roles by providing a site in which to reveal her inner self,[6] they seldom achieve the transgressive potential feminist authors later explore.

In Italian literature, women authors have created compelling and even potentially subversive portraits of friendships between women. In some cases, however, they remain drawn along conventional lines. In Matilde Serao's short story "La virtù di Checchina" [Checchina's Virtue] (1884), for example, the relationship between the heroine Checchina and her friend Isabella serves mainly as an impetus for the heterosexual union.[7] Meanwhile, in Natalia Ginzburg's novella *Sagittario* [Sagittarius] (1957), the relationship is presented as a negative one of competition. In Alba De Céspedes' 1963 epistolary novel *Il rimorso* [The Remorse], on the other hand, the friendship between Francesca and Isabella, though in its own way tense and problematic for both women, becomes an outlet for their thoughts and feelings. Its strength lies in the women's acknowledged differences ("We are very different; so you're the only one I can talk to with absolute honesty"[8]). It also lies in the fact that, because it originated in their youth, the relationship allows them to reconstruct their histories as women and friends.

Later feminist texts have countered these portrayals, reappropriating female friendships as potential sites of entrustment and *autocoscienza* and as reformulations of family relationships. In Gigliola Franco's play, *La bambola woo-doo* [The Voo-Doo Doll] (1979), for instance, the mother is transformed into the protagonist's friend. Contradictions between the mother and daughter arise when the daughter rejects her mother's advice over the breakup of her love relationship as inadequate and antiquated. In order for the conflicting perspectives between the two women to be corrected, the mother must become the daughter's friend, a physical transformation occurring when the mother casts off the veil she is wearing and becomes her daughter's feminist friend. Franco's text focuses on the younger woman's liberation, as it does not free the mother from her traditional role (she is even only identified as *Madre*—mother), and thus fails to provide a beneficial alternative for the mother herself. The mother, however, is not altogether eliminated, but rather remains a symbolic presence through sisterhood in the daughter's life. Rossana Campo's novel *Mai sentita così bene* [Never Felt Better] (1995) is an extended dialogue between Italian women living in Paris. The friendship between the women has a complex identity: It is at once the site of *autocoscienza*, taking place through the women's lively and revealing dialogue, and the purveyor of ties to the women's native culture in a foreign and alienating setting.[9] Barbara Garlaschelli's novella, *Tre amiche e una farfalla* [Three Girlfriends and a Butterfly] (1998), meanwhile, features three young women whose friendship develops as a site of self-expression. Although their differences bring tension to the relationship, their understanding of each other, cultivated over a long period of time, allows them to convert their different opinions into edifying perspectives.[10] All three texts demonstrate the continuing significance of sisterhood as a topos in literary explorations of women's experiences.

Sisterhood has also been the focus of numerous other cross-genre investigations of women's lives, a testament to the weight it carries in the diverse feminist discourses on women's liberation. Exemplary among these are the issue of the journal *Nuova dwf* entitled "Solidarietà, amicizia, amore" [Solidarity, Friendship, Love] (January–June 1979); the issue of the journal of women's culture *I quaderni* entitled "Relazioni tra donne" [Relationships between Women] (1990); the issue of the journal of women's history *Memoria* simply titled "amicizie" [friendships] (1991); the volume of feminist theatrical performances *Il teatro delle donne* [Women's Theater] (1980); and the edited volume of life narratives *Care, carissime donne: racconti di vita e di lavoro* [Dear, Dearest Women: Stories of Life and Work] (1995). Theoretical works by, for example, Maria Luisa Boccia ("L'identità nella relazione" [Identity in Relationship]) (1990); Jolanda Insana ("Essere o fare l'amica" [Being a Friend]) (1991); and Gabriella Paolucci ("Amiche" [Friends]) (1991) define sisterhood as an indispensable tool for the development of women's subjectivity and the fulfillment of their repressed desire for an alternative "sociability."[11] While these texts delineate and analyze various models of sisterhood, literary works such as those noted above and the edited collection of feminist theater depict women's actual involvement in female friendships and explore the way these bonds are played out in women's lives. The result of such a varied focus on this bond is, ultimately, the creation of a sisterhood of women beyond the literary enunciation, a community succinctly captured by the open address of the title *Care, carissime donne* [Dear, Dearest Women].[12]

In the postwar period of Italian feminism, this literary investigation became coupled with women's greater participation in politics, a marriage that has engaged the private as a political debate and has ushered the discourse of a revised Symbolic order into the public realm. Earlier feminist groups such as *UDI* (Unione delle donne italiane), formed in 1944, and *Movimento femminista romano* [Roman Feminist Movement], formed in 1971, helped bring about momentous political and legal changes safeguarding women's rights in both private and public spheres. Symbolically, the groups' tangible goals brought to light the empowering potential of women's unification. However, the impact these groups had on the private sphere went beyond their work in the public sphere. Together with other groups with a more theoretical focus, such as *Rivolta femminile* [Female Revolt], formed in 1970, the Milan Women's Bookstore Collective (formed in 1975), and *Diotima* (formed in 1983), they outlined several practices of sisterhood considered among the most important contributions of Italian feminism to women's liberation both on a domestic and an international scale.[13]

The models these groups advanced both in theory and practice were instrumental in revising the place of sisterhood in society. Women of different backgrounds and ideologies were now united through practices of *autocoscienza* and *affidamento*. Both *autocoscienza* and *affidamento* redefine the presence of the "other" woman in women's lives, as *autocoscienza* allows the individual to reinterpret her personal *storia* through another woman and *affidamento* allows her to rechart it with new points of reference. In these practices of communal recognition and validation, one woman mirrors herself in another woman, who reflects back potentialities the first woman did not know she owned.[14]

The Italian feminist concept of *rispecchiamento* [mirroring] as defined by Gabriella Paolucci, is a fragmentary process that promotes a greater understanding of the whole self: Emphasis is placed on differences between women, for they reveal the untapped in the reflected subjects.[15] This complex configuration of mirroring encompasses the discourses on development put forth both by Lacanian psychoanalysis and feminist theory on friendship. It reflects the essence and implications of the essential role the mirror phase plays in identity formation in Lacanian psychoanalysis.[16] *Rispecchiamento* does not imply a static mirroring of one individual in another, but rather a gradual discovery of oneself through and made possible by the other. In the configuration of sisterhood shaped by this practice, emphasis is placed on differences between women which one individual reflects back to the other, for differences can reveal aspects of the self previously uncovered or ignored.[17]

Because of the emphasis on difference, the union between two women as played out in these practices has engendered debates problematizing such differences as age, socioeconomic status, and education, disparities particularly evident in the relationship with the Symbolic Mother. Elizabeth Abel and Judith Gardiner have engaged in a discussion on the discrepancy of power between one participant in sisterhood and another that clarifies the problem. In her examination of the depiction of female friendships in the fictional works of such authors as Doris Lessing and Toni Morrison, Abel notes that female friendships generate "psychic wholeness." Based on the identification of one member with another, these bonds are fundamental in the development of heroines' identities.[18] Gardiner's response to Abel's analysis perceptively warns against perceiving these relationships as wholly reciprocal: As played out in women's literature, she asserts, "one woman . . . is more of a knower; the other one is to be known."[19] Reading these divergent views through the lenses of Italian feminism, we can say that Gardiner's conclusion is akin to *affidamento*, and mirrors the controversy over the practice voiced by Italian feminists. Although *affidamento* is indeed instrumental in creating a sense of historical situatedness, it can prove problematic in its accordance of power to the older, more "knowing" and experienced woman.

This too, however, can be transgressive and subversive, for assigning equal power to both women would frustrate the articulation of difference. Inequality in the friendship, although a possible source of tension, can actually benefit women by opening them up to another woman's expression of her difference.[20] The sisterhood purposefully forged out of these differences and out of the collective action of Italian feminist groups is, therefore, one of complicity.[21]

In her study of the political nature of sisterhood, bell hooks argues that the success of sisterhood depends upon women's willful and therefore complicitous agreement to join together on "the basis of shared strengths and resources" to achieve common and/or diverse goals.[22] The complicitous bond of sisterhood hook envisions and Italian feminist groups practice has the potential of developing into a site for the exploration of the self in relation to the "other." In their own investigations of the bonds' "alternative" reality, Beauvoir and Rossanda recognize the propitious transgressive nature of their marginalized status. For Beauvoir, the bonds' "behind the scenes" nature also produces a "kind of counter-universe" in the domestic sphere. Indeed, the "confidences and recipes" exchanged herein have situated women into a veritable oral tradition passed down through generations of women. For Rossanda, female friendships have the potential to create a "rebellious identity" because they challenge codified configurations of relationships.[23] The defiant nature of complicitous sisterhood is held up as an empowering symbol of women's solidarity and difference. In the often unpenetrable private sphere these relationships become sites in which women can articulate their experiences, concerns, and identities—Beauvoir's *recipes*. Significantly, these spaces most reveal the realities of women's lives and the potential for successful subjective development.

Dacia Maraini has proven a pioneer in her focus on this relationship and its transgressive potential, since sisterhood is consistently featured as a central theme in her investigation of women's lives. This investigation, coupled with the exploration of new relational spaces, brings to light the importance of female friendships to women's liberation. It leads Maraini's heroines through uncharted territory—from the development of sisterhood in the dark recesses of the private sphere to its impact in the political arena. When moving "behind the scenes" to the sites in which female friendships have historically evolved, the heroines discover that these tucked away, closed spaces are enlightening symbols of difference.

Because as depicted in women's literature friendships between women do occupy exclusionary, historically marginalized spaces, their literary depiction can prove problematic when envisioning a paradigm for women's social liberation. As we shall see in our examination of Maraini's texts, the relationship has immediate regenerative potential only for relationships between the heroine and other women. Although, as our analysis of "Demetra ritrovata" in chapter 1 shows, the extension of the mother-daughter bond into the social sphere of sisterhood can transform the daughter-father relationship as well, this potential is never fully examined beyond the moment of the heroines' epiphanies, which generally involve the discovery of themselves. Indeed, it is still the daughter—in this case the symbolic daughter—who holds the possibility to bring about change.

However, within the economy of Maraini's works, and in their capacity as documents of the women's movement, the heroines' Irigarayan movement toward "underground" sites nevertheless represents a fundamental step in the recuperation of a maternal symbolic order, of a feminine cultural legacy. Eventually, as is proffered in the novel *Donna in guerra*, the heroine's "underground" journey can guide her in reshaping the public sphere. We can ultimately conclude that these underground practices of sisterhood provide a map for our own investigation of the spaces Maraini's texts create for the development of a sisterhood of female subjects.

In the 1970 play *Il Manifesto* this underground voyage is made possible by the then burgeoning *autocoscienza* sessions, which not only put the play's protagonist in touch with the silenced spaces of women's history and her own, but also help map out her own plan for women's liberation. The play's insistence on the importance of these sessions, and its conscious transportation of them onto the public stage, anticipates the structure and purpose of later 1970s-era Italian feminist dramatic productions. Indeed, in this period, as we have noted in the introduction to this book, Italian feminist theater groups often performed in the streets to bring theater to a general audience. In order to create an illuminating experience, they fashioned their street pieces on rap sessions to create a sort of consciousness-raising theater. Groups such as the Milanese *Comitato Donne di Villa San Giovanni* [Women's Committee of Villa San Giovanni], *Le Streghe* [The Witches], and Maraini's own *La Maddalena* transformed both the actual creation of a play and its execution into a collective act of *autocoscienza*. This was done so that the pieces would develop out of dialogues between writers and so that the actual performances would raise the audience's own consciousness about the issues presented.[24]

While Maraini's *Il Manifesto* is not the result of collective creation through *autocoscienza*, it nevertheless is a complex early piece of feminist street theater that showcases *autocoscienza* as an essential cultural and individual experience. *Autocoscienza* shapes the play's plot and character development as well as its structure. As a plot device, it determines characters' actions at the same time that it provides the forum through which characters reveal themselves to the audience and to themselves. As a structural device, it determines the play's relationship to the audience, creating a sort of metatheatrical setting in which the audience becomes participant—albeit a passive one—to the *autocoscienza* sessions represented through the female protagonists' conversations. By showcasing the practice at these various levels, *Il Manifesto* becomes a revelatory experience for both characters and viewing public: The play not only becomes a *manifesto* of the importance of sisterhood and collective action in women's lives, but also of the role feminist theater can play in raising the audience's consciousness to the historical plight of women.

In the play, the friendships between female characters also anticipate the practice of *affidamento* which evolved from *autocoscienza*. The various feminist manifestos produced in the 1960s and 1970s redefined women's relationships according to their experiences inside and outside familial spaces and presented friendships as sites of self-exploration and change. Maraini's play begins to chart new relational territory, forecasting later feminist practices. As the protagonist Anna journeys through the terrain of women's sanctioned social and cultural life and her *storia pellegrina* [pilgrim history] leads her to pen her manifesto of women's rights, the play itself essentially becomes a manifesto for sisterhood. While later works such as the poem "Demetra ritrovata" and the film *Mio padre amore mio* negotiate broader familial spaces for Maraini's characters, *Il Manifesto* focuses its relational discourse on other women, "sisters" if you will.

The play's focal point of sisterhood is, again, the practice of *autocoscienza*, which informs and frames it: As Anna is exhorted to (re)tell her story by a Greek-like chorus of four deceased women, who, in turn, divulge aspects of their own lives, the audience is witness to typically obscured histories.[25] At the same time, through the play's calculated intertwining of past and present dialogue, Anna's own history is reconstructed. During the expository dialogue, the women, who lived under common historical institutions but experienced them differently, prompt each other as well as Anna to remember and recount them. The result on one level is self-revelation, while on another it is the grounding of the heroine's identity in a female cultural context, something missing in her life until now.[26]

Presented in a text that serves as forum for obscured voices, the women's dialogues politicize their private lives and ultimately help politicize Anna. They set up a dichotomy between a life bereft of meaningful female friendships and the reformulation of a personal history through interaction with other women. In life, Anna clashes with the tenets of femininity she is forced to uphold and assimilate. Without the support of friendships with other women who understand her struggle and could even guide her, she is restricted to living on society's fringes. Within the *autocoscienza* sessions of the play's frame, however, she can interpret her own life and later inspire other women to do so as well.

Through the practice of *autocoscienza* and as the female authoritative figure central to the relationship of *affidamento*, Anna motivates her prison companions to discuss and think through their enforced situations. Thus, for example, when the prisoner Pia attempts to rigidly structure a meeting using bureaucratic jargon incomprehensible to the others, Anna interjects and solicits her companions' opinions on their treatment in prison.[27] Later, at work in a factory she informs her co-workers about birth control and abortion, subjects on which they are ill-informed. In the first example of sisterhood, Anna struggles to discuss issues in a language accessible to everyone, while destabilizing the hierarchal format of the prison institution. In the second case, the women around her actually entrust themselves to her for information which creates new choices and new ways to control their lives:

> PINA: [H]ow do you avoid getting pregnant? I force Mario to wear a condom. But he says he can't stand it and we end up fighting.
> ANNA: Condoms are antiquated.
> . . . .
> PINA: So what do we do?
> ANNA: The best thing is the diaphragm.
> PINA: What is it?
> ANNA: It's a rubber cap that closes the uterus. You can't feel it and neither can he, you put it on and take it off when you want and you won't get pregnant. [You can buy it] in a pharmacy. But . . . you can also go to Planned Parenthood. They'll fit you with one there. (247–49)

In instances such as this one, dialogue and Anna's guidance open the women up to rights, choices, and possibilities they did not know or were little aware they had. Similarly, through Anna's example of the power of the written word and of direct action, they are exposed to an alternative practice of revindicating women's rights.

The manifesto Anna pens is a culmination of her relationships with these women and of her own life experiences, while at the same time it is a distillation of several feminist manifestos and writings of the period. Manifestos such as Demau's *Il Manifesto* (1966), Rivolta Femminile's *Il Manifesto* (1970), and Carla Lonzi's treatise *Sputiamo su Hegel* (1970) all advocated overhauling existing social and cultural structures and restructuring relationships in order to develop theories and practices of female subjectivity. As a literary representation of the defining documents of postwar Italian feminism, Anna's manifesto within a manifesto (Maraini's play) also anticipates another writing, the feminist group Anabasi's *Donna è bello* [Woman is Beautiful] (1972). Anabasi's piece strongly advocates the practice of *autocoscienza* as a form of communication between women and as a site in which women understand that the imposed, conventional model of femininity is a social and political problem, not a personal one. Anna's own manifesto casts such issues as femininity, sexuality, work, the family and motherhood as social, political, and cultural dilemmas. Likewise, in a phrase that opens and sets the tone of her manifesto as it anticipates the title *Donna è bello*, it retrieves womanhood from its subservient position and recasts it as a "beautiful" mode of being that does not include the negative characteristics of subordination, "There is nothing embarrassing about being a woman. Actually, it's beautiful" (272).

As her manifesto reflects and anticipates feminist issues and writings of the 1970s, Anna's organization of the rebellion against the prison institution and the traditional family it represents continues the relationship of *affidamento* she has with co-workers such as Pina. Although in other scenes Anna expresses her opinion over the women's condition in prison, it is during the play's climax that the dynamics of entrustment are actually played out. Gathering other women prisoners around her, she, representing the female authoritative figure, articulates for them the realities of their oppression. While this relational dynamic may seem problematic today, at the time of its writing the play anticipated the fundamental relationships of 1980s Italian feminism. Therefore, while in later works the bonds between Maraini's female characters are more balanced even among women with significantly different experiences, in *Il Manifesto* Anna, as an early feminist, raises women's consciousness and makes available to them the necessary tools for articulating that consciousness. The bonds of sisterhood forged out of this manifesto create the rebellious identity Rossanda identifies in sisterhood and that ultimately manifests itself through their rebellion against prison and, symbolically, familial authority. Aware of this, Anna, like Clitennestra after her, calls to women to unite and find strength in and among themselves: "Women, you must be aware . . . // Take the freedom you desire into your possession with force and violence" (281).

The journey underground into the folds of sisterhood leads into a more personal, though no less political sphere of its development in the 1975 novel *Donna in guerra*. A virtual feminist manifesto itself, this work represents the heroine Vannina's journey across the geography of her life and to her eventual liberation, made possible predominantly by her friendships with women. Vannina recounts and, more significantly, interprets her personal narrative through her journal, which is transformed into a *Bildungsroman*.[28] This act of self-narration creates an itinerary of her developing consciousness and enscripts her story onto a literary map of 1970s feminism.

Significantly, Vannina's evolution from compliant housewife and school teacher to assertive and independent woman occurs at the hands of her female friends, who prove instrumental in guiding her toward liberation. The women's relationship is a complex one involving the interpretation of familial relationships and, therefore, the return to the stage of the daughter's psychosocial development into adulthood. The friends recreate the daughter's evolution by reintegrating the primary female presence—the maternal—into her life and inviting her to participate in sisterhood—all fundamental steps, as we have seen, in the Italian feminist project for women's liberation.

In exploring the essential role female friendships play in Vannina's liberation, Maraini's novel creates a panoramic view of this relationship, from the mother-daughter bond to entrustment. This broad view, as subjectively described by the heroine, showcases the impact of sisterhood on identity and on fostering the individual's quest for change. The device Maraini uses to achieve this panorama is to set the novel on the small southern island of Addis at the height of summer season. The island, with its blend of natives and tourists, is a social microcosm bringing together traditional and contemporary views of the issues highlighted. Although later, as Vannina approaches the moment of liberation, the plot shifts to Naples and then Rome, the groundwork for her liberation is set on Addis, where she explores and experiences different facets of sisterhood.

The friendships the heroine develops encourage her to redimension the way she lives her life and permit her to nurture and fulfill a repressed part of her self. While on Addis, Vannina meets the island laundress Giottina and her friend Tota. Through their friendship, she ventures out of the Symbolic sphere and (back) into the pre-Oedipal sphere of the mother-daughter relationship, a journey that motivates her communion with other women, something lacking in her life until now. She also meets the Anglo-Turkish feminist Suna and subsequently moves into the political arena in which Suna works. Here, she discovers the political neglect of women's concerns. Finally, with her colleague Rosa Colla at home in Rome, she forms a bond of entrustment that uncovers issues of difference and motherhood with which she herself grapples. Through these forms of sisterhood, Vannina is forced to confront problems whose resolution is made possible by other women and eventually sets the path for her liberation.

Vannina's friendship with Tota and Giottina replays significant experiences the daughter has in her relationship with the mother, at once illustrating the benefits and shortcomings of this bond in the adult woman's life. The friendship features moments of affection and mutual reliance while replaying the tension the daughter feels toward the mother in moments of individuation. This pre-symbolic-like relationship cleverly takes place in the cave- and theater-like laundrette where Giottina works and Tota visits. As Vannina herself describes it, the laundrette, enveloped in steam and therefore secluded from the outside world, resembles a cave, a prehistoric dwelling. But despite the fact that the two Addis women occupy this space and despite their position within the novel, they are not frozen in time, stuck in the pre-Oedipal. The laundrette represents the obscure Beauvoirian spaces in which female friendships have historically been played out, the world of women's customs silenced in the Symbolic. It functions as the site for the two women's theatrics: In the secluded shop, Tota and Giottina create their own language of gestures to subjectively express themselves to each other, thus securing their bond through commonality.

As it unfolds in the interior spaces of the laundrette, the relationship introduces Vannina, the symbolic daughter, to the customs upon which the women's friendship is rooted, and thus to an unfamiliar world of women's lives and traditions. In this rather one-sided version of the mother-daughter bond in which the daughter develops, Tota and Giottina attempt to bring Vannina back into a complicitous union with women. While their metaphorical warnings attempt to dissuade her from "immoral" sexual behavior, their expressions, gestures, and stories initiate the daughter into their "secret" world. To Vannina these women interact in an enigmatic and mysterious way. Their comportment is undomesticated ("selvatico") as they divulge and indulge their imaginations through the stories they tell.[29]

Despite the fact that this relationship helps put Vannina back in touch with the primary female presence in her life, it nevertheless suffers the same problems the actual mother-daughter union suffers as the daughter strives to separate herself from the mother. While the three women's relationship consistently remains within the pre-Oedipal sphere, Vannina, having already acceded to the Symbolic sphere, is the wary daughter who resists the cryptic warnings the "mothers" express to protect her from outside influences. Significantly, at moments the two women's affection overwhelms the heroine, who is at once attracted and repulsed. Vannina values the women's tales and their friendship. From the beginning, she is bewitched by their earthy friendship and their mode of expression and interaction: "I won't go back there again, I told myself. But I knew I would. It's like a dark theater where they improvise disturbing fantasies, reckless games full of bitter sensuality that fascinate me in spite of the nausea" (14); and again, "Their savage, possessive, friendship gives me a sense of elation. They wanted to tell me that they were jealous, that they needed me" (87). But while she is indeed bewitched by the women, the daughter's return to the mother is by no means an effortless one. Psychoanalytically, this return to another woman is defined as a regression backwards into a narcissistic mode of being. Socially, it symbolizes the surrender to a weighty and entrapping gendered (maternal) role represented by effacement in and subservience to the family. In this scenario, the two Addis women represent the mother who, in Irigarayan terms must go back "under the ground" as the daughter strives to individuate.[30] When Vannina thinks about returning to the cavelike laundrette, she symbolically feels a loss of the adult social identity she has cultivated, experiencing what the French theorist describes as the "opening to the mother": "threats of contamination, . . . madness, death."[31]

The mother's overbearing attitude does not allow the resistant Vannina to understand yet that in the feminist model of regenerated relational spaces, the return to the maternal realm Tota and Giottina represent can actually lead to the re-evaluation of the pre-Oedipal mutuality in the daughter's life. It will take her subsequent friendships with Suna and Rosa Colla—her social sisters—to ultimately awaken Vannina to the possibilities of liberation. In the meantime, while Suna and Rosa Colla provide a relationship of entrustment, or the social extension into adulthood of the symbiotic bond, Tota and Giottina initiate the heroine to her awakening, offering her foremost a site of communion with the Beauvoirian "behind the scenes" side of the social sphere: "By now I no longer take persuading. Indeed, it's me who makes the first move to go to the laundrette" (46). This final dynamic of the relationship is ultimately set later, when, in a moment that mirrors the mother's induction of the reluctant daughter into the world, Tota and Giottina's "due mani amiche" (two friendly hands) help her negotiate movement in the outdoors, an impressive place for a woman who daily lives and works in the confinement of the domestic sphere, "Accustomed as I was to being shut in between the walls of my courtyard, I was overcome by the sense of space" (76).

It is when Vannina enters into entrustment with Suna that she ultimately reads her friendship with the two Addis women as overwhelming and suffocating. As the ambivalent daughter who attempts to free herself from the mother's influence, she experiences a liberating relationship with Suna. This friendship highlights the role entrustment plays in raising a woman's consciousness about the conventional gendered spaces she inhabits. Within the economy of the novel, it exposes Vannina both to the 1970s' feminist discourse on liberation, and, in anticipation of the more developed discourse put forth in Maraini's 1978 poetry collection *Mangiami pure*, to the importance of individual—as opposed to party—action. In addition, while Suna awakens Vannina to her rights in her relationship with her husband Giacinto, she further exposes her to the role sisterhood plays in opening her up to new possibilities. In short, while the friendship with Tota and Giottina integrates Vannina into an exclusive community of women, Suna introduces her to contemporary feminist concerns of social liberation.

Concerns of political achievement, sexual liberation, and theories of subjectivity at the heart of 1970s feminism intersect in Suna. While the practice of *autocoscienza* proved successful as a foundation for relationships in which women could examine their concerns, it proved too personal and too limiting for women entering the more general political arena. Therefore, by the late 1970s women recognized the need to negotiate their concerns through *doppia militanza* [double militancy]; that is, in both women's collectives and political institutions. While *doppia militanza* proved successful in legally enforcing and protecting women's rights, through Suna we foresee an allegorical picture of the problems women faced when working within political institutions. Indeed, as Suna's beautiful "leontine" face represents her adamant, self-assured advocacy of women's rights, her disabled legs symbolize the shortcomings of achieving liberation without a milieu in which to articulate pressing issues. The result is crippling marginalization.

While her physical condition and ethnic origin cast her as a social outsider, Suna's lack of a support group developing out of practices of sisterhood makes it difficult for her to resolve basic problems of belonging.[32] Her choice to participate in the political group *Vittoria proletaria* [Proletarian Victory], for example, exasperates her, since here even her most elemental concerns are met with resistance. This party symbolizes the patriarchal (even if alternative) political arena women tried to penetrate to make women's liberation a reality. It is mainly concerned with class issues rather than the advancement of women's rights and employs traditional political discourses to plan its war against working class subservience. However, while fighting this social problem, the party refuses to recognize women's own subservience in society and within such patriarchal institutions as the family, an issue not dealt with at length even in such leftist ideologies as Marxism.[33] Thus, unlike other members, Suna, a keen proponent of women's rights, is not allowed to express or even represent women's (and her own) concerns. When she does attempt to enter conversations, group leader Vittorio dismisses her comments and objectifies her. His mellifluous—and thus incongruous—response to her interests, "Do you know how gorgeous you are?" (121)—repositions the politically conscious woman into a position of inferiority and underscores her physicality rather than her intellectual concerns. As a result, she is as marginalized within the party as she is in society.

While Suna's struggle serves as an example of the difficulties women face without a forum in which to articulate their ideas, the relationship of entrustment between Suna and Vannina transforms it into a beneficial influence on Vannina's life. As Vannina's friend, Suna taps into her inclination to feel comfortable with her own body. Although Vannina's journal entries reveal early on her unhappiness with the sexual relationship with her husband Giacinto, Suna guides her to an understanding of the ideological roots of that unhappiness. Her assertions (based first on observation and later on knowledge) about Vannina's marriage help Vannina put the relationship into perspective according to her own repressed needs. At first, Vannina resists Suna's assertions. Later, however, as the friendship progresses and Vannina assimilates the tools of inquiry needed to investigate her own life, she examines the marriage and perceives its oppressive nature.

Two examples illustrate the friendship's benefits. Early on in their relationship, Suna observes that Giacinto does not fulfill Vannina's desires and that their marriage functions because she fulfills her prescribed passive role. As the friendship progresses, Vannina becomes more perceptive of her needs and pursues an affair with the much younger Orio, a relationship founded on reciprocity and mutual desire.[34] Later, when Suna invites her on a trip to Naples without Giacinto, Vannina wavers, uneasy about leaving her husband. Suna, however, points out to Vannina that she can indeed exercise agency. Suna's lesson is a successful one, for Vannina not only takes the trip to Naples, she asserts her own independence in the face of her husband's objections: [G.]: "Since we got married this is the first time you've acted off your own bat . . . you're going against your nature." [V.]: "But I feel like acting this way, so this too must be part of my nature" (144–45). As these examples show, true to the dynamics of entrustment, Vannina translates Suna's assertions into her own life.

As she slowly musters up the courage and self-assertion needed to express herself in her marriage, Vannina progresses toward effecting social change as well by implementing tenets of women's liberation advanced in the 1970s. While moments with Suna illustrate the advantages of sisterhood in a woman's life, they also paint a rich portrait of the union that goes beyond this one-dimensional trajectory. The friendship charts alternatives to the feminist involvement in conventional politics. Although Vannina appears the more passive, unenlightened character, the weaknesses of the more overtly politicized Suna soon surface. By operating in a group that enforces traditional ideologies and conventional relational dynamics, Suna loses her ability to understand the plight of those women she endeavors to help.[35] Vannina, on the other hand, working on the fringes of the political arena, successfully unites Suna's guidance with her own experiences, thus achieving an understanding of the women's situations that can result in more substantial change.

At the same time, and true to *rispecchiamento*, it is through her friendship with Vannina and Vannina's own tactics in dealing with other women that Suna herself comprehends her problematic situation and learns to communicate with other women: "I'm better now, I don't scare off the women with my prying: I sit down, I chat and laugh; I'm learning to get information out of them without asking too many questions, I make myself familiar with their problems and gain their trust" (252). The moment of *rispecchiamento*, however, also exposes Suna to weaknesses she cannot fathom rectifying because she is deprived of the female collectivity and support so fundamental to women's liberation. Suna's suicide is a powerful symbol of the tragic consequences of this lack in a woman's life. However, within the economy of the novel, such a tragic solution is not proffered as the only alternative to a situation like Suna's. Instead, it becomes a regenerative symbol through which Vannina can carry out a more enlightened plan of women's liberation. Vannina takes the act as a sign for her to carry Suna's teachings outside the institutions in which her friend worked. This revelation is succinctly encapsulated in a dream sequence that is the culmination of Vannina's experiences in her friendships with Suna, Tota, and Giottina, and, later, Rosa Colla. Through Suna, Vannina learned the importance of loving other women and has become wary of the problems of working within conventional groups, while Tota and Giottina's admonition, "beware of the wings of those who can't fly," warned her of the impending dangers of Suna's predicament. The dream appropriates this warning and converts it into the image of Vannina's own liberation, as she soars above the houses that represent the domestic sphere from which she will eventually be liberated.[36]

While the Addis friendships reintroduce the female presence into her life through a return to the maternal sphere and the development into entrustment, Vannina's relationship with her colleague Rosa Colla in Rome is the culmination of this return and reinstates the maternal presence securely in her adult life. The heroine as daughter, in fact, finally gains the strength necessary to transform her life through this friendship. Significantly, this bond centers on the question of motherhood and of the role sisterhood plays in redefining it. Motherhood assumes an important role in Vannina's development, as it represents the traditional female identity in the novel.[37] When Vannina entrusts herself to Rosa Colla and a complicitous bond develops, she is able to apply Suna's politicized views to her own life. Rosa's independent and eccentric lifestyle, symbolic of her difference, offers her proof that a woman can happily and productively shape her own life.

Rosa's experience in motherhood reveals the consequences of its institutionalization and confirms Vannina's fears of women's subordination to this gendered role.[38] Rosa became pregnant through her relationship with a young homeless man, whom she housed and fed. When he deserted her, she terminated her pregnancy. But upon returning and learning of the abortion, the man beat her in an act of possession and dominance. Vannina faces a similar situation when confronted by Giacinto on the position of motherhood, a narrative technique emphasizing the *rispecchiamento* between the protagonist and Rosa. Giacinto is unable to reconcile himself to his wife's psychic evolution. In an attempt to keep Vannina from rejecting tradition, he tries to convince her to accept the notion of motherhood that up until now has defined her womanhood in the domestic sphere. Giacinto even sets the parameters of her existence within a traditional maternal context, "I hate the house without you, . . . the bed is empty. I'll take you back . . . with your whims. . . . If you want to continue teaching, I'll let you. . . . Why don't we try to have a baby? when you go back to being the sweet Vannina I used to know" (268). When Vannina resists his views, he imposes them on her, exerting a control over her body that is stronger than his will alone. Giacinto rapes her, impregnating her and physically forcing her to embody the maternal ideal identified as both natural and submissive.

Both Rosa and Vannina's experiences not only motivate Vannina's rejection of the institution of motherhood, but, in keeping with *affidamento*, also inform the assistance Rosa offers her. By entrusting herself to Rosa, she is able to make choices regarding her life that she otherwise would not have had the strength to make. She exercises independence by leaving her husband, whom she still loves, terminating her imposed pregnancy, and striking off on her own. Vannina does not ultimately reject motherhood, but rather its imposition and institutionalization. Her position, as well as the situation of the conventional maternal characters in the novel, forces the reader to recognize the predicament of embodying the traditional maternal role and to rethink the possibility of a new maternal experience, where women exercise choice and define the parameters of their own existence.

When combined with the transformation fostered by the friendships on Addis, Rosa's friendship also assists Vannina in extending her transformation to the social sphere of public education. Through her role as schoolteacher, Vannina implements her personal development to effect social and cultural change. Education exposes the idealized "biosocial program" of gendered relationships and ushers motherhood into the realm of knowledge and, consequently, choice. In order to demystify the socialized roles of male dominance and female submission her eight-year-old students have already assimilated and demonstrated in a scene of simulated rape, Vannina decides to give a lesson in sex education excluded from the school curriculum: "I started to draw plants, seeds, animals, eggs. My hand moved securely.... For the first time ... I did not feel frustrated and empty, but charged by feverish happiness" (258).

The diverse friendships Vannina chronicles in her journal have all advanced her subjective development. Her friendship with Tota and Giottina recasts her as daughter, allowing her to begin exploration of her self as a woman within a community of women. The bond with Suna politicizes her, raising her consciousness not only of her immediate situation, but also of the possibilities for political change for other women as well. These friendships converge in the relationship with Rosa. This bond of entrustment with someone unconventional situates Vannina in a female space of difference. The strength gained through these bonds of sisterhood prompts the heroine to leave the confines of her marriage and to challenge the archaic educational system she has complacently supported until now. In changing her life and in raising her students' consciousness to issues of gendered domination and repression, she indeed begins to build a model for women's liberation.

The 1970s feminist discourse on sisterhood which informs Anna and Vannina's rediscovery of female presences in their lives, informs their challenges to the confining spaces of the familial sphere developed in part outside the mainstream political arena and in the "behind the scenes" sites of female collectivity. The poetry collections *Donne mie* [My Women] (1974) and *Mangiami pure* (1978) bring together the practices of sisterhood fundamental to Anna and Vannina's transformation. They also focus on the actual dynamics of *autocoscienza* as played out in women's collectives; the issue of *doppia militanza*; relationships between liberated and nonliberated women; and the significance of entrustment and *rispecchiamento* to women's liberation.

The poems I examine from these collections contain some of the most salient themes of Maraini's discourse on sisterhood. Significantly, in their diversity these pieces all highlight the value to women's liberation of complicitous bonds between women.

The result of the collections' investigation is a rather extensive analysis of conventional roles and of feminist practices designed to transform them. *Donne mie*, a work that like *Il Manifesto* and *Donna in guerra* is a virtual feminist manifesto itself, provides an in-depth study of the cultural codification of women's subordination as it outlines possible means of overcoming it. It begins with poems that consider the collective nature of women's social status and experiences, and ends with five poems whose title female characters recount their own personal experiences in such areas as work and intimate relationships.[39]

Two poems in *Donne mie* are exemplary of the feminist emphasis on collectivity and its benefits for the individual. "L'arte di amare" [The Art of Love] and "Donne mie" focus on the ways in which women can overcome and subvert the silence, fear, invisibility, and powerlessness historically attributed to femininity. To borrow bell hooks' prescription for a successful sisterhood, whether in the political or cultural arena collectivity unifies the means and strengths necessary to make an impact in both public and private spheres.[40] The result is equally the reevaluation and empowerment of the individual within the group, something Suna, for example, could not achieve within the political movement *Vittoria proletaria*. In *Donne mie*, this practice of sisterhood encourages independence as it creates for women a site of mutual understanding through common historical (though not necessarily similar) experiences.

"L'arte di amare" and "Donne mie" proffer a call-to-action intended to strengthen the individual woman's sense of self and purpose in a wider historical context. "L'arte di amare," the opening poem of *Donne mie*, assumes Ovid's *Art of Love* as a metaphor for the cultural model of women's objectification.[41] The poem stands as a rebuttal to Ovid's prescription for courtship, which employs well-known stereotypes of a man's active courtship and a woman's passivity that hides her true desire. The result is a stripping away of the woman's agency as well as the undermining of her will within the relationship. The feminist reading retraces, through the different stages of a woman's life, the consequences this prescription has on her. At the same time, however, it also puts forth a model for changing women's subservient position in such matters as sex, education, and motherhood. Thus, while asserting that "[a] woman can find liberation only by herself, with her head / and her hands" (19), the poem is almost immediately framed by the theme of collectivity, so dear to Anna in *Il Manifesto* and Clitennestra in *I sogni*. Unity is the means through which women reacquire power: "[L]et's look each other in the eyes / fearful and depraved from too much servitude, my beloved women" (6).

In the poem "Donne mie," the text continues the outline begun in "L'arte" as well as its impassioned call-to-action, highlighting, however, the need to surmount class differences through *rispecchiamento*. The piece's analysis cuts across class lines, offering a portrait ranging from housewives secluded in the domestic sphere ("they taught you to work, obey, remain silent, produce offspring"), to emancipated bourgeois women ("wearing mink coats hung / on your shoulders, poor coat hangers of masculine pride"), to university students versed in patriarchal culture ("What good is history when it teaches you that man is the subject and woman is the passive object of all / times?") The poem's call for an alliance between women of different classes warns against socially destructive separatism. It cautions that for a transformation to occur, a dialogue should be opened up not only with men but also with those women who have been coopted and passively enjoy the fruits of their objectification. This open dialogue is constructed through one woman mirroring herself in her interlocutor. In this process of reciprocity, she discovers her thoughts and ideas as aspects of the other woman's life are revealed to her and she responds to them. In reference to its cultural context, the work assumes sisterhood as the solution to issues of class oppression.[42] It is through sisterhood and collective action that women seize governance of their lives and reverse their socialized destiny.

While *Donne mie* develops a call to action to destroy the cultural models of subordination, *Mangiami pure* examines the sites (more specifically the *autocoscienza* groups) and relationships created in the feminist movement to carry out the struggle. The result is a frank look at the social dynamics of women's bonds. Born out of the conditions outlined in *Donne mie*, the dynamics do not always prove constructive. Rather, class-based prejudices and ideological differences can indeed frustrate sisterhood, a situation that clearly arose in the 1970s in *autocoscienza* sessions. As a reflection of its historical context, *Mangiami pure* replies to the unhappy realities of women's relationships within the women's movement. Indeed, when the collection appeared in 1978, the impassioned ideals of women's unified struggle for change put forth by Carla Lonzi and others had already begun to collapse under the weight of centuries of cultural socialization, which, to ensure social stability, stressed solidarity not to each other but to the family, "inside the enervating emptiness / of familiar/familial inertia."[43]

To counter this regression, *Mangiami pure* recuperates elements of traditional culture and/or women's lives as banners for the role of collectivity in women's liberation. While underscoring the significance of unity as a compassionate sisterhood, it focuses on issues that empower the individual as well as the collective. Developing the project begun as early as *Il Manifesto* in 1970, the text as a whole validates aspects of women's historical and physical experiences by proposing them as emblems of courage and fortitude.

The poems "ricamare" and "ad una sorella timida," for example, translate elements and symbols of women's history into a contemporary sisterhood. As we have seen in the introduction to this chapter, "ricamare" features the domestic sphere and the female practice of weaving as symbols of both the condition of women's lives and of their collective experience. The activity of the title refers not only to traditional female work, but also to their creativity: Shut away in domestic spaces women challenge their situation by weaving thoughts of defiance as well as models for change. In keeping with Maraini's acknowledgment of similarities in women's historical situation, the literal as well as figurative activity of *ricamare* becomes a gentle yet symbolically and historically charged call for intellectual action.

Moments in women's history are similarly recuperated in the poem "ad una sorella timida," which borrows imagery from the traditional Witch's Sabbath to symbolically portray the activities the women's movement undertook to challenge female oppression. The Witch's Sabbath represents the activities of women who were knowledgeable about the body and healing methods, thereby posing a threat to the medical as well as religious establishments.[44] The use of this particular imagery is significant in a discourse on women's liberation and sisterhood. Nineteen-seventies feminist groups reappropriated the image of the witch and placed themselves directly into her historical legacy. One theater group, for example, called itself *Le Streghe* [The Witches], while the popular feminist slogan "Tremate le streghe son tornate!" ("Tremble the witches have returned!") announced women's defiant stance against mainstream culture by recalling their earlier defiant ancestors. By paralleling women's collective action with the witches' activities, Maraini herself not only links women to their historic past, but also emphasizes the challenge—mirroring that of their fifteenth- and sixteenth-century sisters—they pose today to the establishment, defined by Maraini as "a new Middle Ages" for its oppressive legal and social systems (38).

Although a source of symbolic placement and cultural identity, the historical legacy of femininity can equally hinder this subversive call for collectivity. Negative aspects of femininity have shaped women's notion of themselves within social discourse and, as several *Mangiami pure* poems show, it has been difficult to extricate this impression even from personal dialogues. Rap sessions were considered successful in the 1970s, but they failed under the weight of tensions between participants, who struggled to accommodate both personality- and class-based differences. Maraini uses these tensions to challenge the attributes of passivity and love deemed natural to women, but which frustrate the goals of women's liberation. The short poem "riunione di gruppo" [group reunion], whose concise, crisp verses echo a tone of desperation, showcases the counterproductive exploitation between women who, instead of entering into supportive bonds of *affidamento*, succumb to feelings of animosity, "an irascible evening / ... / we ferociously searched / in each other's bellies" (41). This issue comes to the fore in the impassioned poem "non mi dire che le donne sono buone" [don't tell me women are good], which counters the traditional notion of women's unwitting essentialist tendency to be pacifists with examples of their cruel attitudes toward each other:

> our friendship is so fragile / don't say / that women are naturally nice and candid and open anymore / it's not true / we don't channel our aggression into wars / ... or in ascensions to power / ... instead under the guise of female gentility / we torture each other with curved needles / we're so good with sons and husbands and lovers / so deceitful with each other / our love is so fragile / we are just born and already we kill each other / in the name of non-violence and female solidarity. (43–44)

These attitudes prove destructive to the principles of sisterhood Italian feminism upholds. While women struggle to unify and redefine traditional qualities of femininity (such as non-violence) as a mark of their difference, they allow historical rifts born of socioeconomic differences to frustrate progress.

These differences and the necessary dependence of one woman on the other for effecting social change propitious to both becomes the focus of the poem "non sappiamo amarci" [we don't know how to love each other]. The poem, however, also indirectly confronts the potentially problematic differences in bonds of entrustment. Addressing a housewife, the poet contemplates how their friendship could possibly survive in the context of the diversity in their individual situations. While both are silenced as women, the housewife depends on the poet for the feminist tools necessary to transform both their situations, "you need me / but you think you hate me . . . why are you and I together?" (49). However, by highlighting their similarities as women, which arise from shared domestic spaces, the poet proposes a solution to the conflicts depicted in earlier poems. Focusing on love between women, she offers a redeeming model of friendship which transcends all considerations of class and gender, "give me your hands they are like mine, / and what if we tried . . . accepting each other as we are?" (49–50).

Both *Donne mie* and *Mangiami pure* offer insight into the feminist discourse on women's collectivity and the viability and success of the practices it defined. For readers of Maraini's works and scholars of Italian feminism, these texts are invaluable documents of the practices and reality of the women's movement. They showcase the importance of recuperating and appropriating moments and events in women's history to reinterpret and redelineate a female cultural legacy that legitimizes women's experiences. At the same time, by combining pieces that illuminate the not always positive "other side" of women's collectives and investigate the remote spaces of *autocoscienza* sessions, the collections also reveal the consequences of socialization on sisterhood and formulate ways to reverse or subvert that socialization. Ultimately, they present clues for developing new practices of sisterhood.

In the 1981 epistolary novel *Lettere a Marina* [Letters to Marina], Maraini provides answers to the dilemmas presented in *Donne mie* and *Mangiami pure* and ponders the effects of the implementation of some of the practices they showcase. With its focus on the protagonist Bianca's search for personal meaning, the novel investigates the effects of sisterhood on the individual woman and highlights the importance, in processes of subjective development, of reconstructing her past in communion with other women. Her letters, which comprise the novel, focus her gaze backwards into her past, and thus place her on the path defined by Vegetti Finzi as essential to the construction of subjectivity.

Tracing a Kristevan trajectory, Bianca delves into her past in search of the prediscursive self repressed in the acquisition of social roles. Although this search is an impossible endeavor, for the prediscursive self is ultimately unknowable, the process itself nevertheless proves regenerative. Through the letters, Bianca reexamines her network of relationships with other women, including her mother, her sister, and her lover Marina, and chronicles her growing friendship with her next-door neighbor Basilia. This movement between past and present reconstitutes Bianca's history from a subjective position, "a woman . . . without a past new-born and naked out of the dark womb of time," and inscribes her through her own hand onto history.[45] It also, however, defines her future, thus fulfilling the project set up in the *Mangiami pure* poem "una testa di medusa" [medusa's head], "I want to go back / towards future happiness / my face is marked by / the deep shadows of memory" (80–81).

In charting the geography of the self, Bianca's letters examine different sites in which her friendships with other women are played out. From the mother-daughter bond defining her relationship with Marina first and then the friendship with Basilia, Bianca's epistles investigate the significance of the different unions to her self-exploration.[46] Significantly, the relationship of *affidamento* that defines these bonds becomes extension of Bianca's cherished *autocoscienza* sessions. Throughout her relationship with Marina, Bianca participated in these sessions with her friends. While these meetings became a point of contention for her lover, who considered them an escape into an area of herself unknown to Marina, Bianca suffers the consequences of not expressing herself anymore through them. Even her thoughts on the sessions are a testament to their original ideation as spaces in which women can explore and articulate themselves: "It is the small group that has given me back the desire to write has brought back to the surface things I thought dead and buried. And if it were not for the small group which made me used to talking about me with a woman's face in front of me I would not be writing to you now [Marina]" (sic 40).

The *autocoscienza* sessions are integral to Bianca's developing identity as a woman, and this importance is reflected in her letters. Written with minimal punctuation in a stream-of-consciousness style, the letters challenge the dictates of formal grammar. As letters written to Marina, they open up a communication between Bianca and the destinator. The fact that they are never sent highlights their function as intermediaries, or interlocutory spaces that bridge the gap between her present self and the past she explores through them. Without the stream-of-consciousness-like *autocoscienza* sessions, the protagonist suffers from writer's block, and it is only their extension into the friendship with Basilia that allows her to relocate her voice.

An extension of these sessions and, more specifically, based on *affidamento* and *rispecchiamento*, the friendship between Bianca and Basilia is instrumental in replacing the historical context of women's socialization with a cultural legacy founded on women's traditions. Tellingly, the relationship results in the reintegration of the mother (Basilia) into the daughter's (Bianca's) life. "Writing beyond the ending" of "Demetra ritrovata," this adult bond carries DuPlessis' proposal of exploring the territory beyond conventional narrative closures even further. It is through the complicitous friendship, unfolding in an*other* space—in Bianca and Basilia's apartments—that we witness the reciprocal, regenerative possibilities of the symbolic mother-daughter relationship central to the liberatory paradigms set up by Luciana Percovich, Luisa Muraro, and Silvia Vegetti Finzi. It situates the protagonist in a legacy of women's customs and traditions, as does Vannina's with Tota and Giottina, but does not vacillate between acceptance and rejection. Rather, the bond is based on mutual growth.[47]

As "symbolic" mother to Bianca, Basilia personifies the complexities of motherhood examined in Maraini's previous works while at the same time it reinforces the maternal role in Bianca's life. She is at once the member of the family who is most exploited and the fundamental purveyor of life and transmitter of women's past, represented by the stories she tells.[48] As mother within her family, Basilia embodies those self-effacing traits of motherhood challenged in the works discussed in chapter 2. When Bianca meets her, the thirty-six-year-old Basilia is unquestioningly dedicated to her role as wife and mother. True to the traditional maternal role, this dedication manifests itself physically through her body, which prematurely ages and decays as it becomes fodder for her two young sons.[49] Likewise, the self-effacement demanded by the role causes Basilia to lack a sense of self separate from her family and the roles she fulfills within that realm. Even in Bianca's apartment, where Basilia does not function in the capacity of wife and mother, she does not lose her posture of self-effacement: "She concealed herself as much as she could behind this sad laughter begging pardon for being in the world" (79).

It is through friendship with another woman in a separate sphere that the mother can ultimately unleash her inner self and subjectively articulate her thoughts.[50] While it is true that in this relationship of *affidamento* it is more Bianca who entrusts herself to the maternal Basilia, Basilia is nevertheless longingly called upon by the heroine to reveal herself, to transmit her knowledge to the searching daughter. In this configuration, the neighbor can articulate herself as well as cherished traditions passed down through generations of female ancestors. This puts Bianca, the *tabula rasa* represented by her very name, in touch with a female ancestral identity—the past she lacks at the beginning of the novel. But it also ensures that Basilia reappropriates those stories and interprets and recounts them herself.

Basilia is an important figure in Bianca's life, for she dispels any conventional notion the protagonist might have about her as a woman and mother. Bianca's notions evolved in part out of a class division which *autocoscienza* and *affidamento* should ideally overcome. While at first the protagonist perceives only the painful aspects of Basilia's life, much like the daughters in *L'età del malessere* and "Madre canina," as the relationship progresses, she recognizes the richness of her friend's character. By entrusting herself to Basilia, she understands the value to women of comprehending the mother, of heeding Irigaray's plea to "not again . . . kill the mother."[51] As the protagonist slowly grows to know Basilia, she, though still recognizing her exploitation within the family, celebrates her physical and emotional strength as procreator of life and of bewitching sagas.

Through Basilia, Bianca is able to glimpse the ancient roots of a maternal discourse based on women's agency, the power Clitennestra tried futilely to maintain. Hearing her neighbor sing a song "just like her peasant mother must have done" (119), the protagonist appreciates the value of possessing and being in touch with a female legacy.[52] Through *rispecchiamento*, and thus by translating Basilia's experiences into her own life, she realizes that in this maternal discourse she will no longer have a "tendenza perversa alla maternità" (perverse tendency towards motherhood), in which she subsumes all her desires under her desire to mother. Bianca's words illuminate her transformation: "As she sang I all at once longed to be her with her swelling breasts her melancholy dark-ringed eyes her decaying teeth and that carefree voice. *She was so entirely herself.* I envied her. . . . I was amazed to find her majestic and very beautiful" (119; emphasis added).

As we have seen in chapter 1, the daughter has the potential to rewrite women out of historical oblivion. In *Lettere*, it is the maternal figure of Basilia who gives life to Bianca and makes an imprint on her "white" slate. While her storytelling abilities bring the daughter in touch with women's oral tradition, kneading her shoulders symbolically ensures the daughter's physical placement within the present. The neighbor's link to the past and her articulation within the *friendship* of stories steeped in ancient beliefs result in a subjective expression through which she speaks, as Percovich notes with regard to women's self-expression, "not only of herself but from her self,"[53] and Basilia does indeed recount her tale "from her self," uniting past, present, and future into a unified frame of reference.

For her part, Bianca is—tellingly—as captivated as she was as a young girl listening to her own mother's tales and as enchanted as Vannina is when listening to Tota and Giottina's. But while Basilia tells stories "from her self," Bianca is still writing letters that speak "of herself," causing her to experience writer's block, connected with her past. The *autocoscienza* sessions with her friends allowed her to "tell of myself," but through the more profound, more involved relationship of *affidamento* she can reenergize at novel's end. Opening Bianca up to women's oral tradition through her stories, and symbolically (re)creating her through a technique transmitted from grandmother to mother to daughter, Basilia helps Bianca replant her roots in the dark recesses of women's history, reclaiming the "history" that "Madre canina" lacked. Therefore, by the end of the novel, Bianca is ready to go to Sicily, the land of her roots, and, by remembering the history that "[m]aybe [she'd] forgotten" (7), Bianca revisits herself.

But the friendship, as noted earlier, is not a one-way process of development from Basilia to Bianca. Basilia has not simply and predictably slipped into the maternal role. On the contrary, she also symbolically figures as Basilia's daughter, completing the *rispecchiamento* of sharing knowledge and experiences. As daughter herself, Basilia grows through the relationship, which helps her develop a sense of self outside her family. She is slowly able to extricate herself from her family, to redefine her self, and to communicate her rich tales. By novel's end, she has the confidence and courage to invite Bianca out for dinner. By expressing her desire for pleasure, and by leaving the home to fulfill it, she is able to strive for wholeness, to strive to be "entirely herself." The relationship between the two women proves beneficial because they have allowed each other to bring their strengths to it. While Basilia helps Bianca recover her past, Bianca helps Basilia recover the voice within her. Thus, while Bianca will set off in the morning for Sicily, Basilia has just begun to allow her inner strength to be spoken, "she was laughing like a woman who feels beautiful and confident of herself" (206). Along with the relationships examined in *Il Manifesto* and in *Donna in guerra*, Bianca and Basilia's friendship demonstrates how essential sisterhood is to women's liberation and in their attempts to situate themselves within a legacy of women's culture.

Decades after feminism began to map out practices of sisterhood and to reconfigure them into a revised family, the union continues to play a significant role in women's exploration of experiences and in the feminist model for alternative female development. As we have seen, works by Franco, Campo, and Garlaschelli prominently feature sisterhood as an essential component in the development of a woman's identity. Maraini's short story "Cinque donne d'acqua dolce" [Five sweetwater women], written in the early 1990s, focuses on the type of *autocoscienza*-like dialogue between women as a liberatory practice.[54] Significantly for Maraini's model, although by the 1980s *autocoscienza* was integrated into *affidamento*, the author still focuses on the first practice as a means for women to discover themselves and each other and to draw strength from their communality.

Tellingly, the short story is not set in the present, but rather in the late 1970s, a time when rap sessions were a common feature of the feminist landscape. The story's narrator designates this period as a fruitful one, as "a year of new seeds that everyone launched with open hands . . . sure that they would take and grow roots and massive stems that then would be transformed into fruit trees."[55] Continuing the metaphor of planting the seed of hope and reshaping its results, however, she also lamentably notes the failure of this plan, as overriding cultural factors played a role in frustrating its development.[56] Nevertheless, the short story not only illustrates the benefits of a feminist practice of sisterhood, but also provides an allegory of the importance of reapplying and reliving it today.

The focus of "Cinque donne" lies in the similarity and communality between the women, as well as in the reconstruction of their past, linking this tale and its characters to Maraini's earlier explorations of womanhood. While the five characters are different in class, age, and occupation, through their group discussions they discover that beneath the apparent diversity they have all inhabited similar gendered spaces, "They were friends, of a soft friendship born among plates full of pasta and red-radicchio salad, among whole wheat bread and small chocolate pastries" (148). While the narrator, echoing the *Mangiami pure* poem "riunione di gruppo," notes that the dissimilarities between the women can and do generate discord, the fact that women of different backgrounds can actually dialogue and reap the personal as well as collective benefits of their union is, in Maraini's text and overall vision of this discourse, a testament to the potential of sisterhood.

Notably, the discussions born of this union take the women through the geography of their experiences as women, and, consequently, revolve around their past and present roles. The women's friendship—and the practice of *autocoscienza* that is a part of that bond—becomes the site where discourses on womanhood converge. The text stresses the illuminatory function of these discussions, as conversations on the women's background reveal formative and telling moments of their socialization. At the same time, these revelations also spark recollection in the other women of long forgotten but transformative moments in their lives. One of the women, for example, reveals sexual abuse as a child, a topic which strikes a mnemonic chord in others, prompting them to remember their own childhood abuse: "Maybe it was Viola. . . . Recounting how one day a tender uncle made his hand slither up his little niece's skirt. . . . Rosaria immediately recalled a memory that she thought she had buried well enough to be free of it forever" (146). The women's pasts are imbedded in unspoken moments shaped by the conventions of the gendered spaces they occupy—silence, passivity, femininity, guilt—and through dialogue each becomes conscious of their similar experiences. "And they all knew it happened just like this. The little girl kept quiet, her tongue glued to her palate, her modesty gripping her throat, a stubborn fear, an inability to say, to reveal that which seemed to sully their trivial female destiny" (147). The process of recollection sparked by *autocoscienza* and, subsequently, *affiatamento* [understanding] not only serves to reconstruct the individual women's pasts, but also their collective past as women, occurring in the Beauvoirian backstage of their apartment in which the women boldly and openly express themselves:

> They knew they were dissimilar, and yet they'd found a bond, a common path. The rhythm of a conversation that digs into their buried memories, inside the dead moments of individual histories. It was mostly there that they recognized themselves, in those first moments of affection and emotions, in the blind love for their mothers, their fathers, just like it was for the thousands of other little girls like them, in the belly of history. It was there that they discovered they were as alike as sweetwater fish, with their silent gasping for air . . . , their swimming wide-eyed in the tepid waters of a common dream for peace. (152)

In the short story's vision, sisterhood and the fundamental familial relationships it extends ultimately offer the possibility of change to traditional gender roles.

The transformation of Maraini's heroines occurs through the symbiotic relationship between women, where through *autocoscienza, affidamento*, and *rispecchiamento* they play an essential role in each other's development. At the same time, Maraini's works inscribe the presence of this fundamental bond in women's cultural history and document its development through the 1970s, 1980s, and 1990s. Anna's consciousness in *Il Manifesto* develops through sisterhood in her life, and, equally critical she has a lasting impact on the women around her. Through the play's frame of *autocoscienza* and entrustment, the dialogue between Anna and the four dead women reconstructs their past, and through the heroine's own "manifesto," she defines the challenge to past subservience. Vannina in *Donna in guerra*, meanwhile, develops through different facets of friendship. In her relationship with Tota and Giottina, she relives the pre-Oedipal bond with the maternal women and thus taps into an aspect of women's lives hidden and silenced. In her relationship of sisterhood with Suna and Rosa Colla, she gains the strength and confidence to embark on a journey of change in both private and public life. Her journal, meanwhile, documents the effects of these bonds on the development of her own voice. In *Donne mie* and *Mangiami pure*, the author examines the problems arising between women during moments of *rispecchiamento*, obstacles easily overcome through complicity. Meanwhile, in *Lettere a Marina*, female friendship creates the possibility for change in motherhood and in a woman's ability to create meaning. Finally, in "Cinque donne di acqua dolce," the benefits of *autocoscienza*, the site of self-articulation and *rispecchiamento*, is narrated from the perspective of the 1990s.

The reconfigured relational spaces carved out for Maraini's heroines include practices of sisterhood executed through unity with other women, described by Giuliana Bruno as a decentralized site that stands as an alternative to conventional familial bonds. The revelation of "micro-histories" surfacing through dialogue between women ultimately leads to self-knowledge and to new interpretations of their situatedness in history.[57] Despite the fact that the relational practices developed in these sites are not necessarily free of tensions, narrating life experiences prove beneficial for Maraini's heroines, including the unnamed subjects of *Donne mie* and *Mangiami pure*. It is a liberating practice of self-articulation and -definition, and creates for them a sense of female community not out of common victimization, but rather out of the perception of a shared historical past and collective action in the present.

Conclusion

THE EXPLORATION OF MOTHERHOOD, DAUGHTERHOOD, AND SISTERhood in Dacia Maraini's writings and films results in documents of the developing Italian feminist debate on women's experiences in familial spaces. The author's early texts deconstruct traditional notions of the family to show the social and cultural construction of women's roles. Later works produced at the height of the women's movement reconstruct possible experiences from new roles and out of women's subjectivity. Maraini's redefinition of familial spaces has roots in the Italian feminist use of familial metaphors to redirect women's experiences and redefine their identities. Thus, the three relationships that form the basis of this study—motherhood, daughterhood, and sisterhood—are deconstructed and reconstructed as symbolic relationships forged out of women's agency.

In Maraini's works, these newly reconstructed relational spaces of the symbolic mother-daughter relationship, the daughter-father bond, and female friendships extract the invisible realities of identity politics. By posing a challenge to such rigid discourses on gender as Freudian psychoanalysis, the philosophical systems of Aristotle and Hegel, and structural anthropology, Maraini's texts construct a discourse on women's social placement based on subjectivity and a system of identification that reinstates female reference points. They investigate the conventional Western discourses on womanhood in order to understand the roles established for women and in order to reconstruct beneficial roles for them. Their examination of relational spaces opens Maraini's readers up to experiences within the Italian domestic and public spheres. By implementing the early feminist slogan "the private is political," her works play an important role in raising public consciousness to the formulation of relationships, and in developing an analysis of familial spaces.

One of Italy's most important and influential authors allows us to better understand advances made in Italian society for women. In early works, Maraini's examination of motherhood includes a tragic portrayal of a role relegated to domestic spaces and rendered ahistorical, invisible, and untouched by the public forces that determine history and social change. At this period in postwar Italian feminism, groups such as *Demau* and *Rivolta femminile* were just beginning to develop a theoretical discourse on women's relationships. This discourse informed later works, in which Maraini develops a maternal discourse which not only reappropriates motherhood's procreative power, but also reinstates the maternal figure as fundamental to women's subjective and social advancement.

The development of women's subjectivity is also an underlying question in Maraini's investigation of daughterhood. This investigation traverses the two most important relationships in the daughter's life, the relationship with the mother and the relationship with the father. The bond with the mother represents, in early works, something to move away from in order to achieve emancipation. Thus, Enrica in *L'età* and the narrative voice of "Madre canina" see the mother as a symbol of women's subordination and sacrifice. Later heroines, such as Proserpina in "Demetra ritrovata," the little girl in *Giochi di latte*, and Bianca in *Lettere a Marina*, however, see the mother as a positive force in their lives, as someone to reintegrate into their lives as they seek emancipation for all women. But the daughterly discourse also includes, for Maraini, the painful contemplation of the daughter-father relationship. This bond represents, in such works as the poetry collection *Crudeltà all'aria aperta* and the film *Mio padre amore mio*, a crossroads in the daughter's investigation of women's subjectivity. The father in these works occupies the social sphere of language and power and the daughter must move toward identification with him to enter those spheres. In order for the daughter to challenge this system and to rewrite the laws of subjectivity, she must deconstruct and then reconstruct her *storia* in relation to her father. The result is a relationship of reciprocal social and cultural agency.

Friendships with other women also play a fundamental role in the development of subjectivity. In the Italian feminist movement, these relationships can become bonds of *affidamento*, or entrustment, which allow members to achieve cultural and social symbolic placement. Symbolically mirroring the Lacanian mirror stage in development, friendships help women gain new perspectives on their lives by coming face to face with other women's experiences. In Maraini's works, these relationships are instrumental to her heroines' journey to self-knowledge. In narratives such as *Donna in guerra* and *Lettere a Marina*, women's friendships put her heroines in contact with women's history and tradition and raise their consciousness about ways to effect social and cultural change.

Familial relationships provide, as we have seen, a fertile field for female artists exploring women's social and cultural situations. Understanding them is fundamental to comprehending what shapes identity and how women can ultimately effect change in their lives. Together with other women artists, Maraini's depictions of these relational spaces creates a genealogy of women's voices within the family. Her works join a legacy of novelists such as Natalia Ginzburg and Fausta Cialente, filmmakers such as Lina Mangiacapre and *Le Nemesiache*, and poets such as Ada Negri and Franca Maria Catri who have focused on familial relationships in their investigations of womanhood. For its complexity and extensiveness, Maraini's opus also stands as reference point in this genealogy for recent family portraits in the continuing legacy of women's culture, represented by, for example, novelists Elisabetta Pierallini, Clara Sereni, and Isabella Bossi Fedrigotti, and poet Rosita Copioli. By bringing family relationships to light, Maraini opens readers up to the cultural and social construction of women's experiences. Her writings and films offer profound insight into the development of the Italian feminist—artistic and theoretical—discourse on women's subjectivity. Ultimately, their investigations of relational spaces are indispensable tools in our understanding of the developmental model upon which women's lives are built.

Notes

Introduction

1. Vannina in Dacia Maraini, *Woman at War*, trans. M. Benetti and E. Spottiswood (New York: Italica Press, 1988), 76.

2. Salvatore Samperi, "Introduzione," *Cuore di mamma* (Milan: Ranzani and Aglieri, 1969), 9. Unless otherwise noted, all translations in this book are my own.

3. Barrie Thorne notes the trend in feminist theory on the family of focusing on issues of gender. An investigation of gender leads to a more sophisticated understanding of principles governing the family and of how the family functions. See *Rethinking the Family* (Boston: Northeastern University Press, 1992), esp. 10–11.

4. Because they strive to establish Maraini's place not only in women's literature but also within Italy's literary pantheon, these critical analyses have to some degree paid attention to the more general aspects of her work. Karen Badt, Gualtiero De Santi, Maryse Jeuland-Meynaud, Bruce Merry, and Grazia Sumeli Weinberg, to name a few, for example, have showcased Maraini's efforts at writing women's voices into literary culture. Others, including Beverly Ballaro, Anna Camaiti Hostert, and Robin Pickering-Iazzi, have focused on more specific themes central to her production, such as motherhood, daughterhood, and the definition of women's subjectivity. These latter works foreground the power and impact of Maraini's exploration of traditionally elided issues on the feminist perception of women's relationships. See Badt's *The Ethics of the Body in American and Italian Women's Fiction* (Dissertation, The University of Chicago, 1994. Ann Arbor: University of Michigan, 1994); De Santi's "La poesia d'amore in Italia (1960–83)," *Testuale* 5.3 (1985): 11–35; Jeuland-Meynaud's "Dacia Maraini: Polémique ou littérature?" in *Les femmes écrivains en Italie aux XIXe et XXe siècles* (Aix-en-Provence: Publications de l'Université de Provence, 1993), 205–38; Merry's *Dacia Maraini and the Written Dream of Women in Italian Literature* (North Queensland: James Cook University, 1997); Sumeli Weinberg's *Parole e impegno nelle opere di Dacia Maraini* (Dissertation, The University of South Africa, 1988. Ann Arbor: University of Michigan, 1988) and *Invito alla lettura di Dacia Maraini* (Pretoria: University of South Africa Press, 1993); Ballaro's "Making the Lesbian Body: Writing and Desire in Dacia Maraini's *Lettere a Marina*," in *Gendered Contexts: New Perspectives in Italian Cultural Studies*, ed. L. Benedetti, J. Hairston, and S. Ross (New York: Peter Lang, 1996), 177–87; Hostert's "Potere dell'alterità-alterità del potere: Una lettura del libro di Dacia Maraini *La lunga vita di Marianna Ucrìa*," *RLA* 5.4 (1992): 204–8; and Pickering-Iazzi's "Designing Women: Images of Motherhood in Novels by Aleramo, Morante, Maraini, and Fallaci," *Annali d'Italianistica* 7 (1989): 325–40.

5. In an essay on her work in film, Maraini explains her choice of themes. This explanation can be applied to her work in other genres as well, "The womanly theme flourishes from those historical bowels that lack a female cultural identity." See

"Tema," in *Cinema, letteratura, arti visive: Lessico politico delle donne*, ed. B. Frabotta, N. Fusini, and A. M. Boetti (Milan: Edizioni Gulliver, 1979), 58. In her own assessment of Maraini's expression of female experiences critic Sumeli Weinberg notes, "Through figurative language, . . . which reveals an intimate and secret world, myths of the sacredness of the family and of institutionalized love crumple." See "All'ombra del padre: la poesia di Dacia Maraini in *Crudeltà all'aria aperta*," *Italica* 67, no. 4 (winter 1990): 453.

6. I use the term *liberation* to recall the historical context of the women's movement in which the works I examine took shape. More importantly, however, I extend its definition to include the notion that developing women's subjectivity and agency and freeing women's relational possibilities can ultimately liberate them from restrictive historical paradigms.

7. Cited in Gillian Rose, *Feminism and Geography: The Limits of Geographical Knowledge* (Minneapolis: University of Minneapolis Press, 1993), 19.

8. Ibid., 144.

9. For studies of the reconfiguration of the relationship between women and space, see *Body Space: Destabilizing Geographies of Gender and Sexuality*, ed. Nancy Duncan (London: Routledge, 1996).

10. Judith Butler, "Performative Acts and Gender Constitution: An Essay in Phenomenology and Feminist Theory," *Performing Feminisms: Feminist Critical Theory and Theater*, ed. S. E. Case (Baltimore: Johns Hopkins University Press, 1990), 273.

11. Victorian models of biology "associated (women) with an unchanging biological role," while men "were imaged as the agents of all social process." Victorian morality, meanwhile, saw the family as a " 'moral' unit" and the domestic sphere as in "opposition to a politics shaped outside the home." See Collier, et al, "Is There a Family: New Anthropological Views," in *Rethinking the Family*, 39 and 40.

12. See Elisabeth Badinter, *Mother Love: Myth and Reality* (New York: Macmillan, 1981).

13. Historically, women primarily occupied the domestic sphere, sometimes even endowed with economic power, while men occupied both domestic and public spheres. The change delineated by sociologists, however, transformed the way children were perceived. This, in turn, expanded the function of motherhood, demanding greater responsibility and sacrifice. Today, according to Saraceno, the division is preserved through differences between male and female activities, including, for example, time organization of work in the public versus domestic spheres and the nonremuneration of housework. For data on this division, see C. Saraceno, *Il lavoro mal diviso* (Bari: De Donato Editore, 1980) and L. Balbo, "Tre interventi sulla famiglia," *Quaderni piacentini*, 16, no. 6 (1977): 139–52. This situation is slowly changing, however. In 1997, the Italian *Corte di Cassazione* deemed housewives managers. As managers, they can be compensated for loss of work in the house due to, for example, personal injury.

14. Chiara Saraceno, *Sociologia della famiglia* (Bologna: Il Mulino, 1988), 8–9.

15. Saraceno, *Il lavoro mal diviso*, 6.

16. Saraceno, "The Italian Family: Paradoxes of Privacy," trans. R. Rosenthal, in *A History of Private Life*, vol. 5, ed. A. Prost and G. Vincent (Cambridge: Harvard University Press, 1991), 501.

17. Balbo, "Tre interventi," 140–41.

18. Mass culture of the immediate postwar period reinforced and perpetuated these insidiously conventional notions of the family. The new and immensely popu-

lar *fotoromanzi* (photonovels), for example, featured conventional stories of love and romance that safely lead to the familial sphere. Recently formed women's groups such as *UDI (Unione dell donne italiane* [Italian Women's Union]) endeavored to counter these ideals in their own publications. Alternative publications such as *UDI*'s *Noi donne* [We Women] focused on issues ranging from universal suffrage to equal opportunity. However, to reach its female readers, the magazine also reflected their social position, catering to concerns in the private sphere reproduced in the *fotoromanzi*. Besides presenting articles on various national and international events, however, it also prominently featured columns on beauty, fashion, and cooking, realistically reflecting the emphasis on domesticity and assumed needs of women in the immediate postwar period. Articles such as "Le donne italiane hanno votato bene" [Italian Women Have Voted Well] (1952) recorded women's progress in the public sphere, articles such as "due novità per essere belle" [Two ways to be beautiful] (1950s) reflected the importance of extending the performance to this realm by offering tips on how to dress and act properly. Clearly, in the society *Noi donne* mirrored, women had to assume a specific feminized persona when entering the public sphere to exercise their newly gained right to vote. And, as is clear even in enlightened literature such as this, women's participation in social discourse, even when gains were made, still entailed personifying the conventional attributes of femininity: beauty, a sweet, submissive disposition, a shapely body put on display through the proper clothing. See *Noidonne*, February 1993. Today, debates that concern feminist issues and counter the persistently conventional portrayal of gender roles in mass culture populate mainstream newspapers, magazines, and television programs. For a discussion of this trend, see Mimma De Leo and Fiorenza Taricone, eds., *Le donne in Italia: Diritti civili e politici* (Naples: Liguori Editore, 1992).

19. Saraceno, *Sociologia*, 10.

20. For a historical look at these social and political changes in women's status, see De Leo and Taricone, *Le donne in Italia*. Despite these significant advances in legislation and lifestyle, however, inequities still exist, as the title of Saraceno's *Il lavoro mal diviso* [Poorly Divided Work] asserts. These inequities endure especially in the family, where women continue to perform the majority of household and child rearing duties. Referring to statistics published by the UN on women's responsibilities inside and outside the family, Maraini herself draws a similar conclusion, noting how even if women have entered the public sphere in full force, their involvement in the domestic sphere has altered little. See Maraini, "Se esser donne vi sembra poco," *L'unità* on internet (23 September 1995). Italian sociologists have also confronted the problems outlined by Maraini. Nora Federici, for example, examines the way political, economic, and demographic factors have changed the family. She notes that despite the fact that factors such as legislative advances, equal rights in the workforce, and a decreasing birthrate have transformed women's roles within the home, cultural and social prejudices based on gender and the division of labor work against extricating women from the domestic sphere. See *Procreazione, famiglia, lavoro della donna* (Torino: Loescher Editore, 1984). For even further analysis of the changing family in Italy see Alfieri and Ambrosini, *La condizione economica, sociale e giuridica della donna in Italia* (Torino: Paravia, 1975), in which the historical and theoretical foundations of the modern family are discussed and which includes a list of earlier legislation; Bimbi, "Three Generations of Women: Transformations of Female Identity Models in Italy," in *Visions and Revisions: Women in Italian Culture*, ed. M. Cicioni and N. Prunster (Providence: Berg, 1993), 149–66; Dal Pozzo, *Donna 70* (Milan: Teti

Editore, 1977); and Giuseppina Malerba and Giovanna Rossi, *La donna nella famiglia e nel lavoro* (Milan: Franco Angeli, 1993). Since the 1980s, women have attained considerable political successes that must be noted. These include an increase in the number of women in political office and administrative positions. For a statistical examination of women in these positions, see De Leo and Taricone, *Le donne in Italia*, and the supplement to the June 1999 issue of *Noi donne* entitled "per un'Europa di donne e uomini."

21. Rosi Braidotti, *Nomadic Subjects: Embodiment and Sexual Difference in Contemporary Feminist Theory* (New York: Columbia University Press, 1994), 183.

22. In her discussion of Maraini's production across genres, Sumeli-Weinberg draws a genealogical line that reflects the Milan Women's Bookstore Collective's notion of symbolic placement. Asserting that Maraini's choice of genre is tied to her position vis-à-vis history, Sumeli-Weinberg notes, "Always excluded from official historiography, woman, for Maraini, lives her absence by trying to impose her own sense of time on the linearity of social time." See "Dacia Maraini e il teatro femminista come modello di trasgressione," *Studi d'Italianistica nell'Africa Australe* 3 (1990): 22.

23. The Milan Women's Bookstore Collective, *Sexual Difference: A Theory of Social-Symbolic Practice*, trans. Teresa De Lauretis (Bloomington: Indiana University Press, 1990), 25.

24. See "Alla ricerca di una soggettività femminile." *La ricerca delle donne: studi femministi in Italia*, ed. Maria Cristina Marcuzzo and Anna Rossi-Doria (Torino: Rosenberg and Sellier, 1987), 228–48.

25. Maraini, interview by author, tape recording, Rome, 26 November 1992.

26. Maraini has argued the benefits of reevaluating the mother-daughter bond: "It can be the daughter who convinces the mother that her place in the family is unhappy, that she had to sacrifice all of her self. Or, it can be the mother who convinces the daughter that she was wrong. In other words, the mother-daughter relationship can always be a very positive encounter. At times, even just supporting each other emotionally, affectionately, can help give the daughter or mother a certain sense of self-confidence, because without this sense of confidence you cannot change your own position of inferiority and subordination. The mother is the reference point to which women can aspire. Motherhood has often been subordinate to fatherhood; but I don't think that there are other roads to take to achieve a certain freedom—that is, recognizing in us the roots of the mother, and of the mothers before her." (Interview by the author, 1992.)

27. Sally Robinson, *Engendering the Subject: Gender and Self-Representation in Contemporary Women's Fiction*, (Albany: State University of New York Press, 1991), 17–19. In her analysis of Italian feminist narratives of the 1970s, Lazzaro-Weis argues that while many women writers—Maraini included—introduced new thematic concerns, they did not break free of conventional generic constraints, such as the romance. The tension between the representations of gender in the works and the works' conventional structure ultimately underscores the difficulty in breaking free of gendered molds. See *From Margins to Mainstream: Feminism and the Fictional Modes in Italian Women's Writing, 1968–1990*, (Philadelphia: University of Pennsylvania Press, 1993) and "Gender and Genre in Italian Feminist Literature in the Seventies," *Italica*, 65, no. 4 (winter 1988): 293–307.

28. Rachel DuPlessis, *Writing Beyond the Ending: Narrative Strategies of Twentieth-Century Women Writers* (Bloomington: Indiana University Press, 1985), 4.

29. See Elisabetta Rasy, *Le donne e la letteratura: Scrittrici, eroine, e ispiratrici nel mondo delle lettere* (Rome: Editori Riuniti, 1984). According to Susan Gubar, the exclusion of women from mainstream artistic arenas has diminished the distance between women's lives and their artistic creations. She argues in "The 'Blank Page' and the Issues of Female Creativity" that "[t]he attraction of women writers to personal forms of expression like letters, autobiographies, confessional poetry, diaries, and journals points up the effect of a life experienced as an art or an art experienced as a kind of life." In *Writing and Sexual Difference*, ed. E. Abel (Chicago: University of Chicago Press, 1982), 81–82.

30. For its originality in content and intention, Nozzoli defines these writers' style as *degree zero*, "The modest, anti-rhetorical, anti-lyrical uses of the language, which suggest a stylistic 'degree zero', can be linked to the reasons behind a direct, anti-literary, polemically bare rendition of reality." See *Tabù e coscienza: La condizione femminile nella letteratura italiana del novecento* (Florence: La Nuova Italia, 1978), 72–73.

31. Lazzaro-Weiss, *From Margins to Mainstream*, 40.

32. Translated by Beverly Kittiel and Jane Jewell, *The Defiant Muse: Italian Feminist Poems from the Middle Ages to the Present* (New York: The Feminist Press, 1986), 97.

33. For Maraini's own views on theater, see *Fare teatro: Materiali, testi, interviste* (Milan: Bompiani, 1974).

34. For a discussion of *La Maddalena*, see "Women's Theatre: Teatro La Maddalena and the Work of Dacia Maraini," *Western European Stages* 1, no. 1 (fall 1989): 27–29. Maraini's quest for theater as a performative site continues today, after the demise of *La Maddalena*. Not only does she continue to produce plays and offer theater workshops to aspiring playwrights, but she has also published a study of theater culture in Palermo. See *Il sommacco: Piccolo inventario dei teatri palermitani trovati e persi* (Palermo: Flaccovio, 1993).

35. For example, *Maria Stuarda* and *I sogni di Clitennestra*, both of which appeared in US and other international venues. For further information on the history of Maraini's involvement in theater, see Jane House, "Interview: Dacia Maraini," *Western European Stages* 1, no. 1 (fall 1989): 39–43; Rhoda Helfman Kaufman, "Introduction," *Only Prostitutes Marry in May*, Dacia Maraini, trans. R. H. Kaufman (Toronto: Guernica, 1994), 9–29; and Tony Mitchell, " 'Scrittura femminile': Writing the Female in the Plays of Dacia Maraini," *Theater Journal* 42, no. 3 (1990): 332–49.

36. Dacia Maraini, panel discussion, Chicago, 5 April 1994.

37. See Maraini's preface to the study of women's theater, "Una lunga storia di esclusione," in *La scena delle donne: presenza e partecipazione della donna al rito scenico occidentale, dalle origini ai giorni nostri*, Emilia Costantini and Mario Moretti (Rome: Editori e Associati, 1992), 3–6.

38. Maraini, "Una lunga storia di esclusione," 3. For histories of women's theater see *La scena delle donne* and *Il teatro delle donne*, ed. M. G. Silvi (Milan: La Salamandra, 1980).

39. Costantini, *La scena*, 128.

40. See Silvi, *Il teatro*, 36–37.

41. Ibid., 40.

42. These works were filmed in super-8 and are not available to the general public. In the 1970s, the most intense period of Maraini's filmmaking, feminist filmmakers shifted, like Maraini, from conventional film to super-8. This choice of a smaller for-

mat allowed them to investigate and ultimately create new spaces of filmmaking. Filmmaker Annabella Miscuglio defines this choice as "a more direct and immediate cinematic 'writing' . . . [which] offers the most accessible and cheapest means of representing one's own fantasies and expressing one's own creativity." See Bruno, *Off Screen*, 157. Lina Mangiacapre used this technique herself to film, for example, *Il mare ci ha chiamate* [The Sea has Called Us], an examination of the female body in Greek myth and Neapolitan oral culture. See Bruno, *Off Screen*, 157. Maraini herself used it because it allowed her to "approach faces, discover them, unveil them, preserve them, touch them." See Bruno, *Off Screen*, 157. For an account of Maraini's involvement in and approach to filmmaking, see "Tema."

43. According to Stephen Heath, classic cinema endorses male subjectivity and agency by tightening and virtually obliterating the distance between spectator and male protagonist. It creates a relationship between spectator and screen (and the images on screen) that mirrors the Lacanian imaginary stage, thus ensuring the spectator's identification with the character who embodies the values underlying the film's intent. See *Questions of Cinema* (Bloomington: Indiana University Press, 1981), 87–88. Teresa De Lauretis, borrowing Foucault's notion of the "technology of sex," also recognizes the potential of film to reinforce gender roles in the spectator, who, as passive receptor of the action on screen, is in a position to assimilate the values presented. See *Technologies of Gender: Essays on Theory, Film, and Fiction* (Bloomington: Indiana University Press, 1987). For other studies of classic Hollywood cinema, see Patricia Erens, ed., *Issues in Feminist Film Criticism* (Bloomington: Indiana University Press, 1990); Annette Kuhn, "Textual Politics," in *Issues in Feminist Film Criticism*, 250–67; Laura Mulvey, *Visual and Other Pleasures* (Bloomington: Indiana University Press, 1989); and Kaja Silverman, *The Acoustic Mirror: The Female Voice in Psychoanalysis and Cinema* (Bloomington: Indiana University Press, 1988).

44. See Claire Johnston, "Women's Cinema as Counter-Cinema," in *Notes on Women's Cinema*, ed. Claire Johnston (London: Society for Education in Film and Television, 1973).

45. Kuhn, "Textual Politics," 254.

46. Maraini, interview by author, 1992.

47. See "Women's Cinema: A Look at Female Identity," trans. Jane Dolman, in *Off Screen*, 24–35.

48. Over the past several decades, a debate over the focus of women's cinema (and feminist film criticism) has called for looking beyond the film's deconstructive aspects and considering the film's relationship to the spectator, the film's awareness of its spectator, and the discourse the film creates in relation to its spectators. Because my study is concerned with Maraini's interpretation and reworking of relational spaces and construction of new modes of representation for the female subject, I will focus on the deconstructive aspects of her work in film. For more on the issues outlined above, see De Lauretis, *Alice Doesn't: Feminism, Semiotics, Cinema* (Bloomington: Indiana University Press, 1984) and *Technologies of Gender*; and Paola Melchiori, *Crinali*.

49. Maraini, *Perché scrivete? Rispondono 109 scrittori italiani*, ed. Ferdinando Camon (Milan: Garzanti, 1989), 97–101.

50. Terry Eagleton, *Literary Theory: An Introduction* (Minneapolis: Minnesota University Press, 1983), 167–68.

51. Maraini herself notes, "We must begin our trip in the world of the written word from the mother's body, which is the source of all our dissatisfactions and our

delights, and which we reject as the remains of our past of dependency." See Camon, *Perché scrivete?*, 100. In another interview, she reiterates the powerful link between the act of writing and the experience of motherood, "Women would express themselves more in writing if they were to express themselves in motherhood, and I include in motherhood, besides procreation, the bonds between woman and daughter, mother and daughter." See "Les femmes et la créativité," in *Dialogues franco-italiens*, ed. Roger Pillaudin (Paris: Institute culturel italien, 1978), 79. When describing women's writing in an interview with Sumeli Weinberg, Maraini notes, "For me the need to ascertain a truly feminine writing involves ... a comprehensive vision of the world which entails taking a particular stand with regard to philosophy, history, religion, medicine, everything, including mythology." See "An interview," 65–66.

52. Laura Di Nola, ed., *poesia femminista italiana* (Rome: Savelli, 1978), 9.

53. See Linda Boose, *Daughters and Fathers* (Baltimore: Johns Hopkins University Press, 1989). Subsequent references to the work are indicated parenthetically in the text. I use the dyads "father-daughter" and "mother-daughter" when referring to the more conventional configuration.

54. This "reality," it must be noted, is in constant mutation. This has been true especially in the years since the 1980s, which have seen a rise in the number of immigrants living in Italy and who have been assimilated into Italian society.

55. *Autocoscienza* was introduced into Italy in 1970 by philosopher Carla Lonzi, who during a trip to the United States participated in consciousness-raising rap sessions and used her experiences to define the Italian practice. Although helpful in enlightening women about themselves and about other women of similar or different backgrounds, *autocoscienza* as a formal practice was all but abandoned as it proved the site of tensions underscored by differences in class, opinions, and ideologies. Maria Luisa Boccia, however, maintains the importance of *autocoscienza* as a formal practice of sisterhood and identifies it as the site of the development of the theory of sexual difference. Boccia argues that *autocoscienza* should still be considered "another way of producing ideas and facts," because it allows the individual to create a relational network and to explore its importance in her life. See "L'identità nella relazione," *I Quaderni dell'associazione culturale Livia Laverani Donini* 3, no. 6 (May 1990): 17, 25.

56. The practices of *autocoscienza* and *affidamento* are the focus of many studies of Italian feminism. See, for example, *Sexual Difference*, including De Lauretis' informative "Introduction"; Lucia Chiavola Birnbaum, *Liberazione della donna: Feminism in Italy* (Middletown: Wesleyan University Press, 1986); Paola Blelloch, "Il femminismo italiano: una diversa prospettiva del rapporto fra donne," *La fusta: Journal of Italian Literature and Culture* 10 (fall 1993–spring 1994): 227–39; and *Italian Feminist Thought: A Reader*, ed. P. Bono and S. Kemp (London: Basil Blackwell, 1991).

Chapter 1. Daughterhood

1. Lucy Gilbert and Paula Webster, *Bound by Love: The Sweet Trap of Daughterhood* (Boston: Beacon Press, 1982), xvii–xviii.
2. William Shakespeare, *King Lear* (New York: Simon and Schuster, 1957) 9.
3. Dacia Maraini, interview by author, tape recording, Rome, 6 April 1993.
4. Boose, *Daughters and Fathers*, 20–21.

5. Lévi-Strauss defines women, and more specifically daughters, as "the most precious possession" for their status as intermediaries between two kinship groups. As subject to this system, women are the grounds that make culture possible, since their exchange is essential to the transition from nature to culture. See *The Elementary Structures of Kinship*, trans. & ed. James H. Bell, John R. von Sturmer, and Rodney Needham (Boston: Beacon Press, 1969), 25. Deprived of agency in cultural production, women stand in a position outside culture, an issue addressed by anthropologist Sherry Ortner in her landmark article "Is Female to Male as Nature is to Culture?" When assessing Lévi-Strauss' definition, she argues that in his conception of the creation of culture women must be " 'socialize[d]' and 'culturalize[d]'." In *Woman, Culture, and Society*, ed. Michelle Z. Rosaldo (Stanford: Stanford University Press, 1974), 76 and 73. Luciana Percovich, when discussing the daughter's development in light of the structural anthropological view, notes that as the object of the law of exogamy, she learns to repress the desire for agency. See "Relazione," in *L'etica necessaria: eredità materna e passione politica* (Milan: Melusine, 1993), 84.

6. Sigmund Freud, "Femininity," *Freud on Women: A Reader*, ed. E. Young-Bruehl (New York: W.W. Norton, 1990), 342–62. This reality is, of course, self-perpetuating in the daughter's development into "normalcy." As the adult daughter reoccupies the domestic sphere as mother and wife, she will repeat this pattern in her relationship with her own daughter. When examining this situation, Sandra Gilbert calls this inheritance "an empty pack." Because the ideology the daughter must follow implies that "culture is by definition both patriarchal and phallocentric" she "must . . . transmit the empty pack of disinheritance to every daughter." See "Life's Empty Pack: Notes toward a Literary Daughteronomy," in *Daughters and Fathers*, 258. For Freud's further discussion of the relationship between daughter and family, see "Three Essays on the Theory of Sexuality," *Freud on Women: A Reader*, ed. E. Young-Bruehl (New York: W.W. Norton, 1990); and *Totem and Taboo*, trans. J. Strachey (New York: W.W. Norton, 1950).

7. Maraini, interview, 1992.

8. Messina, *Casa paterna* (Palermo: Sellerio, 1990), 27. Subsequent references to the work are indicated parenthetically in the text.

9. Mariolina Graziosi has surveyed the regime's gender program. Because during WWI women had entered the workforce and the emancipation movement had begun to grow, she concludes, in the interwar period political and cultural gender warfare was waged to reestablish the earlier division between domestic and public spheres. See "Gender Struggle and the Social Manipulation and Ideological Use of Gender Identity in the Interwar Years," in *Mothers of Invention: Women, Italian Fascism, and Culture*, ed. Robin Pickering-Iazzi (Minneapolis: University of Minnesota Press, 1995), 26–51. For a detailed source on the development of women's social status in the interwar period, including changes in behavior and appearance, see Michela De Giorgio, *Le italiane dall'Unità ad oggi* (Bari: Editori Laterza, 1992). For an analysis of the Fascist regime's regulation of gender, see also Victoria De Grazia, *How Fascism Ruled Women: Italy, 1922–1945* (Berkeley: University of California Press, 1992).

10. Carla's brother Michele also represents the effects of the mores of this period. Unlike his sister, Michele is plagued by inertia, a characteristic mirroring the existential crisis of the postwar years and key to his inability to control the sexual tension Carla creates within the family.

11. Both Ancona and Magrini also examine other significant relationships with female friends, men, siblings, and so on. However, the recurring relational element with

which the protagonists of both works must deal is the mother-daughter/father-daughter bond.

12. In her excellent reading of the text, Daria Valentini notes that the father is the figure that sets the pace for her journey back into her history: "[Manzini] . . . pay[s] homage to a great man, while at the same time measuring herself against her father's expectations of her. . . . The novel assumes the tone of a confession, in which the narrator seeks to relieve her remorse at not being able to be more like her father." See "Father-Daughter Reflections in Gianna Manzini's *Ritratto in piedi*," *RLA* 9 (1998): 368.

13. Although Chiara loves her mother and recognizes the importance of that bond in her childhood, it is the relationship with her father that most speaks for her image of her life and for her sense of identity. For example, Chiara entitles the section in which she recounts the most idyllic moments of their relationship "La vita è una cosa meravigliosa" ("Life is a marvelous thing"). In the same section, she notes how emotional the bond was and how it shaped her sense of self, "It often happened that between us there would develop small misunderstandings due to an excess of tenderness, to the desire to please each other, to agree with our reciprocal thoughts before they were even expressed, not only to each other but especially to oneself" (86).

14. When defining the ambivalence of Eva's situation, the narrator notes, "Eva understands that she should not have considered her father her light, her guide. A blinding light, a sure guide she need not doubt. She asked herself why she married. Even though she married she continued loving her father as when she lived dedicated to him. . . . Her love would not have changed: until the end of her days, until the end of her days" (46).

15. Carla Cerati, *La cattiva figlia* (Piacenza: Frassinelli, 1990), 29. Subsequent references to this work will be indicated parenthetically in the text.

16. See "Era là dall'inizio," *Diotima. Il cielo stellato dentro di noi: L'ordine simbolico della madre* (Milan: La Tartaruga edizioni, 1992), 21–47.

17. Percovich notes, "It is we daughters who, discovering this common origin and love for the body of the woman who generated us, overthrow, deconstruct, and invent diverse possibilities of relationship and representation. Only as daughters can we establish our individuality and commonality, which will permit us to enter the world . . . and to tell *our* experiences." See "Relazione," *L'etica necessaria: eredità materna e passione politica* (Milan: Melusine, 1993), 15.

18. Even though, as noted in the introduction, the immediate postwar period saw a definitive rise in the mobilization of such women's groups as *Cif* and *Udi*, women's periodicals continued to feature articles on women's domestication. See also De Giorgio *Le italiane*, esp. 515.

19. Maraini's first novel *La vacanza* [The Holiday] (1962) also traces the daughter's development, but focuses at greater length on the fourteen-year-old Anna's burgeoning sexuality and her more insular relationship with her father, a single parent. Therefore, we can read *L'età del malessere* as an extension of *La vacanza*, and it is for this reason that I focus only on the later text.

20. Fenoglio's protagonist Ettore, returned from combat in WWII, finds himself in a transitional phase between violent action and everyday routine. This in-between stage results in an inertia aimed at establishing normalcy, "I can't get used to this life because I fought in a war, and war changed me, it alienated me from this life. I understood even then that I would not be used to this life anymore. And now I spend the entire day not doing anything because I want to become used to this life again, I concentrate myself on that." See *La paga del sabato* (Torino: Einaudi, 1969), 9–10.

21. Although it is Cesare who first suggests the abortion, Enrica agrees with the decision, recognizing the impossibility of raising a child at this point in her life. Furthermore, her contemplations while pregnant and her experience of the abortion mark a turning point in her life, revealing, as we have seen, her growing awareness of her situation as woman.

Given the import of this event in Enrica's life, I will describe it here in detail. Enrica confronts the experience alone, not confiding in her father or accepting Carlo's offer to accompany her to the abortionist. When Enrica arrives at the abortionist's, she meets the abortionist's daughter, Patrizia, who is Enrica's age. Patrizia accompanies Enrica into the operating room, equipped with a bed, implements for the operation, and a picture of womanly and motherly perfection, the Madonna. The abortion scene introduces a mother-daughter relationship that is similar, though ultimately antithetical to Teresa and Enrica's relationship. Patrizia is similar to Enrica in age and activity. However, she is physically different from her. While Enrica wears resoled shoes and can only afford imperfect sweaters, and while Teresa hands her own clothing down to her daughter, Patrizia can afford lipstick, chic pants, and high-heeled shoes. The implication of this difference is, given the fact that there is no mention of a father, that abortion, though illegal, is much in demand and a very lucrative business for her mother.

22. I borrow this notion from Adrienne Rich, who reads the conventional mother-daughter relationship in Western culture as fundamental to the perpetuation of the patriarchal social order. She notes, "Many daughters live in rage at their mothers for having accepted, too readily and passively, 'whatever comes.' A mother's victimization does not merely humiliate her, it mutilates the daughter who watches her for clues as to what it means to be a woman." See *Of Woman Born*, 243. Marianne Hirsch, in her discussion of representations of conventional familial relationships, argues that the daughter distances herself from the mother when she understands the reality of the conventional role the mother represents. See *The Mother/Daughter Plot: Narrative, Psychoanalysis, Feminism* (Bloomington: Indiana University Press, 1989), 11.

23. Dacia Maraini, *L'età del malessere* (Turin: Einaudi, 1963), 13. Subsequent references to the work are indicated parenthetically in the text.

24. Teresa's indoctrination of her daughter assumes a physical dimension when Teresa alters her clothing for Enrica. Although Teresa passes her clothing to her daughter out of financial necessity, the action also serves as a symbol of the transmittal of tradition from mother to daughter: Enrica will em*body* her mother's role. The daughter's unwillingness to follow suit, however, reveals an awareness of the implications of the mother's offer.

25. Jenijoy La Belle, *Herself Beheld: The Literature of the Looking Glass* (Ithaca: Cornell University Press, 1988), 2.

26. Cerati, *La cattiva figlia*, 7.

27. When Enrica is ready to approach the mother, it is at the moment in which their experiences coincide and are visibly inscribed on their female bodies—pregnancy. Pregnancy ultimately compels Enrica to confront both her reproductive powers as a woman and her similarity, as a woman, to her mother, the person she thought she could not "imagine." In this sense, the pregnancy prompts Enrica to rethink the bond with her mother, to re-conceive her mother as a woman like her, and to understand the choices available to her as a woman.

28. As Enrica eschews her prescribed behavior and progresses toward her final decision to set off on her own, the father becomes even more absorbed in building his

cages, abandoning all other work. Indeed, early in the novel, when Enrica returns home after a sexual encounter with her classmate Carlo, her father furtively hides a birdcage he had been building. Although Enrica had already been having sex with Cesare, the man her family believes she will eventually marry, her relationship with Carlo, whom she has no intention of marrying, carries her even further outside the limits of her socially mandated code of behavior. Thus the cage, which she describes as "the most complicated cage he'd ever made" (25), is built at a time when the daughter even more willfully (because committed outside a relationship based on love) eschews traditional femininity. For Tonia Riviello, Enrica's confinement is the result of her father's indifference toward her and to the desire for love and attention that indifference breeds in her. See "The Motif of Entrapment in Elsa Morante's *L'isola d'Arturo* and Dacia Maraini's *L'età del malessere*," *Rivista di Studi Italiani* 8.1–2 (June–December 1990): 74. See also Edera Ciambellotti, "Una stanza tutta per sè: Intorno a *L'età del malessere di Dacia Maraini*," in *Nel passato presente degli anni sessanta* (Urbino: Montefeltro), 1981.

29. In the introduction to her collection of essays *La bionda, la bruna e l'asino*, Maraini defines the father in similar terms, "He is the architect who decides how the house will be built in which mothers and daughters will live, prisoners for life" (Milan: Rizzoli, 1987), xvi.

30. Tonia Riviello, "The Motif of Entrapment," 70.

31. Dacia Maraini, *Bagheria* (Milan: Rizzoli, 1993), 62. Subsequent references to the work are indicated parenthetically in the text.

32. Maraini herself makes the link between memory loss and her place in history, reading the loss of memory as a deliberate rejection of a history in which she has no symbolic placement because there is a lack of a thoroughly documented female legacy. See the poem "Mancanza di memoria" in *Crudeltà all aria aperta* (Milan: Feltrinelli, 1966), 51.

33. According to Grazia Sumeli Weinberg the collection can be divided into two sections. While in the first the daughter narrates the relationship with her father, in the second she tries to move beyond it through self-reflection. It is the first part of the collection that will be discussed here. See "All'ombra," 455.

34. In her assessment of the father's role in the daughter's life, Sumeli Weinberg also argues that the father facilitates the development of the daughter's vision of herself. See "All'ombra," 461–62. As the poems themselves show, and as is often clarified in the interviews Maraini has given on her autobiography, the elusiveness of the father occurs on two levels. The first is the physical level, where the father leaves the daughter for trips to far-away lands and for trysts with lovers, while the second is the mnemonic level, where the father escapes the daughter because she can only draw up so many memories from the depths of her subconscious.

35. The father's (and, symbolically, culture's) disconcert over the daughter's reminiscences were subsequently expressed by Fosco Maraini in an interview after the publication of *Bagheria* in 1993. When asked if he knew of his daughter's love for him, "that intense, child's love," his response foregrounds his familial role and their political differences: "No, I didn't know about it, I couldn't even imagine it. . . . I thought everything was fine, between us, I didn't see this fervor, I wasn't touched by such a strong attachment. In fact, when she grew up I felt she was against me, us, because she was on the extreme left." See Natalia Aspesi, "Quall'intenso amore di mia figlia Dacia," *La Repubblica* 13 February 1993, 34–35.

36. In Italian, *volere bene* is used to express love to family and friends. *Amare* has

more rigid parameters, reserved, in its strictest sense, for partners in a love relationship.

37. For a discussion of the relationship between women, both characters and actual spectators, and visual agency in cinema, see Mulvey, *Visual and Other Pleasures*.

38. In her discussion of this poem, Sumeli Weinberg notes, with regards to vision, that "the verses . . . turn on the semantic dislocation of the 'eye'." See "All'ombra," 457.

39. For Althusser's definition of *ideological state apparati* and discussion of the role institutions play in social regulation, see "Ideology and Ideological State Apparatuses (Notes towards and Investigation)," in *Lenin and Philosophy and Other Essays*, trans. Ben Brewster (New York: Monthly Review Press, 1972).

40. Dacia Maraini, *Il Manifesto*, in *Il ricatto a teatro e altre commedie* (Turin: Einaudi, 1970), 192. Subsequent references to this work are indicated parenthetically in the text.

41. The differences between maternal and paternal roles in birth is succinctly depicted in Maraini's 1984 novel *Il treno per Helsinki*. Here, the protagonist Armida Bianchi describes her pregnancy as a struggle that pits her and her unborn son against those who lay claim to the fetus. Of the relationship between her and her fetus she says, "There is an understanding between me and my son. . . . Even before being born this much awaited son mocks whomever considers him already his. . . . He is sure only of me." Of her husband she says, "Euphoric enthusiastic he would like to immediately pull him out of my womb and take him for a walk. . . . He would watch over him better than me because I'm distracted by pain and maybe even not that maternal. He would educate him scientifically according to the latest pediatric discoveries." See *Il treno per Helsinki* (Turin: Einaudi, 1984), 71, 67–68; sic.

42. When Anna and her father Gaetano take a Sunday stroll, his friends make lewd remarks about her, such as "[a]ll it takes if you're not careful . . . is for one like her to turn her head and you'll find her pregnant" (195). Control of a social discourse defining the daughter's sexuality therefore comes in the form of quips between the men, who, in turn, define ways in which the father should oversee her behavior. When one friend proclaims, " 'What a beautiful daughter, Gaetano! Keep a tight grip on her or she'll escape'," the father possessively replies, " 'I know how to take care of my own flesh and blood' " (195) and " 'I know how to take care of my own things' " (196). The men's cryptic and therefore "tasteful" linguistic description of femininity reifies the daughter's sexuality, rooting it in a conventional description that at once divests it of its threatening potential and renders it a "precious possession" to be passed on from father to husband. Later, these descriptions of female behavior will be upheld and further inculcated by two social institutions, both with hierarchical structures similar to the family, the *collegio* Anna attends, and the prison to which she is condemned for theft. In the *collegio*, the female students' sexuality is controlled by strict rules of conduct. In prison, the paternal director lays out ground rules of female behavior, comparing the prison to a family and himself to the father who regulates the female prisoners' conduct.

43. One such daughter is Marianna Ucrìa, of the eponymous novel. Both deaf and mute, Marianna transforms her physical condition into an*other* and alternative linguistic perspective. For a perceptive analysis of Marianna Ucrìa's relationship to language, see Anna Camaiti Hostert, "Potere dell'alterità-alterità del potere: Una lettura del libro di Dacia Maraini *La lunga vita di Marianna Ucrìa*."

44. To more clearly render Anna's act of appropriation, I will cite the Italian, " 'Cazzo! . . . Perché non lo mandi a farsi fottere?' "

In Italian, the word *cazzo* ("damn") is literally "prick," and renders even more evident Anna's usurpation of authority.

45. For Maraini's discussion of her journey through this film, see *Lessico*.

46. Luce Irigaray, *Speculum of the Other Woman*, trans. Gillian C. Gill (Ithaca: Cornell University Press, 1989), 142.

47. Judith Butler, in her analysis of socialized roles, uses a theatrical metaphor analogous to Irigaray's concept of social stage. She defines gender as "a corporeal field of cultural play" whose "legacy [is] sedimented acts." See "Performative Acts and Gender Constitution," 282 and 274.

48. Irigaray, *Speculum*, 141; emphasis added.

49. See, for example, Irigaray, "Body Against Body: In Relation to the Mother," trans. Gillian C. Gill, in *Sexes and Genealogies* (New York: Columbia University Press, 1993); Ileana Montini, *Parlare con Dacia Maraini* (Verona: Bertani Editore, 1977); and Hirsch *The Mother-Daughter Plot*.

50. See Luisa Veroli, "Il divino femminile," in *Dee fuori dal tempio: vivere e pensare la relazione madre-figlia* (Milan: Melusine, 1992).

51. DuPlessis, *Writing Beyond the Ending*, 105, 107, and 108.

52. In a note to her discussion of *Crudeltà*, Sumeli Weinberg focuses on the return to the mother in "Demetra ritrovata" as Maraini's attempt to "recuperate feminine authenticity." See "All ombra," 465n15. Maraini has rewritten other myths and tales to expose the development of women's subordination and the institutionalization of female power. These include the 1981 revision of Aeschylus' *Oresteia*, *I sogni di Clitennestra*, in which she explores the institutionalization of Clitennestra's sexuality and power; the use of the father-daughter story in Verdi's *Rigoletto* as a metaphor for the heroine's own story in *Lettere a Marina*; the 1978 poem "le cinquanta sorelle" (in *Mangiami pure*), a retelling of the Hypemnestra myth; and the 1966 poem "Cordelia," a rereading of Shakespeare's *King Lear* as a parallel for her own daughterly story.

53. DuPlessis, *Writing Beyond the Ending*, 105.

54. Silvia Vegetti Finzi, "Relazione," in *Dee fuori dal tempio: vivere e pensare la relazione madre-figlia* (Milan: Melusine, 1992), 19.

55. Dacia Maraini, "Demetra ritrovata," in *Mangiami pure* (Torino: Einaudi, 1978), 5. Subsequent references to the work will be indicated parenthetically in the text.

56. Instruction in mathematics, governed by Pythagoras' "logica sibillina" ("sibylline logic"), provides the metaphor for the daughter's apprenticeship into her gendered role and the institutionalization of the daughter-father bond. In the *Crudeltà* poem "La rosa del buon senso," images of this socialization surround the father and daughter, through the father's apartment, the army barracks next door, and the school where she is educated. Her resistance to this system, however, is glimpsed, for example, in the *Crudeltà* poem, "Il Circolo Chaplin," in which she resents the rigid laws her father represents and upholds. In "Demetra ritrovata," as she enters numbers into her schoolbooks, she *uneasily* acquiesces to a conventional system of logic from whose creation she is absent: Her hand, an instrument in this initiation, but with the potential of expressing (in writing) her self, betrays that uneasiness, "a soft hand / that sleeps *restlessly* on the paper," 7; emphasis added.

57. This placement within patriarchal order is codified through the education at the basis of the father-daughter relationship. The father endorses the mathematical laws she identified in "Circolo di Chaplin" and that she must learn as a member of

society. These, however, set her apart from the mother, as they create a gateway to the public sphere of which the mother is clearly not a part. Thus Proserpina identifies that element of the father-daughter relationship that results in the insidious enforcement of social law, "feet in shoes walk by themselves / towards a street without roses where / Pythagoras sings his song of / sibylline logic, his eel's voice wound itself / in her marble ear and there made a nest / in the warmth of feminine fatality" (8). The poet defines herself as an unformed Pygmalion statue, whose ear (gateway to the intellect) is subject to conventional education (Pythagoras's sibylline logic). The father's habitation of the world of logic and mathematical laws represents a recurring trope in women's literature. Cerati's *La cattiva figlia* serves as clear example. When reading the father, the daughter places him in his "natural" authoritative role, "he was authoritative by nature . . . in my eyes he . . . represented intelligence and therefore reason." The father occupies the world of books and, like Maraini's father, the world of logic, represented by mathematics, "I remember him, for the most part, buried in reading or concentrated on strange calculations for which he used a pocket slide rule that he always carried with him." See *La cattiva figlia*, 24–25 and 10.

58. Percovich, "Relazione," 81.

59. While the daughter's use of blood as a metaphor for the mother's subordinate position is consonant with the historical image of women's frailty and powerless alterity, it is a subversion of the feminist reading of blood as a metaphor of artistic creativity. In her analysis of Dinesen's story "The Blank Page," in which blood assumes currency in women's cultural production, Susan Gubar notes "one of the primary and most resonant metaphors provided by the female body is blood, and cultural forms of creativity are often experienced as painful wounding. . . . The stained pages are . . . biographical remnants of otherwise mute existences, a result of and response to life." See " 'The Blank Page' and the Issues of Female Creativity," 78.

60. Rich, *Of Woman Born*, 218.

61. Dacia Maraini, interview by author, 1992.

62. Irigaray, "Body Against Body," 15.

63. See Percovich, "Relazione," 15.

Chapter 2. Motherhood

1. Rich, *Of Woman Born*, 11.

2. Judith Wilt, *Abortion, Choice, and Contemporary Fiction: The Armageddon of the Maternal Instinct* (Chicago: University of Chicago Press, 1990), 1.

3. Irigaray, "Body Against Body," 18.

4. Maraini, interview by author, 25 November 1992.

5. "A woman," Kristeva argues, "has only two choices: either to experience herself in sex *hyperabstractly* (in an 'immediately universal' way, as Hegel would say) so as to make herself worthy of divine grace and assimilation to the symbolic order, or else to experience herself as *different*, other, fallen (or, in Hegel's terms again, 'immediately particular')." See "Stabat Mater," *Poetics Today* 6, no. 1–2 (1985): 142. Besides "Stabat Mater," which intertwines considerations of cultural representations of the maternal with her own experience of motherhood, see also Kristeva's "Motherhood According to Bellini," *Desire in Language: A Semiotic Approach to Literature and Art*, trans. Thomas Gora, Alice Jardine, and Leon S. Roudiez, ed. Leon S. Roudiez

(New York: Columbia University Press, 1980), which also examines the cultural reproduction of motherhood. In her own discussion of motherhood and sexuality, Adrienne Rich concludes, "Women are permitted to be sexual only at a certain time of life, and the sensuality of mature . . . women has been perceived as . . . threatening and inappropriate." See *Of Woman Born*, 183. The image of asexuality and purity that most informs the Western understanding of motherhood is the Virgin Mary. Laura Bosio's *Annunciazione* represents an important contribution to the feminist analysis of women's identity in Western culture: It traces the development of the image of the Virgin Mary through analyses of, among other things, celebrated paintings and written documents. At the same time, it evolves into a sociocultural investigation of the self, demonstrating the impact of tradition on a woman's understanding of her relationship to womanhood. See *Annunciazione* (Milan: Mondadori, 1997).

6. See "Motherhood according to Bellini." Maraini has investigated women's response to this biosocial program in a nonfiction forum. In *Un clandestino a bordo*, she examines the role abortion plays in this response and explores the relationship between women and the female body, taking into consideration such issues as pornography and the cultural objectification of the female body. This book is also Maraini's participation in and response to women's discussion of these issues, clearly rendered by the use of section titles that recall other works, such as "Corpo a corpo," which recalls Luce Irigaray's famous essay on women and motherhood, "Body against Body, in Relation to the Mother." See *Un clandestino a bordo: Le donne, la maternità negata, il corpo sognato* (Milan: Rizzoli, 1996), and Luce Irigaray's "Body against Body."

7. For analyses of these changes, see Alfieri and Ambrosini, *La condizione economica, sociale e giurdica della donna in Italia*, and De Leo and Taricone, *Le donne in Italia: diritti civili e politici*.

8. In her own reading of these theories, Maraini asserts that they have rendered gendered roles "absolutes," making it difficult to challenge them: "It is very difficult to rebel against scientific arguments, but it is above all difficult to challenge 'absolutes' based on nature. . . . Nature is what it is, immutable." See "Quale cultura per la donna," *Donna, cultura e tradizione* (Milan: Gabriele Mazzotta editore, 1976), 64.

9. Marianne Cline Horowitz, "Aristotle and Women," *Journal of the History of Biology* 9, no. 2 (fall 1976): 183.

10. Aristotle, *G.A.I* 51 (729a 10–12) and 52 (29–31), and *G.A.II* 58–59 (4–9). Women from diverse fields have recognized the enduring import of Aristotelian theory on the definition of issues challenged by the women's movement. Historian Gerda Lerner has investigated the implications of this theory on the relationship between biology and gender. Lerner notes, "Aristotle elevated the counterfactual account of the origin of human life from the level of myth to the level of science by grounding it in a broad-ranging philosophical system." See *The Creation of Patriarchy* (New York: Oxford University Press, 1986), 206.

11. G. W. Hegel, *Phenomenology of Spirit*, trans. A. V. Miller (Oxford: Clarendon Press, 1977), 274.

12. In one of the founding documents of Italian feminism, *Sputiamo su Hegel* (Let's Spit on Hegel), Carla Lonzi disputes Hegel's theory. She underscores the impossibility in Hegelian dialectics for women to extricate themselves from the family, their natural domain, and enter the community, where it is possible to reach a state of self-awareness. Hegelian theory, Lonzi notes, creates a distinction between a "divine feminine principle and a virile human principle" and thus defines woman as universal.

See *Sputiamo su Hegel, La donna clitoridea e la donna vaginale, e altri scritti*. Scritti di Rivolta Femminile 1, 2, 1987), 25.

13. Badinter, *Mother Love*, 260.

14. For Freud's theory on female sexuality, see his articles "Female Sexuality" and "Femininity." There have been countless studies of Freud's theory of women's psychology. See, for example Luce Irigaray, *Speculum* and *This Sex Which is Not One*, trans. Catherine Porter with Carolyn Burke (Ithaca: Cornell University Press, 1985), and Contardo Calligaris "Sessualità femminile: Che ti dice Freud?" *Il piccolo Hans* 5 (January–March 1975): 31–67. Feminist psychoanalyst Nancy Chodorow has authored an important revision of Freudian psychoanalysis, of which object-relations theory is a central focus. For Chodorow, this theory, according to which the child assumes the mother as the object against which it develops, places the mother at the center of identity formation. See *The Reproduction of Mothering: Psychoanalysis and the Sociology of Gender* (Berkeley: University of California Press, 1978). See also Chodorow's *Feminism and Psychoanalytic Theory* and Vegetti Finzi's "La maternità negata: Alle origini dell'immaginario femminile," *Memoria* 7 (September 1983): 45–55.

15. For a discussion of this location and management, see chap. 1 of this study.

16. See Percovich's "Relazione" (15–21) and "Relazione" (77–91).

17. See Paola Melchiori, *Crinali: Le zone oscure del femminismo* (Milan: La Tartaruga, 1995). Anna Maria Piussi similarly notes, "Women's liberation would result in revealing what the mother really is, a real subject with an independent existence: a subject on whom others should have to measure their limits and the limits of their identity." See "Era là dall'inizio," 25. Many other theorists have considered this subject in their own projects for women's liberation. Luce Irigaray's deconstructive investigation of the family in "Body against Body" exposes the cultural censorship of the maternal and of the primary bond with the mother. In response to the institutionalization of motherhood, Adrienne Rich for her part uncovers archeological evidence of procreation and motherhood as elements of social agency. See *Of Woman Born*. In what is a fundamental text of the analysis of motherhood in literature, *The Mother-Daughter Plot*, Marianne Hirsch looks at the cultural sedimentation of subordinate motherhood and women's literary responses to it. Finally, in *The Modernist Madonna*, Jane Silverman Van Buren examines the way women have challenged the "values of language and signification" in their efforts to defy their displacement as "other" in social discourse. See *The Modernist Madonna: Semiotics of the Maternal Metaphor* (Bloomington: Indiana University Press, 1989), 14. These theorists all explore the consequences on women of the traditional maternal discourse, as well as new approaches to (re)establishing the mother's social and cultural primacy.

18. Diane Fuss, *Feminism, Nature, and Difference* (New York: Routledge, 1989), 1.

19. This exclusion, according to Jane Gallop, forces women into an essentialist "realm of love and the body" outside history and politics. See Gallop's *Thinking through the Body* (New York: Columbia University Press, 1988), 2. See also Teresa De Lauretis, "The Essence of the Triangle or, Taking the Risk of Essentialism Seriously: Feminist Theory in Italy, the U.S., and Britain." *Differences* 1 (1989).

20. de Beauvoir, *The Second Sex*, xv.

21. Irigaray, *This Sex*, 28.

22. For an investigation of the trajectory taken by the Italian women's movement from the 1960s to the 1970s in creating a theory of motherhood, see Roberta Fossati and Immacolata Mazzonis, "La maternità come destino," *Donna, cultura e tradizione* (Milan: Gabriele Mazzotta editore, 1976).

23. Irigaray, "Body against Body," 18.

24. Examples of these texts are Ancona's *Una famiglia normale* and Cerati's *La cattiva figlia*, in which, as discussed in chapter 1, the mother is in part blamed for the daughter's confinement to a narrow identity.

25. See Michela De Georgio, *Le italiane dall'unità ad oggi*, 309.

26. Their feelings touch upon different areas of restrictions placed on the mother, the body, sexuality, their psychic development: "The children found it strange that they were born from her. It would have been much less strange being born from grandmother or Diomira, with their big warm bodies that protected them against fear, that defended them against storms and thieves. It was strange to think that she was their mother." See "La madre," in *Novelle del Novecento: An Anthology*, ed. Brian Moloney (Manchester: Manchester University Press, 1966), 52.

27. Franca Rame, "L'uomo incinto," in *Coppia aperta, quasi spalancata* (Turin: Einaudi, 1991), 101–13. Subsequent references to this work are indicated parenthetically in the text. Even though the mother admits not being as knowledgeable at seventeen as her daughter is at eighteen, the fact that she was married overrode her naiveté.

28. The *Industriale* becomes pregnant because he mistakingly took his wife's birth control pills, resulting in a physiological change that led to self-impregnation.

29. Dacia Maraini, "Quale cultura per la donna," 61.

30. Rich, *Of Woman Born*, 237.

31. For the "Manifesto," see Paola Bono and Sandra Kemp, ed., *Italian Feminist Thought*, 34–35.

32. These terms are linked to the traditionally feminine description, examined by Robin Pickering-Iazzi, of the "natura dolce" ("sweet nature") of the mother in Aleramo's novel. The echoes between Aleramo and Maraini's descriptions show a distinct legacy linking one woman's examination of the traditional representation of motherhood to the other. See "Designing Mothers."

33. In her reading of this poem, Grazia Sumeli Weinberg attributes the daughter's polemic against the mother to the mother's reflection of her destiny as a woman. See "All'ombra del padre."

34. Dacia Maraini, interview by author, 6 April 1993.

35. Dacia Maraini, interview by author, 6 April 1993. For its construction of the mother-daughter relationship as one with liberating potential, Maraini's film subverts the conventional representation of this relationship. When discussing this representation in cinema, Paola Melchiori notes, "The self-confidence which women represent for each other at the start of 'the journey of life' often turns into a nightmare of disillusion, the 'fall of the gods'." See "Women's Cinema: A Look at Female Identity," trans. Jane Dolman, in *Off Screen*, 31. Maraini's film reinstates the goddess into the relational equation and as a result the relationship into history.

36. Michelle Citron's feminist film *Daughter Rite* similarly uses repetition to uncover different levels of meaning behind a gesture. In the film, the mother's willful adjustment of her daughter's hair represents her transmittance of traditional values of femininity. The gesture is repeated several times to deconstruct its place within this narrative of female development.

37. Like Sally Potter's landmark 1979 film *Thriller*, which deconstructs Puccini's *La Bohème*, *La bella* is deconstructive in its examination of the female protagonist's position in the narrative. In her feminist masterpiece, Potter deconstructs the film's heroine into several Mimis, and analyzes through each one the different ideological

codes that have determined Mimi's objectification within the narrative vis-à-vis the male protagonists. For an insightful analysis of Potter's film, see Ann Kaplan, "Dora; Thriller; Amy!" *Women and Film: Both Sides of the Camera* (London: Metheun 1983).

38. The themes of the reality of motherhood and the mother's desire were a growing focus of feminist cinematic inquiry of this period. Anna Carini and Annabella Miscuglio, for example, produced a documentary on these topics called *"Il rischio di vivere"* [The Risk of Living]. See Giuliana Bruno, ed., *Off Screen*.

39. Claude Akerman's film *Jeanne Dielman, 23 Quai du Commerce, 1080 Bruxelles* demystifies the traditional portrait of the housewife represented in classic Hollywood cinema. In the classical portrait, housework is almost never present as part of the narrative because it is much less "important" within the context of the characters' lives than work in the public sphere, which, in Hegelian terms, is considered the locus of meaningful activity. Ackerman's film uses real time to showcase a day in the life of its heroine. By allowing the heroine to perform her tasks and live out her daily life in real time, each gesture gains currency within the text. For an insightful reading of Akerman's film, see Marsha Kinder, "Reflections on 'Jeanne Dielman'," *Film Quarterly* 30, no. 4 (1977).

40. In a discussion of the film, Maraini describes this connection: "Cuts of an onion . . . in her hands . . . become magical and sexualized events. . . . They reveal the energetic imagination needed for the capricious and personal manipulation of nourishment for the family." See "Fra le mura," in *La bionda, la bruna e l'asino*, 33–34.

41. Dacia Maraini, post-screening discussion, Rome, 19 November 1992.

42. Bruno and Nadotti, *Off Screen*, 12–13.

43. There is a debate as to whether or not a matriarchy ever existed. *The Oresteia* has been referred to in many feminist readings of this debate. See, for example, Françoise D'Eaubonne, *Les femmes avant le patriarcat* (Paris: Payot, 1976); Lerner, *The Creation of Patriarchy*; and Irigaray, *Sexes and Genealogies*. Outside the realm of feminism see S. Freud, *Totem and Taboo*.

44. In her interview with Grazia Weinberg, Maraini clarifies why she chose to interpret *The Oresteia* and not represent history itself. Women's actions and accomplishments are absent, she contends, from official history. In such symbolic representations of history as Aeschylus' tale, however, women are an important presence. See "An Interview with Dacia Maraini," 69. Daniela Cavallaro has also analyzed the relationship between Maraini and Aeschylus' texts. For Cavallaro, the purpose of Maraini's play is to showcase various relationships between female characters. See " 'I sogni di Clitennestra': *The Oresteia* According to Maraini," *Italica* 72, no. 3 (1995): 340–55.

45. In her study of the importance of dreams to women's liberation, Lella Revasi Bellocchio concludes that dreams represent the transcendental quality of myth, analogous to Jung's notion of collective unconscious. In this capacity, dreams begin as a collective experience and transcend to the individual, helping to create a sort of personal history within a larger historical context. See "Relazione," in *Dee fuori dal tempio: vivere e pensare la relazione madre-figlia* (Milan: Melusine, 1992), 44.

46. Aeschylus, *The Oresteia*, trans. Robert Fagel (New York: Penguin Classics, 1979), 112, 293. Subsequent references to the work are indicated parenthetically in the text.

47. Robert Fagles and W. B. Stanford note that dreams in *The Oresteia* are used by Clytemnestra to "manipulate her listeners [and] undermine her victims." See Ae-

schylus, *The Oresteia*, 288. In contrast, in Maraini's revisionist play Clitennestra's dreams constitute a symbolic link with women of the past and future.

48. Maraini, *I sogni di Clitennestra*. In *I sogni di Clitennestra* (Milan: Bompiani, 1981), 9. Subsequent references to the work are indicated parenthetically in the text.

49. Dacia Maraini, in Montini, *Parlare con Dacia Maraini*, 131.

50. With regards to Clytemnestra's anger in *The Oresteia*, Marianne Hirsch notes, "[Since] maternal anger at separation and betrayal takes on deathly proportions, . . . it must be domesticated or eradicated if the structure of civilization is to be maintained." Hirsch also argues that nonmaternal anger is instead considered reasonable and logical: Agamemnon's anger is legitimized by the Trojan war, which initiates the "legitimate battle of culture," while Electra and Orestes' anger is rendered by Athena a "legitimate expression of filial loyalty to the father." See *The Mother/Daughter Plot*, 38, 37.

51. Silvia Vegetti Finzi, "Relazione," *Dee fuori dal tempio: vivere e pensare la relazione madre-figlia* (Milan: Melusine, 1992), 114. Vegetti Finzi concludes, "Women . . . have to find the courage to . . . continue being in relation with every part of themselves in order to avoid accepting a social image created by others. . . ." See "Relazione," 114. Similarly, with regard to Clytemnestra, Luce Irigaray notes, "Clytemnestra does not conform to that image of the virgin-mother which has been promoted as our ideal for centuries. She is still a passionate lover." See *Sexes and Genealogies*, 11.

52. Tensions over the mother's sexuality and, more specifically, over the expression of her sexuality have informed the articulation of this sexuality in the Aeschylian tale. The Aeschylian text expresses and then neutralizes it by representing the split between the pure, beneficent mother and the sexual mother, now the fear-inspiring Gorgons. In his description of the relationship between Clytemnestra and the Gorgons, William Blake Tyrell defines this neutralization as a sort of Freudian movement away from the mother: "[Aeschylus removes] sexuality from the mother in order to make her solely a virginal nurse. . . . He confronts Orestes with Clytemnestra's sexuality and then moves her away from him as mother. Since sex is part of Clytemnestra, she must be dissociated from the mother." See *Amazons: A Study in Athenian Mythmaking* (Baltimore: Johns Hopkins University Press, 1984), 110–11.

53. An example of this dichotomy is depicted in De Cespedés' *Quaderno proibito*. Valeria, the wife and mother, is contained within the two roles by her family. Her husband calls her "mamma," enclosing the husband-wife relationship within the roles set by the children and thus ridding it of sexual overtones. He, in the meantime, is distraught over a failed romance with Valeria's friend. Valeria's daughter, who will not acknowledge that her mother can feel desire, is having an affair with an older married man.

Chapter 3. Sisterhood

1. Sylvia Plath, *Collected Poems* (London: Faber and Faber), 174.

2. Dacia Maraini, "ricamare," in *Mangiami pure* (Turin: Einaudi, 1978), 25. Subsequent reference to works in this collection will be indicated parenthetically in the text.

3. For Nancy Chodorow, the pre-Oedipal relationship with the mother is extended through female friendships, which "resolve and recreate" it and become "an

expression of women's general relationship capacities and definition of self in relationship." Chodorow concludes, however, as we have already noted, that a woman's quest for relational fulfillment is completed only when she has a child. See *The Reproduction of Mothering*, 200 and 201. Maria Luisa Boccia's theory on these unions implies a similar return to the maternal. When delineating her theory on identity formation in her article "L'identità nella relazione," Boccia argues that the union between women allows them to "return to themselves," to identify themselves—and here the function is like that of the pre-Oedipal bond—in relation to other women (16). The movement Boccia defines recalls Maraini's own vision of a family of human beings who subjectively regenerate themselves in relation to each other. For Maraini, who maps out this regeneration in the poem "Demetra ritrovata," this return constitutes a movement toward change.

4. Simone De Beauvoir, *The Second Sex*, 604–5.

5. Rossana Rossanda, *Anche per me: Donna, persona, memoria dal 1973 al 1986* (Milan: Feltrinelli, 1987), 140. Italian theorist Gabriella Paolucci also links the secondary status of female friendships to women's historical marginalization. Like Rossanda, Paolucci maintains that their legitimization is instrumental in helping women transcend centuries of subjugation. See "Amiche: Figure dell'amicizia femminile e femminismo," *Memoria* 32, no. 2 (1991): 56–66.

6. Janet Todd, *Women's Friendship in Literature* (New York: Columbia University Press, 1980), 306.

7. For an excellent analysis of friendship in this short story, see Laura Salsini, "Checchina and Isolina: Female Friendship in Matilde Serao's 'La virtù di Checchina'," *RLA* 3 (1991): 309–13.

8. Alba De Cespedes, *Il rimorso* (Milan: Mondadori, 1963), 13.

9. For an examination of female friendship in Campo's novel, see Giovanna Bellesia, "*Mai sentita così bene*: Solidarietà fra donne nei romanzi di Rossana Campo," *Italian Culture*, 10, no. 1 (1998):157–67. Bellesia informs her analysis by placing the text's consciousness-raising setting within the context of Italian feminism.

10. Garlaschelli's novella was actually published as part of a series aimed at a young adult readership. Its significance to our study of sisterhood is its focus on friendship between younger female characters as a unique relationship that is integral to identity formation.

11. Paolucci, "Amiche," 59. Underscoring the notion that subjectivity develops through the individual's participation in social relationships, Janice Raymond argues that female friendships are essential to the formation of a woman's sense of self and purpose: "Female friendship helps create the woman of woman's own inventiveness. . . . Only the woman who is Self-created can be an original woman . . . and a friend to other women." See *A Passion for Friends: Toward a Philosophy of Female Affection* (Boston: Beacon Press, 1986), 5. For an excellent historical study of the way women have experienced alternative sociability, see Lilian Faderman, *Surpassing the Love of Men: Romantic Friendship and Love between Women from the Renaissance to the Present* (New York: William Morrow, 1981).

12. In her own work, Nina Auerbach attests to the power of unions between women in bringing about change. She asserts that female communities growing out of relationships between women were instrumental in creating "a drama of widening cultural consciousness . . . [sweeping] across official cultural images of female submission, subservience, and fulfillment in a bounded world." See *Communities of Women: An Idea in Fiction* (Cambridge: Harvard University Press, 1978), 6.

13. Paola Blelloch, "Il femminismo italiano," 227. Analysts of Italian feminism recognize its uniqueness in its emphasis on the reintegration of female friendship into women's lives. Paola Blelloch, for example, asserts that the history of Italian feminism is essentially "the history of relationships between women." See "Il femminismo italiano," 227. See also Cicioni, " 'Love and Respect, Together': The Theory and Practice of 'Affidamento'" in Italian Feminism," *Australian Feminist Studies* 10 (summer 1989): 71–83.

14. Paolucci, "Amiche," 58.

15. Ibid., 58.

16. In her study of friendship in women's (English and American) literature, Gillian Firth draws a link between the centrality of mirroring in female friendships and Lacanian psychoanalysis. See *The Intimacy which is Knowledge: Female Friendship in the Novels of Women Writers*, (Dissertation, University of Warwick, 1988. Ann Arbor: University of Michigan, 1988), 12. During this stage, the child perceives its reflection in the mirror as an other apart from him/herself. Later, as the child develops, this reflected self is incorporated into his/her identity. In her own study of this process, Jacqueline Rose explains the mirror stage in terms interesting to our study of sisterhood and the *rispecchiamento* that occurs in *autocoscienza* and *affidamento*: "The mother does not . . . mirror the child to itself; she grants an image *to* the child, which her presence instantly deflects. Holding the child . . . is to be understood not only as a containing, but as a process of referring, which fractures the unity it seems to offer." See "Introduction II," *Feminine Sexuality: Jacques Lacan and the école freudienne*, ed. J. Mitchell and J. Rose (New York: W. W. Norton, 1985), 30; emphasis added. This fracturing is what allows women to discover themselves. For Lacan's own reading of this process see *Il seminario: Gli scritti tecnici di Freud, 1953–54*, 5.1, (Torino: Einaudi, 1978). For a feminist critical reading of Lacan's theory, see also Elizabeth Grosz *Jacques Lacan: A Feminist Introduction*, (London: Routledge, 1990).

17. My decision to begin this chapter with a quote from Sylvia Plath's poem "Mirror" is based on the symbolic role the mirror plays in a woman's life. The subject of Plath's poem is indeed a mirror, which reflects the woman's image back to her. But through the poem's narrating voice, the mirror is anthropomorphized. We can thus extend its agency of reflection to another woman, whose position in sisterhood is to reflect another woman's image back to her.

18. Elizabeth Abel, "(E)Merging Identities: The Dynamics of Female Friendship in Contemporary Fiction by Women," *Signs* 6, no. 31 (spring 1981): 418.

19. Judith Gardner, "The (US)es of (I)dentity: A Response to Abel on '(E)Merging Identities'," *Signs* 6, no. 31 (spring 1981): 441.

20. For analyses of the power structure and transgressive nature of *affidamento*, see *Feminine Feminists: Cultural Practices in Italy*, ed. Giovanna Miceli Jeffries (Minneapolis: University of Minnesota Press, 1994).

21. Commonality—shared experiences shaped under common cultural and social institutions—can also bring women together in bonds of sisterhood. However, it is ultimately problematic in its limitations and implications. Bell hooks, in her study on the political nature of sisterhood, notes that women have traditionally unified out of a perceived shared victimization, a bond whose unfortunate consequence is the perpetuation of a woman's perception of herself as victim. Hooks' argument is based in part on victimization as a condition defined by the hegemonic class along class and racial lines. See "Sisterhood: Political Solidarity Between Women," in *A Reader in Feminist Knowledge*, ed. Sneja Gunew (London: Routledge, 1991), 27–41.

22. hooks, "Sisterhood," 31.
23. Rossanda, *Anche per me*, 140.
24. Maria Grazia Silvi, *Il teatro delle donne*, 109. While this collective activity was indeed beneficial for the women involved, it was also the site of tensions growing out of, among other things, bare, open dialogues. Two former members of *Le Streghe*, known simply as Marina and Gemma, noted the two sides of this process. Although she recalls the creative sessions as very positive moments in her life, Marina admits that misunderstandings and contradictions often led to frustrating results. For Gemma, it was the practice of *autocoscienza* itself that kept the theater group alive and creative. For personal accounts of the creative process arising from *autocoscienza*, see *Il teatro delle donne*, especially pages 109–22.
25. In the play Maraini portrays several different women's relationships, including, for example, Anna's relationships with Colomba, who runs a prostitution house, with Gina, a submissive wife, and with the various female guardians in the prison in which she serves time for theft. I will focus exclusively on those relationships that use as a paradigm the practice of *autocoscienza*.
26. Taken together, the women's histories form a sort of female genealogy: They transcend time to incorporate such experiences as the witch hunts, illegal abortion, and their fulfillment of traditional feminine codes of behavior within their families.
27. The play's representation of the prisoners' squalid conditions, including insufficient, often rotted food and harsh treatment, is based on studies and interviews Maraini conducted on women's prisons in the late 1960s. These studies ultimately culminated in Maraini's novel *Memorie di una ladra*, whose protagonist, Teresa, is a prisoner the author befriended during her investigation. See the preface to the novel for a discussion of Maraini's study, *Memorie di una ladra* (Milan: Bompiani, 1972). In *Il Manifesto*, *autocoscienza* is instrumental in revealing to the women the mechanisms of their subordination. After Anna is sent to prison for theft, the interaction between the women during the play's *autocoscienza* sessions is the antithesis of the prison's instruction on proper feminine behavior. While in the former the women discuss and render opinions on their experiences and relationships inside and outside the prison, during the periods of instruction they are forced to reply in memorized phrases to the questions on femininity put forth by the warden. These instances expose the indoctrination of women by social institutions which codify womanhood: The prison is defined by the director as "one big happy family," in which he is the father and the prisoners his daughters; the nuns who run the prison therefore symbolize the maternal figure who transmits social law within the family. At the same time, they offer the feminist alternative of interaction as a model for change.
28. For a reading of this novel as *Bildungsroman*, see Carol Lazzaro-Weiss, *From Margins to Mainstream*.
29. Although Tota and Giottina still negotiate their expression through social convention, the stories used to express themselves uncover to Vannina a language of symbols hidden behind the gendered spaces Beauvoir identifies. While entertaining, the purpose of the tales is to communicate beliefs and warnings to the developing daughter and, codified in stories of Boccaccian sexual intrigue, impart their knowledge of sex. For example, when Vannina becomes involved with political activists, Tota and Giottina relay a story about political activist Faele and the young woman he attempted to rape. The story serves to warn against the political arena Faele represents, which while the site of struggle against social injustices, is also the site of injustice against women, and in fact does little to advance women's social status. While, how-

ever, the stories expose Tota and Giottina's attitudes towards sex, the women must still couch their message in metaphorical language to avoid breaking the social code of women's propriety. This is common in women's storytelling, as Jan Radner emphasizes in her analysis of women's folk narratives: "*code* . . . designate[s] . . . a set of signals—words, forms, behaviors, signifiers of some kind—that protect the creator from the consequences of openly expressing particular messages." See "Strategies in Coding Women's Culture," in *Feminist Messages: Coding in Women's Folk Culture.* ed., J. Radner (Urbana: University of Illinois Press, 1993), 3.

For her part, Vannina reads these narratives in connection to the activities performed by women accused of witchcraft in earlier centuries, thus linking the two friends to a period of women's history in which women were persecuted for their subversion of established medical and religious practices. Vannina herself describes the atmosphere created when Tota and Giottina tell their "fantastic and lewd tales" (24) as a spell, "a mysterious and disturbing ceremony" (47). Ultimately and significantly, her own reaction to them is indicative of the effect they have over her, "I will come under the spell of their infamous words" (138). However, even though Tota and Giottina are representatives of obscured women's customs, their differences are nevertheless underscored. When, for example, the two women tell their similar stories, Vannina repeatedly notes that their voices are always distinct, as they narrate "without ever overlapping" (10). Likewise, the two women have distinct tastes in, for example, music: while Giottina prefers opera, Tota enjoys popular music. These differences add greater depth and color to the women's lives, revealing to Vannina the way friendship can indeed foster self-expression.

30. Luce Irigaray, "And the One Doesn't Stir Without the Other," trans. Hélène Vivienne Wenzel, *Signs* 7, no. 1, 1981: 65.

31. Irigaray, *Sexes and Genealogies*, 15. Given the mother-daughter bond at the base of the friendship, Tota and Giottina's imposing sentiments and emotions can be read as the traditional attitude attributed to the "overbearing" mother. And indeed Vannina herself notes that she has tried to extricate herself from the women's "suffocating hugs" by which she feels "engulfed" (146). Luce Irigaray has chronicled the daughter's struggle against this unfavorable aspect of the bond, noting how it represents her struggle not only for identity but also for a redimensioning of this coveted relationship. Irigaray's description of this struggle mirrors Vannina's occasionally negative sentiments toward her two maternal friends: "You [mother] take care of me, you keep watch over me. You want me always in your sight in order to protect me. You fear that something will happen to me. . . . Already full-grown and still in the cradle." See "And the One Doesn't Stir Without the Other," 60.

32. In an interview with Ileana Montini, Maraini discusses Suna's negative experiences without the support of feminism. See Ileana Montini, *Parlare con Dacia Maraini*, esp. 147–48.

33. The resistance of, for example, conventional Marxist ideology to the "woman question" has been the basis of the feminist polemic against conventional political ideologies. See, for example, the essays by *Rivolta femminile* in *Italian Feminist Thought*, pages 36–61. In Maraini's novel, this polemic is represented by members of *Vittoria proletaria*. Faele, for example, bases his understanding of prostitution on stereotypes of women's sexuality, which include the Freudian view of women's "natural" passivity: "I can assure you that [prostitutes] enjoy being treated badly, . . . You must admit that women are servile by nature" (121). For his part, Vittorio has little understanding of the labor-intensive work of a housewife and mother: "[S] 'What

does your mother do?' [V] 'Nothing, she stays at home, . . . she does the housework' " (73).

34. Within the economy of the novel, the young Orio represents someone who, as Anthony Tamburri notes, has not yet been coopted by patriarchy. See "Dacia Maraini's *Donna in guerra*: Victory or Defeat?" in *Contemporary Women Writers in Italian: A Modern Renaissance*, ed. Santo L. Aricò (Amherst: University of Massachusetts Press, 1990), 148. Thus, the conventional dynamics operating in Vannina's marriage are not meant to affect her relationship with Orio.

35. One particular episode examines the difficulty Suna has in communicating with women when operating within the political arena. As Suna and Vannina survey Neapolitan women who do piecework at home, they catch a glimpse of these women's desperate lives, marked by worker exploitation, death, and subservience. Within this scenario, the solution to these women's problems is not simply political consciousness, but rather a reconfiguration of their personal lives as well. But Suna, whose symbolic role in the novel is clearly underscored in this episode, remains detached from the personal concerns of the women she surveys. The women, who seemingly have no political consciousness, resist Suna's rhetoric. They cannot respond to accusations of their subordination because they read their situation as a natural condition. Vannina, on the other hand, creates a successful relationship with them. Augustus Pallotta attributes Vannina's transformation in scenes such as this one to her "taking cognizance of social injustices." See "Dacia Maraini: From Alienation to Feminism," *World Literature Today* 58 (1984): 361.

36. Carol Lazzaro-Weis, who places *Donna in guerra* within the romance tradition, notes that Vannina's dream assumes a significant role within this cultural context. The dream is a liberating force in Vannina's life because it signals a positive ending to an at times strained relationship. See *From Margins to Mainstream*, 77.

37. Pickering-Iazzi, "Designing Mothers," 335.

38. Several mothers, along with their experiences, force the protagonist to reexamine the traditional principles governing this role. The self-sacrificing mothers the protagonist encounters on the island are testimonies to the negative effect of the institution of motherhood on women. Giacinto's friend Santino's nurturing mother, silenced and confined by her family to a position of alterity in the kitchen, and the older neighbor mother, forced by her daughter into submission, represent dismal portraits of the role. By reacting to these maternal experiences, Vannina exposes the loss of individual consciousness and control Kristeva attributes to the "biosocial program." Her compassionate description of Santino's demure, seemingly retiring mother, for example, imparts her understanding of the mother's subordinate position and her growing awareness of the mother's suppressed voice and hidden strengths. During a dinner at Santino's house, the mother, relegated to the stove and enveloped in smoke and steam, objects to her sons' account of their sexual exploits, including rape, but the family angrily silences her. In contrast to the family's reaction, Vannina perceives the mother's self-assertive nature, "The mother . . . draws out a hard, aggressive voice" (35). By narrating the mother's response to the family, Vannina enscripts the mother's voice onto her own narrated history.

39. Although I will not examine these five poems, it should be noted that together they represent a sisterhood of experience and, for their personal expression, create a sort of *autocoscienza* forum.

40. hooks, "Sisterhood," 31.

41. Ovid uses the rape of the Sabines to comment on women's position in the

chase, or courtship. His text dismisses the women's fears as "endowments of charm" and their resistance to their captors as foolish misapprehension: " 'Why do you spoil your beautiful eyes with that crying? Wasn't your mother a wife? That's all I want you to be' " (109).

42. As is the case in *Donne mie*, besides being the psychoanalytic basis of friendships between her heroines, *rispecchiamento* also provides the basis of an inquiry into class roles in other Maraini texts as well. In the play *Maria Stuarda*, for example, the protagonists' desires, emotions, and concerns are all reflected through the figure of their servants, all of whom have stronger personalities in more dire circumstances. The imprisoned Maria Stuarda uses her personal maid Kennedy as the "gaze" through which she garners her own image. Her cousin Elizabeth uses her own personal maid Nanny to do the same. It is interesting to note that in *MS* Maraini offers the option of hiring different actors to play the roles of the queens and the servants, or—in a very telling move—to use only two actors to alternately play the queen and the servant. In the latter, the two queens—although on opposite ends of the political and religious spectrum—become reflections for each other. See also the play *Sor Juana Inès de la Cruz*, where a similar reflection occurs.

43. From "ad una sorella timida," *Mangiami pure* (Turin: Einaudi, 1978), 36. The verse in Italian reads "dentro il vuoto / sfibrante dell'inerzia familiare." The word "familiare" in Italian means both "of the family" and "familiar." The double meaning contained within the verse underscores the strength and stratification of the cultural model. Conventional roles and relationships are fostered and assimilated within the family, and thus become "familiar," a natural part of social existence. Subsequent references to works in this collection are indicated parenthetically in the text.

44. For excellent studies of this period in women's history, see M. T. Bergamaschi, et al, *L'erba delle donne: Maghe, streghe, guaritrici: la riscoperta di un'altra medicina* (Rome: Roberto Napoleone, 1978) and Carlo Ginzburg, *The Night Battles: Witchcraft and Agrarian Cults in the Sixteenth and Seventeenth Centuries*, trans. John and Anne Tedeschi (New York: Penguin, 1985). See also Maraini's play *Zena*, in which this specific moment in women's history is used as a reference point for deconstructing the present.

45. Dacia Maraini, *Letters to Marina*, trans. Dick Kitto and Elspeth Spottiswood (Freedom, CA: The Crossing Press, 1987), 7. Subsequent references to the work are indicated parenthetically in the text.

46. In our examination of sisterhood, Basilia is the ultimate catalyst for the final stages of the part of the journey represented in the novel, and it is the bond with Basilia that contains fundamental elements of the contemporary feminist discourse on sisterhood. Pauline Dagnino offers a sensitive critique of Bianca's journey, identifying it as a search for that part of her self not represented in culture but found in the pre-Oedipal relationship with the mother. For Dagnino, it is the relationship with her lover Marina that fuels Bianca's journey and makes its success possible. See "Fra madre e marito: The Mother/Daughter Relationship in Dacia Maraini's *Lettere a Marina*," in *Visions and Revisions: Women in Italian Culture*, ed. M. Cicioni and N. Prunster (Providence: Berg, 1993), 183–97. However, while Marina does indeed play a primary role in Bianca's mnemonic recreation of her past, she nevertheless remains in the past. For Patricia Dunker, Bianca's relationships with both Marina and Basilia are problematic. According to Dunker, the relationship with Marina, which is devoid of "sister-love," and the relationship with Basilia, whose transgressive tales of sexual intrigue she considers troubling clichés, are not emblems of women's love.

Rather, they form part of an alarming aspect of Maraini's novel, which renders love between women "safe for men." See *Sisters and Strangers: An Introduction to Contemporary Feminist Fiction* (Oxford: Blackwell, 1992), esp. 174–75.

47. Bianca's reaction to one of her favorite stories told by her mother offers an example of the possibilities of this bond. In the fairytale, a king forbids his three daughters from eating the golden apples growing on his property. Two daughters obey and are rewarded with prestigious marriages, while the third daughter, in an action reminiscent of Eve's, disobediently takes an apple and becomes small and evil. Ideally, the tale instills obedience of paternal law in the daughter. Bianca's reaction to it as a child, however, is one of defiance. She remembers, "I ate up the golden apples and with them I ate up my mother's arms and her voice and her throat" (135). Bianca rejects the story's conventional moral because in her mind the golden apples, traditionally symbols of knowledge and life, represent the "knowledge of mother-and- daughterhood" that shapes her female heritage. For a definition of the meaning of apples as symbols in women's history, see Barbara Walker, *The Woman's Encyclopedia of Myths and Secrets* (San Francisco: Harper & Row, 1983), 48. For the quote, see Adrienne Rich, *Of Woman Born*, 225. By eating the apples, she assimilates the maternal heritage she would later lose when abandoning the mother for the father. This knowledge is reacquired, however, in the constructive friendship with Basilia.

48. The name Basilia itself symbolizes this role, as it can be derived from the word "basiliare," or fundamental, basic.

49. Bianca describes the relationship between mother and sons in terms of comestibility: The concrete description the protagonist provides connotes the offspring's appropriation and control of the mother. Thus, the son not only actually devours her, but also beats his stomach to emphasize satisfaction and the integration of the maternal into his own body. But contrary to Bianca's interpretation of the situation and of Basilia's exploitation, the mother proudly accepts the position to which she has been relegated. When Bianca notes the boys' aggression toward her, she recounts Basilia's pride and parallels it to her self-neglect. Only Basilia's smile belies her true physical condition.

50. Bianca's relationship with Marina also occurs in an*other* space, that of the lesbian relationship, which counters the heterosexual union to which the conventional heroine's life narrative leads. Although I read this relationship as an essential one in the novel, its representation is a debated topic. Patricia Duncker, for example, considers this "version of Lesbianism" as troubling and even harmful, in that in its depiction of the relationship there is "a knowing resignation" to heterosexuality. See *Sisters and Strangers*, 175. Beverly Ballaro, on the other hand, asserts insightfully that the relationship highlights Maraini's "larger textual project of clearing an Italian narrative space for lesbian voices." See "Making the Lesbian Body," 186. My own decision to focus exclusively on Bianca's friendship with Basilia is based on the fact that this relationship mirrors the female relationships explored in other Maraini texts, not only in its composition (mother-mother-daughter/mother-daughter-mother), but also in its purpose within the work. This bond functions as a place of development for Bianca—a place she moves toward when her relationship with Marina falters and a place in which she comes to understand her position in other relationships, Marina's included.

51. Irigaray, *Sexes and Genealogies*, 18.

52. Bianca recognizes Basilia's link to a female cultural legacy. She notes, "In another century Basilia would have been a story teller . . . recounting marvelous sagas

and romances. . . . Basilia's voice . . . is like a rock . . . rolling with inexorable power propelled by those profound forces which harmonize time and space past and future!" (80, 164). Even Bianca's physical description of Basilia's voice, which comes from a part deep within her and thus alien to Bianca, attests to its deep roots, "She sang at the top of her voice—a *strange guttural* song" (119; emphasis added).

53. Luciana Percovich, "Relazione," in *L'etica necessaria: eredità materna e passione politica* (Milan: Melusine, 1993), 55.

54. The short story first appeared in *Tuttestorie* between 1990 and 1993, and has since been collected in *Il pozzo segreto: Cinquanta scrittrici italiane* (ed. Maria Rosa Cutrufelli, Rosaria Guacci, Marisa Rusconi; Florence: Giunti, 1993). This is the edition cited here.

55. Dacia Maraini, "Cinque donne d'acqua dolce," in *Il pozzo segreto*, 145. Subsequent references to the work are indicated parenthetically in the text.

56. These cultural factors range from, for example, women entering the work force and adapting to its already existing precepts to the growing number of male and female politicians espousing traditional family values and battling against such legal rights as abortion.

57. Bruno, "Off Screen: An Introduction," in *Off Screen: Women and Film in Italy*, ed. G. Bruno and M. Nadotti (London: Routledge, 1988), 8.

Bibliography

Abel, Elizabeth. "(E)Merging Identities: The Dynamics of Female Friendship in Contemporary Fiction by Women." *Signs* 6, no. 31 (spring 1981): 413–35.

Aeschylus. *The Oresteia*. Translated by Robert Fagel. New York: Penguin Classics, 1979.

Aleramo, Sibilla. *Una donna*. Milan: Feltrineli, 1992.

Alfieri, Paola and Giangiulio Ambrosini. *La condizione economica, sociale e giuridica della donna in Italia*. Torino: Paravia, 1975.

Althusser, Louis, "Ideology and Ideological State Apparatuses (Notes towards and Investigation)." In *Lenin and Philosophy and Other Essays*, translated by Ben Brewster. New York: Monthly Review Press, 1972.

Ancona, Teresa. *Una famiglia normale*. Milan: Edizioni il Formichiere, 1974.

Ariès, Philippe. *Centuries of Childhood*. London: Cape, 1962.

Aristotle. *De Partibus Animalium I and De Generatione Animalium I (with passages from II. 1–3)*. Translated by D. M. Balme. Oxford: Clarendon Press, 1972.

Aspesi, Natalia. "Quall'intenso amore di mia figlia Dacia." *La Repubblica* 13 February 1993, 34–35.

Auerbach, Nina. *Communities of Women: An Idea in Fiction*. Cambridge: Harvard University Press, 1978.

Bacichi, Flavia. *Happening in strada. Il teatro delle donne*. Edited by M. G. Silvi. Milan: La Salamandra, 1980. Badinter, Elisabeth. *Mother Love: Myth and Reality*. New York: Macmillan, 1981.

Badt, Karin L. "The Ethics of the Body in American and Italian Women's Fiction: A Study of Sylvia Plath, Natalia Ginzburg, Dacia Maraini, Milena Milani, and Toni Morrison." Diss., The University of Chicago, 1994. Ann Arbor: University of Michigan, 1994.

Balbo, Laura. "Tre interventi sulla famiglia." *Quaderni piacentini*. 16, no. 6 (1977): 139–52.

Ballaro, Beverly. "Making the Lesbian Body: Writing and Desire in Dacia Maraini's *Lettere a Marina*. In *Gendered Contexts: New Perspectives in Italian Cultural Studies*, edited by L. Benedetti, J. Hairston, and S. Ross, 177–87. New York: Peter Lang, 1996.

Bellesia, Giovanna. "*Mai sentita così bene*: Solidarietà fra donne nei romanzi di Rossana Campo." *Italian Culture*. 16, no. 1 (1998): 157–67.

Bellocchio, Lella Ravasi. "Relazione." In *Dee fuori dal tempio: vivere e pensare la relazione madre-figlia*, 43–48. Milan: Melusine, 1992.

Bergamaschi, M. T., et al. *L'erba delle donne: Maghe, streghe, guaritrici: la riscoperta di un'altra medicina*. Rome: Casa editrice Roberto Napoleone, 1978.

Bimbi, Franca. "Three Generations of Women: Transformations of Female Identity Models in Italy." In *Visions and Revisions: Women in Italian Culture*, edited by M. Cicioni and N. Prunster. 149–66. Providence: Berg, 1993.

Birnbaum, Lucia Chiavola. *Liberazione della donna: Feminism in Italy*. Middletown: Wesleyan University Press, 1986.

Blelloch, Paola. "Il femminismo italiano: una diversa prospettiva del rapporto fra donne." *La fusta: Journal of Italian Literature and Culture* 10 (fall 1993–spring 1994): 227–39.

Boccia, Maria Luisa. "L'identità nella relazione." *I Quaderni dell'associazione culturale Livia Laverani Donini* 3, no. 6 (May 1990): 15–25.

Bono, Paola and Sandra Kemp, eds. *Italian Feminist Thought: A Reader*. London: Basil Blackwell, 1991.

Boose, Lynda E. *Daughters and Fathers*. Edited by L. Boose & Betty S. Flowers. Baltimore: Johns Hopkins University Press, 1989.

Bosio, Laura. *Annunciazione*. Milan: Mondadori, 1997.

Braidotti, Rosi. *Nomadic Subjects: Embodiment and Sexual Difference in Contemporary Feminist Theory*. New York: Columbia University Press, 1994.

Bruno, Giuliana and Maria Nadotti. "Off Screen: An Introduction." In *Off Screen: Women and Film in Italy*, edited by G. Bruno and M. Nadotti, 1–17. London: Routledge, 1988.

Butler, Judith. "Performative Acts and Gender Constitution: An Essay in Phenomenology and Feminist Theory. In *Performing Feminisms: Feminist Critical Theory and Theater*, Edited by S. E. Case, 270–82. Johns Hopkins Universit Press, 1990.

Calligaris, Contardo. "Sessualità femminile: Che ti dice Freud?" *Il piccolo Hans* 5 (January–March 1975): 31–67.

Calvino, Italo. *Il sentiero dei nidi di ragno*. Torino: Einaudi, 1984.

Camon, Ferdinando, ed. *Perché scrivete? Rispondono 109 scrittori italiani*. Milan: Garzanti, 1989, pp. 97–101.

Campo, Rossana. *Mai sentita così bene*. Milan: Feltrinelli, 1998.

Cavallaro, Daniela. " 'I sogni di Clitennestra': *The Oresteia* According to Maraini." *Italica* 72, no. 3 (1995): 340–55.

Cerati, Carla. *La cattiva figlia*. Piacenza: Frassinelli, 1990.

Ceresa, Alice. *Bambine*. Torino: Einaudi, 1990.

Chodorow, Nancy. *Feminism and Psychoanalytic Theory*. New Haven: Yale University Press, 1989.

———. *The Reproduction of Mothering: Psychoanalysis and the Sociology of Gender*. Berkeley: University of California Press, 1978.

Ciambellotti, Edera. "Una stanza tutta per sè: Intorno a *L'età del malessere* di Dacia Maraini." In *Nel passato presente degli anni sessanta*. Edited by Umberto Piersanti Urbino: Montefeltro, 1981.

Daughter Rite. Michelle Citron. Women Make Movies, 1979.

Cicioni, Mirna. " 'Love and Respect, Together': The Theory and Practice of 'Affidamento" in Italian Feminism." *Australian Feminist Studies* 10 (summer 1989): 71–83.

Collier, J., M. Z. Rosaldo and S. Yanagisako. "Is There a Family?: New Anthropological Views." In *Rethinking the Family: Some Feminist Questions*, edited by Barrie Thorne, 31–48. Boston: Northeastern University Press, 1992.

Costantini, E. and Moretti, M. *La scena delle donne: presenza e partecipazione della donna al rito scenico occidentale, dalle origini ai giorni nostri*. Rome: Editori e Associati, 1992.

D'Amico, Maria Luisa Aguirre. *L'ombra del padre*. Florence: Giunti, 1997.

Dagnino, Pauline. "Fra madre e marito: The Mother/Daughter Relationship in Dacia Maraini's *Lettere a Marina*." In *Visions and Revisions: Women in Italian Culture*, edited by M. Cicioni and N. Prunster, 183–97. Providence: Berg, 1993.

Dal Pozzo, Giuliana and Enzo Rava. *Donna 70*. Milan: Teti Editore, 1977.

De Beauvior, Simone. *The Second Sex*. Translated by H. M. Parshley. New York: Vintage Books, 1952.

De Céspedes, Alba. *Il rimorso*. Milan: Mondadori, 1963.

———. *Nessuno torna indietro*. Milan: Mondadori, 1938.

———. *The Secret*. Translated by Isabel Quigly. New York: Simon & Schuster, 1958.

D'Eaubonne, Françoise. *Les femmes avant le patriarcat*. Paris: Payot, 1976.

De Giorgio, Michela. *Le italiane dall'Unità ad oggi*. Bari: Editori Laterza, 1992.

De Grazia, Victoria. *How Fascism Ruled Women: Italy, 1922–1945*. Berkeley: University of California Press, 1992.

De Lauretis, Teresa. "Aesthetic and Feminist Theory: Rethinking Women's Cinema." *New German Critique* 34 (1985): 174–95.

———. *Alice Doesn't: Feminism, Semiotics, Cinema*. Bloomington: Indiana University Press, 1984.

———. "The Essence of the Triangle or, Taking the Risk of Essentialism Seriously: Feminist Theory in Italy, the U.S., and Britain." *Differences* 1 (1989).

———. "The Practice of Sexual Difference and Feminist Thought in Italy: An Introductory Essay." In *Sexual Difference: A Theory of Social-Symbolic Practice*, translated by Teresa De Lauretis, 1–21. Bloomington: Indiana UP, 1990.

———. *Technologies of Gender: Essays on Theory, Film, and Fiction*. Bloomington: Indiana University Press, 1987.

De Leo, Mimma and Fiorenza Taricone, eds. *Le donne in Italia: Diritti civili e politici*. Naples: Liguori Editore, 1992.

De Santi, Gualtiero. "La poesia d'amore in Italia (1960–83)." *Testuale* 5, no. 3 (1985): 11–35.

Di Lascia, Mariateresa. *Passaggio in ombra*. Milan: Feltrinelli, 1997.

Di Nola, Laura. "L'io sottratto." In *poesia femminista italiana*, edited by Laura Di Nola, 9–12. Rome: Savelli, 1978.

Duncan, Nancy. *Body Space: Destabilizing Geographies of Gender and Sexuality*. London: Routledge, 1996.

Duncker, Patricia. *Sisters and Strangers: An Introduction to Contemporary Feminist Fiction*. Oxford: Blackwell, 1992.

DuPlessis, Rachel. *Writing Beyond the Ending: Narrative Strategies of Twentieth-Century Women Writers*. Bloomington: Indiana University Press, 1985.

Eagleton, Terry. *Literary Theory: An Introduction*. Minneapolis: Minnesota University Press, 1983.

Erens, Patricia, ed. *Issues in Feminist Film Criticism.* Bloomington: Indiana University Press, 1990.

Faderman, Lillian. *Surpassing the Love of Men: Romantic Friendship and Love between Women from the Renaissance to the Present.* New York: William Morrow, 1981.

Fallaci, Oriana. *Lettere a un bambino mai nato.* Milan: Rizzoli, 1975.

Federici, Nora. *Procreazione, famiglia, lavoro della donna.* Torino: Loescher Editore, 1984.

Fenoglio, Beppe. *La paga del sabato.* Torino: Einaudi, 1969.

Finzi, Silvia Vegetti. "Alla ricerca di una soggettività femminile." In *La ricerca delle donne: studi femministi in Italia,* edited by Maria Cristina Marcuzzo and Anna Rossi-Doria, 228–48. Torino: Rosenberg and Sellier, 1987.

———. "La maternità negata: Alle origini dell'immaginario femminile." *Memoria 7* (September 1983): 45–55.

———. "Relazione." In *Dee fuori dal tempio: vivere e pensare la relazione madre-figlia,* 13–26. Milan: Melusine, 1992.

———. "Relazione." In *Dee fuori dal tempio: vivere e pensare la relazione madre-figlia,* 111–15. Milan: Melusine, 1992.

Frith, Gillian. *The Intimacy which is Knowledge: Female Friendship in the Novels of Women Writers.* Diss., University of Warwick, 1988. Ann Arbor: University of Michigan, 1988.

Fossati, Roberta and Immacolata Mazzonis. "La maternità come destino." In *Donna, cultura e tradizione,* 67–76. Milan: Gabriele Mazzotta editore, 1976.

Franco, Gigliola. *La bambola woo-doo. Il teatro delle donne.* Edited by M. G. Silvi. Milan: La Salamandra, 1980.

———. *Su da brave bambine. Il teatro delle donne.* Edited by M. G. Silvi. Milan: La Salamandra, 1980.

Freud, Sigmund. "Female Sexuality." In *Freud on Women: A Reader,* edited by E. Young-Bruehl, 321–40. New York: W.W. Norton, 1990.

———. "Femininity." In *Freud on Women: A Reader,* edited by E. Young-Bruehl, 342–62. New York: W.W. Norton, 1990.

———. *Totem and Taboo.* Trans. J. Strachey. New York: W.W. Norton, 1950.

Fuss, Diane. *Feminism, Nature, and Difference.* New York: Routledge, 1989.

Gallop, Jane. *Thinking Through the Body.* New York: Columbia University Press, 1988.

Gardiner, Judith K. "The (US)es of (I)dentity: A Response to Abel on '(E)Merging Identities'." *Signs* 6, no. 31 (spring 1981): 436–44.

Garlaschelli, Barbara. *Tre amiche e una farfalla.* Trieste: Edizioni EL, 1998.

Gilbert, Lucy and Paula Webster. *Bound by Love: The Sweet Trap of Daughterhood.* Boston: Beacon Press, 1982.

Gilbert, Sandra M., "Life's Empty Pack: Notes toward a Literary Daughteronomy." In *Daughters and Fathers,* edited by Lynda E. Boose and Betty S. Flowers, 256–77. Baltimore: Johns Hopkins University Press, 1989.

Ginzburg, Carlo. *The Night Battles: Witchcraft and Agrarian Cults in the Sixteenth and Seventeenth Centuries.* Translated by John and Anne Tedeschi. New York: Penguin, 1985.

Ginzburg, Natalia. "La madre." In *Novelle del Novecento: An Anthology*, edited by Brian Moloney (Manchester: Manchester University Press, 1966).

———. *Sagittario.* Torino: Einaudi, 1957.

Graziosi, Mariolina. "Gender Struggle and the Social Manipulation and Ideological Use of Gender Identity in the Interwar Years." In *Mothers of Invention: Women, Italian Fascism, and Culture*, 26–51. Minneapolis: University of Minnesota Press, 1995.

Grosz, Elizabeth. *Jacques Lacan: A Feminist Introduction.* London: Routledge, 1990.

Gubar, Sandra. " 'The Blank Page' and the Issues of Female Creativity." In *Writing and Sexual Difference*, edited by E. Abel, 73–94. Chicago: University of Chicago Press, 1982.

———. "Mother, Maiden and the Marriage of Death: Women Writers and an Ancient Myth." *Women's Studies: An Interdisciplinary Journal* 6, no. 3 (1979): 301–15.

Guiducci, Armanda. *La mela e il serpente: Autoanalisi di una donna.* Milan: BUR, 1974.

Heath, Stephen. *Questions of Cinema.* Bloomington: Indiana University Press, 1981.

Hegel, G. W. *Phenomenology of Spirit.* Translated by A. V. Miller. Oxford: Clarendon Press, 1977.

Hirsch, Marianne. *The Mother/Daughter Plot: Narrative, Psychoanalysis, Feminism.* Bloomington: Indiana University Press, 1989.

Homer. *The Homeric Hymn to Demeter.* Translated and edited by Helene P. Foley. Princeton: Princeton University Press, 1994.

hooks, bell. "Sisterhood: Political Solidarity Between Women." In *A Reader in Feminist Knowledge*, edited by Sneja Gunew, 27–41. London: Routledge, 1991.

Horowitz, Maryanne Cline. "Aristotle and Women." *Journal of the History of Biology* 9, no. 2 (fall 1976): 183–213.

Hostert, Anna Camaiti. "Potere dell'alterità-alterità del potere: Una lettura del libro di Dacia Maraini *La lunga vita di Marianna Ucrìa. RLA* 5, no. 4 (1992): 204–8.

House, Jane. "Interview: Dacia Maraini." *Western European Stages* 1, no. 1 (fall 1989): 39–43.

Insana, Jolanda. "Essere o fare l'amica?" *Memoria* 32, no. 2 (1991): 7–17.

Irigaray, Luce. "And the One Doesn't Stir Without the Other." Translated by Hélène Vivienne Wenzel. *Signs* 7, no. 1 (1981): 60–67.

———. "Body Against Body: In Relation to the Mother. In *Sexes and Genealogies*, translated by Gillian C. Gill, 7–21. New York: Columbia University Press, 1993.

———. *Sexes and Genealogies.* Translated by Gillian C. Gill. New York: Columbia University Press, 1993.

———. *Speculum of the Other Woman.* Translated by Gillian C. Gill. Ithaca: Cornell University Press, 1989.

———. *This Sex Which is Not One.* Translated by Catherine Porter with Carolyn Burke. Ithaca: Cornell University Press, 1985.

Jeanne Dielman, 23 Quai du Commerce, 1080 Bruxelles. Directed by Claude Akerman, 1975.

Jeffries, Giovanna Miceli, ed. *Feminine Feminists: Cultural Practices in Italy*. Minneapolis: University of Minnesota Press, 1994.

Jeuland-Meynaud, Maryse. "Dacia Maraini: Polémique ou littérature?" In *Les femmes écrivains en Italie aux XIXe et XXe siècles*, 205–38. Aix-en-Provence: Publications de l'Université de Provence, 1993.

Johnston, Claire. "Women's Cinema as Counter-Cinema." In *Notes on Women's Cinema*, edited by Claire Johnston. London: Society for Education in Film and Television, 1973.

Kaplan, E. Ann. "Dora; Thriller; Amy!" *Women and Film: Both Sides of the Camera*. Metheun 1983.

Kaufman, Rhoda Helfman. "Introduction." In *Only Prostitutes Marry in May*. Dacia Maraini. Translated by R. H. Kaufman, 9–29. Toronto: Guernica, 1994.

Kinder, Marsha. "Reflections on 'Jeanne Dielman'." *Film Quarterly* 30, no. 4 (1977).

Kittiel, Beverly and Jane Jewell. *The Defiant Muse: Italian Feminist Poems from the Middle Ages to the Present*. New York: The Feminist Press, 1986.

Kristeva, Julia. "Motherhood According to Bellini." In *Desirein Language: A Semiotic Approach to Literature and Art*, translated by Thomas Gora, Alice Jardine, and Leon S. Roudiez, edited by Leon S. Roudiez. New York: Columbia University Press, 1980.

——. "Stabat Mater." *Poetics Today* 6, no. .1–2 (1985): 133–52.

Kuhn, Annette. "Textual Politics." In *Issues in Feminist Film Criticism*, edited by Patricia Erens, 250–67. Bloomington: Indiana UP, 1990.

La Belle, Jenijoy. *Herself Beheld: The Literature of the Looking Glass*. Ithaca: Cornell University Press, 1988.

Lacan, Jacques. *Il seminario: Gli scritti tecnici di Freud, 1953–54*. 5.1. Torino: Einaudi, 1978.

Lazzaro-Weis, Carol. "Gender and Genre in Italian Feminist Literature in the Seventies." *Italica*, 65, no. 4 (winter 1988): 293–307.

——. *From Margins to Mainstream: Feminism and the Fictional Modes in Italian Women's Writing, 1968–1990*. Philadelphia: University of Pennsylvania Press, 1993.

Lerner, Gerda. *The Creation of Patriarchy*. New York: Oxford University Press, 1986.

Lévi-Strauss, Claude. *The Elementary Structures of Kinship*. Translated and edited by James H. Bell, John R. von Sturmer, and Rodney Needham, Boston: Beacon Press, 1969.

Lonzi, Carla. *Sputiamo su Hegel, La donna clitoridea e la donna vaginale, e altri scritti*. Scritti di Rivolta Femminile 1, 2, 1987, pp. 228–48.

Magrini, Gabriella. *Lunga giovinezza*. Milan: Mondadori, 1976.

Mangiacapre, Lina. *Cinema al femminile*. Padova: Mastrogiacomo Images 70, 1980.

Manzini, Gianna. *Ritratto in piedi*. Milan: Mondadori, 1971.

Mapelli, Barbara. *Care, carissime donne: Racconti di vita e di lavoro*. Rome: Ediesse, 1995.

Maraini, Dacia. *Aborto: parlano le donne*. Rome 1976.

——. *L'amore coniugale*. Rome, 1969.

——. *Bagheria*. Milan: Rizzoli, 1993.

———. *La bella addormentata nel bosco*. Rome, 1978.

———. *La bionda, la bruna e l'asino*. Milan: Rizzoli, 1987.

———. "Cinque donne d'acqua dolce." In *Il pozzo segreto*, edited by Maria Rosa Cutrufelli, Rosaria Guacci, and Marisa Rusconi. 145–52. Florence: Giunti, 1993.

———. *Un clandestino a bordo. Le donne: la maternità negata, il corpo sognato*. Milano: Rizzoli, 1996.

———. *Crudeltà all'aria aperta*. Milan: Felrinelli, 1966.

———. *Donne mie*. Torino: Einaudi. 1974.

———. *L'età del malessere*. Torino: Einaudi, 1963.

———. *Fare teatro: Materiali, testi, interviste*. Milan: Bompian, 1974.

———. "Les femmes et la créativité." In *Dialogues franco-italiens*, 6, edited by Roger Pillaudin, 53–82. Paris: Institute culturel italien, 1978.

———. *Giochi di latte*. Rome, 1978.

———. Interview by author. Rome, 26 November 1992.

———. Interview by author. Rome, 6 April 1993.

———. *Letters to Marina*. Translated by D. Kitto and E. Spottiswood. Freedom, CA: The Crossing Press, 1987.

———. "Una lunga storia di esclusione." In *La scena delle donne: presenza e partecipazione della donna al rito scenico occidentale, dalle origini ai giorni nostri*, Emilia Costantini & Mario Moretti, 3–6. Rome: Editori e Associati, 1992.

———. *La lunga vita di Marianna Ucrìa*. Milan: Rizzoli, 1991.

———. *Mangiami pure*. Torino: Einaudi, 1978.

———. *Il manifesto. Il ricatto a teatro e altre commedie*. Torino: Einaudi, 1970, pp. 187–279.

———. *Maria Stuarda. I sogni di Clitennestra*. Milan: Bompiani, 1981, pp. 213–52.

———. *Memorie di una ladra*. Milan: Bompiani, 1972.

———. *Mio padre amore mio*. Rome, 1979.

———. Panel Discussion. Chicago, 5 April 1994.

———. Post-Screening discussion, Rome, 19 November 1992.

———. "Quale cultura per la donna." In *Donna, cultura e tradizione*. Milan: Gabriele Mazzotta editore, 1976.

———. *Ritratti di donne africane*. Rome, 1976.

———. "Se esser donne vi sembra poco," *L'unità* on internet (23 September 1995).

———. *I sogni di Clitennestra. I sogni di Clitennestra*. Milan: Bompiani, 1981, pp. 5–60.

———. *Il sommacco: Piccolo inventario dei teatri palermitani trovati e persi*. Palermo: Flaccovio, 1993.

———. *Suor Juana*. Torino: Edizioni La Rosa, 1980.

———. "Tema." In *Cinema, letteratura, arti visive: Lessico politico delle donne* 6, edited by M. Frabotta, N. Fusini, and A. M. Boetti, 58–64. Milan: Edizioni Gulliver, 1979.

———. *Il treno per Helsinki*. Torino: Einaudi, 1984.

———. *Veronica, meretrice e scrittora*. Milan: Bompiani, 1992.

———. *Woman at War*. Translated by M. Benetti and E. Spottiswood. New York: Italica Press, 1988.

———. *Zena 1512–1975. I sogni di Clitennestra*. Milan: Bompiani, 1981, pp. 105–47.

Melchiori, Paola. *Crinali: Le zone oscure del femminismo*. Milan: La Tartaruga, 1995.

———. "Women's Cinema: A Look at Female Identity." Translated by Jane Dolman. In *Off Screen: Women and Film in Italy*, edited by G. Bruno and M. Nadotti, 24–35. London: Routledge, 1988.

Merry, Bruce. *Dacia Maraini and the Written Dream of Women in Italian Literature*. North Queensland: James Cook University, 1997.

Messina, Maria. *Casa paterna*. Palermo: Sellerio, 1990.

The Milan Women's Bookstore Collective. *Sexual Difference: A Theory of Social-Symbolic Practice*. Bloomington: Indiana University Press, 1990.

Miscuglio, Annabella. "An affectionate and irreverent account of eighty years of women's cinema in Italy." In *Off Screen: Women and Film in Italy*, edited by G. Bruno and M. Nadotti. 151–64. London: Routledge, 1988.

Mitchell, Tony. " 'Scrittura femminile': Writing the Female in the Plays of Dacia Maraini." *Theater Journal* 42, no. 3 (1990): 332–49.

Montini, Ileana. *Parlare con Dacia Maraini*. Verona: Bertani Editore, 1977.

Moravia, Alberto. *Gli indifferenti*. Milan: Bompiani, 1976.

Mulvey, Laura. *Visual and Other Pleasures*. Bloomington: Indiana University Press, 1989.

Muraro, Luisa. *L'ordine simbolico della madre*. Rome: Riuniti, 1992.

Noidonne. no. 2 February 1993.

Nozzoli, Anna. *Tabù e coscienza: La condizione femminile nella letteratura italiana del novecento*. Florence: La Nuova Italia, 1978.

Ortner, Sherry. "Is Female to Male as Nature is to Culture?" *Woman, Culture, and Society*, edited by Michelle Z. Rosaldo. Stanford: Stanford University Press, 1974.

Ovid. *The Art of Love*. Translated by Rolfe Humphries. Bloomington: Indiana University Press, 1957.

Paolucci, Gabriella. "Amiche: Figure dell'amicizia femminile e femminismo." *Memoria* 32, no. 2 (1991): 56–66.

Pallotta, Augusto. "Dacia Maraini: From Alienation to Feminism." *World Literature Today* 58 (1984): 359–62.

"Per un'Europa di donne e uomini." Supplement to *Noidonne* 6 (June 1999).

Percovich, Luciana. "Relazione." In *L'etica necessaria: eredità materna e passione politica*, 15–21. Milan: Melusine, 1993.

———. "Relazione." In *L'etica necesaria: eredità materna e passione politica*, 55–65. Milan: Melusine, 1993.

———. "Relazione." In *L'etica necesaria: eredità materna e passione politica*, 77–91. Milan: Melusine, 1993.

Picchietti, Virginia. "Symbolic Mediation and Female Community in Dacia Maraini's Fiction." *The Pleasure of Writing: Critical Essays on Dacia Maraini*. Rodica Diaconescu-Blumenfeld and Ada Testaferri, eds. West Lafayette: Purdue University Press, 2000.

———. " 'Tornare indietro verso l'allegria del futuro': Daughterhood and 'Revisionary Mythopoesis' in Dacia Maraini's 'Demetra ritrovata'." *RLA* 6 (1994): 354–59.

Pickering-Iazzi, Robin. "Designing Mothers: Images of Motherhood in Novels by Aleramo, Morante, Maraini, and Fallaci." *Annali d'Italianistica* 7 (1989): 325–40.

Pirandello, Luigi. *Sei personaggi in cerca d'autore*. Milan: Mondadori, 1964.

Piussi, Anna Maria. "Era là dall'inizio." In *Diotima. Il cielo stellato dentro di noi: L'ordine simbolico della madre*, 21–47. Milan: La Tartaruga edizioni, 1992.

Plath, Sylvia. "Mirror." In *Collected Poems*, 173–74. London: Faber & Faber, 1981.

Radner, Joan and S. Lanser. "Strategies in Coding Women's Culture." In *Feminist Messages: Coding in Women's Folk Culture*, edited by J. Radner. Urbana: University of Illinois Press, 1993.

Ramondino, Fabrizia. *Althénopis*. Turin: Einaudi, 1981.

———. *Terremoto con madre e figlia*. Genoa: Il melangolo, 1994.

Rasy, Elisabetta. *Le donne e la letteratura: Scrittrici, eroine, e ispiratrici nel mondo delle lettere*. Rome: Editori Riuniti. 1984.

Raymond, Janice. *A Passion for Friends: Toward a Philosophy of Female Affection*. Boston: Beacon Press, 1986.

Rich, Adrienne. *Of Woman Born: Motherhood as Experience and Institution*. New York: W.W. Norton, 1986.

Riviello, Tonia. "The Motif of Entrapment in Elsa Morante's *L'isola d'Arturo* and Dacia Maraini's *L'età del malessere*." *Rivista di Studi Italiani* 8, no. 1–2 (June–December 1990): 70–87.

Robinson, Sally. *Engendering the Subject: Gender and Self-Representation in Contemporary Women's Fiction*. Albany: State University of New York Press, 1991.

Rose, Gillian. *Feminism and Geography: The Limits of Geographical Knowledge*. Minneapolis: University of Minneapolis Press, 1993.

Rose, Jacqueline. "Introduction II." In *Feminine Sexuality: Jacques Lacan and the école freudienne*, edited by J. Mitchell and J. Rose. New York: W.W. Norton, 1985.

Rossanda, Rossana. *Anche per me: Donna, persona, memoria dal 1973 al 1986*. Milan: Feltrinelli, 1987.

Rossi, Giovanna and Giuseppina Malerba, eds. *La donna nella famiglia e nel lavoro*. Milan: Franco Angeli, 1993.

Salsini, Laura. "Checchina and Isolina: Female Friendship in Matilde Serao's 'La virtù di Checchina'." *RLA* 3 (1991): 309–13.

Samperi, Salvatore. "Introduzione." In *Cuore di mamma*, 9–16. Milan: Ranzani and Aglieri, 1969.

Sanvitale, Francesca. *Madre e figlia*. Turin: Einaudi, 1980.

Saraceno, Chiara. *Sociologia della famiglia*. Bologna: Il Mulino, 1988.

———. *Il lavoro mal diviso*. Edited by C. Saraceno. Bari: De Donato Editore, 1980.

———. "The Italian Family: Paradoxes of Privacy." Translated by R. Rosenthal. In *A History of Private Life*, vol. 5, edited by A. Prost and G. Vincent, translated by A. Goldhammer, 451–501. Cambridge: Harvard University Press, 1991.

Schiller, F. *Maria Stuart*. Translated by Ervino Pocar. Milan: Bompiani, 1986.

Serao, Matlide. "La virtù di Checchina." In *Serao*, edited by P. Pancrazi, 863–911. Milan: Garzanti, 1946.

Shakespeare, William. *King Lear*. New York: Simon & Schuster, 1957.

Silverman, Kaja. *The Acoustic Mirror: The Female Voice in Psychoanalysis and Cinema*. Bloomington: Indiana University Press, 1988.

Silvi, Maria Grazia, ed. *Il teatro delle donne*. Milan: La Salamandra, 1980.

Tamburri, Anthony. "Dacia Maraini's *Donna in guerra*: Victory or Defeat?" In *Contemporary Women Writers in Italian: A Modern Renaissance*, edited by Santo L. Aricò, 139–51. Amherst: University of Massachusetts Press, 1990.

Thorne, Barrie, ed. *Rethinking the Family: Some Feminist Questions*. Boston: Northeastern University Press, 1992, pp. 3–30.

Thriller. Sally Potter. Women Make Movies, 1979.

Todd, Janet. *Women's Friendship in Literature*. New York: Columbia University Press, 1980.

Tyrell, William Blake. *Amazons: A Study in Athenian Mythmaking*. Baltimore: Johns Hopkins University Press, 1984.

Valentini, Daria. "Father-Daughter Reflections in Gianna Manzini's *Ritratto in piedi*." *RLA* 9 (1998): 368–72.

Van Buren, Jane Silverman. *The Modernist Madonna: Semiotics of the Maternal Metaphor*. Bloomington: Indiana University Press, 1989.

Veroli, Luisella. "Il divino femminile." In *Dee fuori dal tempo: vivere e pensare la relazione madre-figlia*, 61–62. Milan: Melusine, 1992.

Vittorini, Elio. *Conversazione in Sicilia*. Torino: Einaudi, 1981.

Walker, Barbara G. *The Woman's Encyclopedia of Myths and Secrets*. San Francisco: Harper & Row, 1983.

Weinberg, Grazia Sumeli. "All'ombra del padre: la poesia di Dacia Maraini in *Crudeltà all'aria aperta*." *Italica* 67, no. 4 (winter 1990): 453–65.

———. "Dacia Maraini e il teatro femminista come modello di trasgressione." *Studi d'Italianistica nell'Africa Australe* 3 (1990): 20–31.

———. "An Interview with Dacia Maraini." *Tydskrif vir letterkunde* 27, no. 2 (2 May 1989): 64–72.

———. *Invito alla lettura di Dacia Maraini*. Pretoria: University of South Africa Press, 1993.

———. *Parola e impegno nelle opere di Dacia Maraini*. Diss., University of South Africa, 1988. Ann Arbor: University of Michigan, 1988.

———. "Women's Theatre: Teatro La Maddalena and the Work of Dacia Maraini." *Western European Stages* 1, no. 1 (fall 1989): 27–29.

Wilt, Judith. *Abortion, Choice, and Contemporary Fiction: The Armageddon of the Maternal Instinct*. Chicago: University of Chicago Press, 1990.

Index

Abel, Elizabeth, 110
Aeschylus, 25, 95–97, 103
affidamento, 109, 110, 136, 139, 147 n. 56; defined, 30–31; in *Donna in guerra*, 119 (as "entrustment"), 120–21 (as "entrustment"), 123; in *Lettere a Marina*, 130–31; in *Mangiami pure*, 124 (as "entrustment"), 129 (as "entrustment"); in *Il Manifesto*, 113–16
Aleramo, Sibilla, 27–28, 38, 41, 44, 70
Alfieri, Paola, 143 n. 20, 155 n. 7
Althusser, Louis, 55
Ambrosini, Giangiulio, 143 n. 20, 155 n. 7
Ancona, Teresa, 40, 63, 148 n. 11, 157 n. 24
Ariès, Philippe, 16–17, 74
Aristotle, 74–75
Aspesi, Natalia, 151 n. 35
Auerbach, Nina, 160 n. 12
autocoscienza, 44, 147 n. 56; defined, 30, 109; history of, 147 n. 55; in "Cinque donne d'acqua dolce," 134–36; in *Donne mie* and *Mangiami pure*, 124, 126, 128 (as "rap sessions"); in *Lettere a Marina*, 130–31; in *Il Manifesto*, 112–15

Bacichi, Flavia, 24–25
Badinter, Elisabeth, 16, 17, 75, 142 n. 12
Badt, Karin L., 141 n. 4
Balbo, Laura, 17, 142 nn. 13 and 17
Ballaro, Beverly, 141 n. 4, 166 n. 50
Barthes, Roland, 27
Beauvoir, Simone de, 78, 106–7, 111
Bellesia, Giovanna, 160 n. 9
Bellocchio, Lella Ravasi, 158 n. 45
Bergamaschi, M. T., 165 n. 44
Bimbi, Franca, 143 n. 20

Birnbaum, Lucia Chiavola, 147 n. 56
Blelloch, Paola, 147 n. 56, 161 n. 13
Boccia, Maria Luisa, 19, 108, 147 n. 55, 159 n. 3
Bono, Paola, 147 n. 56
Boose, Lynda E., 29, 58, 147 n. 4
Bosio, Laura, 154 n. 5
Braidotti, Rosi, 18, 144 n. 21
Bruno, Giuliana, 94, 137, 145 n. 42
Butler, Judith, 16, 142 n. 10, 153 n. 47

Calligaris, Contardo, 156 n. 14
Calvino, Italo, 80, 81
Camon, Ferdinando, 146 nn. 49 and 51
Campo, Rossana, 108
Care, carissime donne, 108–9
Carini, Anna, 158 n. 38
Cavallaro, Daniela, 158 n. 44
Cerati, Carla, 13, 41–42, 46–47, 63, 153 n. 57, 157 n. 24
Ceresa, Alice, 55
Chodorow, Nancy, 156 n. 14, 159 n. 3
Ciambellotti, Edera, 150 n. 28
Cicioni, Mirna, 161 n. 13
cinema: feminist revision of, 25–27, 93–94; classic, 26, 59–60, 158 n. 39; daughter's vision in, 58–62
Collier, Jane, 17, 142 n. 11
consciousness-raising. See *autocoscienza*
contestatory narrative practices, 21–22
constructionism, 77–79
Costantini, Emilia, 24

D'Amico, Maria Luisa Aguirre, 40–41, 49
Dagnino, Pauline, 165 n. 46
Dal Pozzo, Giuliana, 143 n. 20
Daughter Rite (film), 157 n. 36
De Céspedes, Alba, 13, 28, 41–42, 55, 107, 159 n. 53

178

INDEX

D'Eaubonne, Françoise, 158 n. 43
De Giorgio, Michela, 82, 148 n. 9, 149 n. 18
De Grazia, Victoria, 148 n. 9
De Lauretis, Teresa, 78, 146 nn. 43 and 48, 147 n. 56, 156 n. 19
Deledda, Grazia, 38
De Leo, Mimma, 142 n. 18, 143 nn. 19 and 20, 155 n. 7
De Santi, Gualtiero, 141 n. 4
Di Lascia, Mariateresa, 40, 49
Di Nola, Laura, 28
doppia militanza, 120, 124
Duncan, Nancy, 142 n. 9
Duncker, Patricia, 165 n. 46, 166 n. 50
DuPlessis, Rachel, 22, 63, 153 n. 53

Eagleton, Terry, 146 n. 50
entrustment. See *affidamento*
Erens, Patricia, 146 n. 43
essentialism, 77–79

Faderman, Lillian, 160 n. 11
Fallaci, Oriana, 28, 79, 83–84, 85
family: defined, 16–19; daughter's position in Western family, 35–36; feminist revision of daughter's position in, 33–35, 42–43; mother's position in Western family, 72–75; feminist revision of mother's position in, 18–19, 75–79. See also symbolic mother
father: and daughter, 34, 36–37, 40–41; in *Crudeltà all'aria aperta*, 50–55; in "Demetra ritrovata," 64–67, 69–70; in *L'età del malessere*, 48–49; in *Il Manifesto*, 56–58; in *Mio padre amore mio* (film), 59–62
Federici, Nora, 143 n. 20
female friendship. See sisterhood
female-gendered frames of reference. See genealogy
Fenoglio, Beppe, 44, 149 n. 20
Finzi, Silvia Vegetti, 20, 98, 144 n. 24, 153 n. 54, 156 n. 14
Frith, Gillian, 161 n. 16
Fossati, Roberta, 156 n. 22
Franco, Gigliola, 24, 107–8
Freud, Sigmund and Freudian psychoanalysis: and daughterhood, 28–29, 36, 61, 148 n. 6; and motherhood, 29, 75, 158 n. 43
Fuss, Diane, 77–78

Gallop, Jane, 156 n. 19
Gardiner, Judith K., 110
Garlaschelli, Barbara, 108
gaze. See vision and visual language
genealogy, 63, 140; in "Demetra ritrovata," 69–70; in *Giochi di latte*, 90–91 (also as "female legacy"); in *Lettere a Marina*, 132–34 (as "female legacy"); in *Mangiami pure*, 127 (as image of witch); in *Il Manifesto*, 162 n. 26; in *I sogni di Clitennestra*, 96–97 (as "female-gendered frames of reference")
Gilbert, Lucy, 147 n. 1
Gilbert, Sandra, 62, 148 n. 6
Ginzburg, Carlo, 165 n. 44
Ginzburg, Natalia, 13, 79, 82–83, 85
Graziosi, Mariolina, 148 n. 9
Gregory, Derek, 16
Grosz, Elizabeth, 161 n. 16
Gubar, Sandra, 145 n. 29, 154 n. 59
Guiducci, Armanda, 39–40, 70

Heath, Stephen, 146 n. 43
Hegel, G. W., 75
Hirsch, Marianne, 150 n. 22, 153 n. 49, 156 n. 17, 159 n. 50
Homer, 63
hooks, bell, 111, 125, 161 n. 21
Horowitz, Maryanne Cline, 155 n. 9
Hostert, Anna Camaiti, 141 n. 4, 152 n. 43
House, Jane, 145 n. 35

Insana, Jolanda, 108
Irigaray, Luce, 60–61, 78, 154 n. 3, 156 n. 14; and motherhood, 68–69, 80, 132, 155 n. 6, 156 n. 17, 157 n. 23, 158 n. 43, 159 n. 51, 163 nn. 30 and 31

Jeanne Dielman, 23 Quai du Commerce, 1080 Bruxelles (film), 158 n. 39
Jeffries, Giovanna Miceli, 161 n. 20
Jeuland-Meynaud, Maryse, 141 n. 4
Johnston, Claire, 26

Kaplan, Ann, 157 n. 37
Kaufman, Rhoda Helfman, 145 n. 35
Kemp, Sandra, 147 n. 56
Kinder, Marsha, 158 n. 39
Kristeva, Julia, 73, 154 n. 5
Kuhn, Annette, 26, 146 n. 43

La Belle, Jenijoy, 150 n. 25
Lacan, Jacques and Lacanian psychoanalysis, 27, 46–47, 61, 110
Lazzaro-Weis, Carol, 22–23, 144 n. 27, 162 n. 28, 164 n. 36
Lerner, Gerda, 155 n. 10, 158 n. 43
Lévi-Strauss, Claude, 29, 35–36, 148 n. 5
liberation. *See* women's liberation
Lonzi, Carla, 115, 147 n. 55, 155 n. 12

Magrini, Gabriella, 13, 40, 148 n. 11
Malerba, Giuseppina, 143 n. 20
Mangiacapre, Lina, 145 n. 42
Manzini, Gianna, 40, 49
Maraini, Dacia: critical reception, 141 n. 4. Works: *Aborto: parlano le donne* (film), 25; "ad una sorella timida" (*Mangiami pure*), 127–28; *L'amore coniugale* (film), 25; "L'arte di amare" (*Donne mie*), 125; *Bagheria*, 58, 151 n. 31; "Bagheria" (*Crudeltà all'aria aperta*), 51–53; *La bella addormentata nel bosco* (film), 25–26, 89, 91–95, 103–4, 145 n. 42; *La bionda, la bruna e l'asino*, 151 n. 29, 158 n. 40; "Cinque donne d'acqua dolce," 134–36, 137; "Il circolo di Chaplin" (*Crudeltà all'aria aperta*), 54, 153 n. 56; *Un clandestino a bordo. Le donne: la maternità negata, il corpo sognato*, 155 n. 6; "Cordelia" (*Crudeltà all'aria aperta*), 50–51, 53 n. 52; *Crudeltà all'aria aperta*, 29, 49–55, 56, 58, 59, 64, 71, 139; "Demetra ritrovata" (*Mangiami pure*), 30, 58, 63–70, 71, 139; *Donna in guerra*, 13, 44, 116–24, 136, 139–40, 141 n. 1; *Donne mie*, 29, 62, 124–26, 129, 136; "Donne mie" (*Donne mie*), 126; *L'età del malessere*, 30, 43–49, 52–53, 71, 86, 103–4, 139; *Fare teatro: Materiali, testi, interviste*, 145 n. 33; "Les femmes et la créativité," 146 n. 51; *Giochi di latte* (film), 25, 26, 30, 89–91, 103–04, 139, 145 n. 42; "An interview," 146 n. 51; "Interview by author" (26 November 1992), 21, 37, 68, 72, 144 nn. 25 and 26, 146 n. 46, 154 n. 61; "Interview by author" (6 April 1993), 147 n. 3, 157 nn. 34 and 35; *Lessico politico delle donne*, 153 n. 43; *Lettere a Marina*, 129–34, 136, 139–40, 153 n. 52; *Letters to Marina, see Lettere a Marina*; "Una lunga storia di esclusione," 145 nn. 37 and 38; *La lunga vita di Marianna Ucrìa*, 44, 152 n. 43; "Madre canina" (*Crudeltà all'aria aperta*), 30, 86–88, 103–4, 139; "Mancanza di memoria" (*Crudeltà all'aria aperta*), 151 n. 32; *Mangiami pure*, 62, 124, 126–29, 136, 153 n. 52; *Il Manifesto*, 55–58, 71, 112–16, 136; *Maria Stuarda*, 25, 145 n. 35, 165 n. 42; *Memorie di una ladra*, 162 n. 27; *Mio padre amore mio* (film), 25, 26, 29, 52, 59–62, 71, 139, 145 n. 42; "non mi dire che le donne sono buone" (*Mangiami pure*), 128; "non sappiamo amarci" (*Mangiami pure*), 129; "Panel Discussion" (5 April 1994), 145 n. 36; "Perché scrivere," 146 nn. 49 and 51; "Le poesie delle donne," 23; "Quale cultura per la donna," 155 n. 8, 157 n. 29; "ricamare" (*Mangiami pure*), 105, 127; *Ritratti di donne africane* (film), 25; "riunione di gruppo" (*Mangiami pure*), 128; "La rosa del buonsenso" (*Crudeltà all'aria aperta*), 52, 153 n. 56; "Se esser donne vi sembra poco," 143 n. 20; *I sogni di Clitennestra*, 25, 95–104, 145 n. 35, 153 n. 52; *Il sommacco: Piccolo inventario dei teatri palermitani trovati e persi*, 145 n. 34; *Suor Juana*, 25, 165 n. 42; "Tema" (*Lessico politico delle donne*), 141 n. 5, 145 n. 42; *Il treno per Helsinki*, 152 n. 41; *La vacanza*, 149 n. 19; *Veronica, meretrice e scrittora*, 25; "Villa Valguarnera" (*Crudeltà all'aria aperta*), 51–52, 64; *Woman at War, see Donna in guerra*; *Zena 1512–1975*, 165 n. 44
Maraini, Fosco, 151 n. 35

Mazzonis, Immacolata, 156 n. 22
Melchiori, Paola, 26–27, 76–77, 79, 146 n. 48, 157 n. 35
Merry, Bruce, 141 n. 4
Messina, Maria, 37, 38–39
Milan Women's Bookstore Collective, The, 19, 20, 34–35, 76–77, 109, 144 nn. 22 and 23
Miscuglio, Annabella, 145 n. 42, 158 n. 38
Mitchell, Tony, 145 n. 35
Montini, Ileana, 153 n. 49, 163 n. 32
Morante, Elsa, 13, 79
Moravia, Alberto, 37, 39, 44
Mulvey, Laura, 146 n. 43, 152 n. 37
Muraro, Luisa, 18–19, 76–77

Nadotti, Maria, 94
Noidonne, 142 n. 18
Nozzoli, Anna, 22, 145 n. 30

Ortner, Sherry, 148 n. 5
Ovid, 125
Pallotta, Augusto, 164 n. 35

Paolucci, Gabriella, 108, 109, 160 n. 5, 161 n. 14
Percovich, Luciana, 42–43, 66, 70, 76–77, 133, 148 n. 5, 149 n. 17
Pickering-Iazzi, Robin, 141 n. 4, 157 n. 32
Pierallini, Elisabetta, 13
Pirandello, Luigi, 37–38
Piussi, Anna Maria, 42–43, 156 n. 17
Plath, Sylvia, 105, 159 n. 1, 161 n. 17
poetry: feminist revision of, 27–28. See also contestatory narrative practices
prose: feminist revision of, 27–28. See also contestatory narrative practices

Radner, Joan, 162 n. 29
Rame, Franca, 84–85
Ramondino, Fabrizia, 41, 63
rap sessions. See *autocoscienza*
Rasy, Elisabetta, 22
Raymond, Janice, 160 n. 11
Rich, Adrienne, 68, 79, 86, 150 n. 22, 154 nn. 1 and 5, 156 n. 17
rispecchiamento, 30, 122, 124, 126, 136; defined, 109–10; as mirroring, 31–32, 46–48, 61; in *Lettere a Marina*, 131–33
Riviello, Tonia, 150 n. 28, 151 n. 30
Robinson, Sally, 21
Rosaldo, Michelle, 17
Rose, Gillian, 16, 20, 142 nn. 7 and 8
Rose, Jacqueline, 161 n. 16
Rossanda, Rossana, 107, 111
Rossi, Giovanna, 143 n. 20

Salsini, Laura, 160 n. 7
Samperi, Salvatore, 13, 141 n. 2
Sanvitale, Francesca, 13, 41, 79
Saraceno, Chiara, 17, 18, 73–74, 142 n. 13, 143 n. 20
Schiller, Friedrich, 25
Serao, Matilde, 38, 107
Shakespeare, William, 50, 147 n. 2
Silverman, Kaja, 146 n. 43
Silvi, Maria Grazia, 145 nn. 38 and 40, 162 n. 24
space: defined, 15–16
storia: defined, 20, 109
symbolic mediation, 19, 20–21
symbolic mother, 31, 35, 131–33; defined: 19, 77
symbolic placement, 19–21, 35; in film, 26–27; in theater, 24–25

Tamburri, Anthony, 164 n. 34
Taricone, Fiorenza, 142 n. 18, 143 nn. 19 and 20
theater: feminist revision of, 23–25, 56, 62, 112–13
Thorne, Barrie, 16, 141 n. 3
Thriller (film), 157 n. 37
Todd, Janet, 160 n. 6
Tyrell, William Blake, 159 n. 52

Valentini, Daria, 149 n. 12
Van Buren, Jane Silverman, 156 n. 17
Veroli, Luisella, 63
vision and visual language, 25–27 (also as "gaze"); in *La bella addormentata nel bosco* (film), 93–94; in *Crudeltà all'aria aperta*, 52–55; in *L'età del malessere*, 46–48; in *Mio padre amore mio* (film), 58–62
Vittorini, Elio, 80–81

voice, 52–55, 57–58

Walker, Barbara G., 166 n. 47
Webster, Paula, 147 n. 1
Weinberg, Grazia Sumeli: and Maraini, 141 nn. 4 and 5, 144 n. 22, 146 n. 51, 158 n. 44; and *Crudeltà all'aria aperta*, 151 nn. 33 and 34, 152 n. 38, 153 n. 52, 157 n. 33
Wilt, Judith, 154 n. 2
witches, 127–28

women's collectives, 19; *Anabasi*, 115; *Demau*, 86–87, 115; *Diotima*, 109; *Movimento femminista romano*, 109; *Rivolta femminile*, 109, 115, 163 n. 33; *Le Streghe*, 127; *UDI*, 109, 142 n. 18
women's liberation, 16, 19, 20; defined, 142 n. 6; daughter's role in defined, 34; and motherhood, 75–79; and sisterhood, 31, 105

Yanagisako, Sylvia, 17